ROCKING SURREY

A HISTORY OF SUBURBAN ROCK 'N' ROLL

NEIL MACH

To Heart Doe
for delivering the music

and to Barry Dix
for preserving the memories

1

ROCK 'N' ROLL WON'T PASS AWAY...

How did the modest English County of Surrey come to rule rock music, become the soul of pop creation, and satisfy the creative talents of so many superstar celebrities during the golden age of rock 'n' roll?

This is the memoir of a regular guy who, as a child growing up in Rocking Surrey at the height of Western popular music, struggled to make sense of what was happening.

Figure 1Chuck Berry 1957 (Public Domain)

2

TIME AND RELATIVE SPACE

As you read this, the Voyager 2 space probe travels at unfathomable speeds towards the next star system. The silver machine *swooshes* through pitch-black *nothingness* on a road to nowhere.

A gold compact disc is located within the spacecraft along with scientific waste and assorted electronic junk. I'll explain what a compact disc *is* to those readers who were born after 2003: in the 1980s, the music industry created digital optical discs to store & play recordings. If I recall, a bloke named Kieran Prendiville, a scruffy-haired individual, claimed these discs were the *future* because they were *unbreakable*. He fixed a compelling glare into the camera on BBC's popular *Tomorrow's World* science programme, and claimed the compact disc he held in sticky fingers was *indestructible*. We later learned that TV presenters Prendiville, Raymond Baxter, and Judith Hann had fibbed about *many* things. Maybe it's time to put the grudge to bed; but, anyway, we found that compact discs were curiously *susceptible* to damage. Nevertheless, N.A.S.A. scientists chose digital optical data storage over *other* formats because of the conjectural toughness and mythical durability of the storage discs (since disproven — *thanks a lot*, Kieran.)

Anyway, back to the spacecraft whooshing through blackness, a goal of the Voyager 2 mission was to have an alien race intercept the

craft once it left our solar system. Moreover, assuming the interplane-
tary policemen who snared it possessed the prerequisite audio equipment (i.e., a 1980s Walkman with a pack of fresh triple A's,) the
intercepting aliens would be able to play the attached compact disc
and, hopefully, be entertained by the sounds. Ideally, the extra-terrestrials would view the 'cover-mount' disc as a thoughtful offering given
by a peaceful species, so they wouldn't dispatch a battle cruiser forth-
with, to implement orders for our immediate and painful extinction.
The hope was that the songs that were most meaningful to us, as a
culture, would have been played by the aliens (if the disc hadn't been
banjaxed when they shoved it into their second-hand Walkman.)
Conceivably, the most important track on this interstellar freebie was:
'Johnny B. Goode' by a guy named Chuck Berry.

It's mind-boggling to think that the chain-smoking nerds who
sent this probe into deep space with its accompanying disc genuinely
believed that *'Johnny B. Goode'* represented the peak of our carbon-
based success on Earth. Yet, they did! They deemed *'Johnny B. Goode'*
to be the most recognizable song in our shared heritage.

———

Anyway, they recorded *'Johnny B. Goode'* in January 1958 at Chess
Studios, Chicago, Illinois.

I expect you're asking: What connection does this author have
with *that* song? Besides, you're thinking, what has *any of this* got to do
with Surrey? Well, hold your horses, I'm getting around to that,
daddio! When *that song* was released, I was six months old. On my
birthday Chess released Berry's *'Rock and Roll Music.'* Consequently,
like many of the Baby Boomers reading this, I am a *true* rock 'n' roll
kid. I was hatched the *same day* that rock 'n' roll was born. How cool
is that? Also, I'm a native of the Surrey landscape, a genuine Surrey
citizen, so *it all dovetails* (as my Mother often said.)

Please keep in mind these incredible circumstances as you leaf
through this book of *rockin'* memories: I was born at a time when
albums made by unassuming rural kids were good enough to be
launched into space. I'm privileged to say that rock music *began* the

4

very day I was born. I'm even prouder to say I grew up in an era when exchanging records with neighbouring extra-terrestrials was deemed a sensible and logical idea! You see, during the rock 'n' roll years, we understood the concept of taking records around to a neighbour's place to spin. In essence, when they sent Chuck Berry into space, N.A.S.A. scientists were visiting a pal's house to spin a new disc on the neighbour's living room Dansette. That's how we kids behaved in the *rock 'n' roll years*. We shared our sounds! That's how we lived our rock 'n' roll lives.

———

They launched Voyager 2 and the Chuck Berry compact disc from Cape Canaveral in August 1977. They blasted it into space a fortnight after my twentieth birthday. Four days *before* the launch, they found Elvis dead in his bathroom. It was the end of a king: the end of an era.

The rock boomtime lasted approximately two decades, 1957 to 1977. I say that rock 'n' roll died during the steamy summer of '77, though you might dispute the point (it's up to you.)

But this is how I remember the rocking years. It's a first-hand narrative describing how the early years influenced the development of a musically inspired Surrey lad. Naturally, your recollections will vary. My book attempts to illustrate how a uniquely African American kind of dance hall entertainment, which originated from World War II big band sounds, changed suburban life, and ignited a countercultural revolution. I'm interested in learning more about how this music influenced my early years in the unremarkable (and occasionally dreary) County of Surrey. I encourage you to follow along, and maybe we might uncover some answers together.

3

A TALENTED LITTLE COUNTRY BOY

I was born 4,000 miles away from Chess Studios. Curiously, my birthplace is the same distance from Cape Canaveral *too*. But that's purely coincidence. But, yes, I was born in the boring English county of Surrey and, yes, I have a rock 'n' roll narrative to share.

I lived a *promising* childhood. And that's because the history of rock & roll is one *of promise*. In my narrative, the history of the English suburbs becomes a major theme. My tale concerns growing up in a region that is frequently regarded as 'leafy' (often by those who don't live there) yet is a region that's typically *experienced* by teenagers as *deadening*. The optimal word to characterise Surrey is ho-hum! My tale is about entering and exploring this ho-hum environment just as rock caught the attention of the world. We Baby Boomers witnessed the expansion of the rock 'n' roll universe from the front-doors of suburban homes (from boxes *made of ticky-tacky*.) I was amazed at the extraordinary innovation and vision of my generation. The effect that rock had on young people is astounding. And let's be clear from the outset that the influence of rock 'n' roll on the teenagers of Surrey went *way* beyond *diffusion*. The kids of Surrey were *more than* just shoppers and clients of popular sounds. Rock 'n' roll didn't simply just rub-off on us. Oh no! In this book, I'll explain how Surrey kids *made* the world rock! I'll explain how

Surrey kids helped rock 'n' roll become the dominant aesthetic force of the 20th-century. In fact, I'll go further, and I'll suggest that rock *became* the dominant aesthetic force *because* of kids from Surrey! A bold assertion? Over the next pages, I will illustrate how Surrey, an English County, rose to prominence during the height of rock 'n' roll, on a par with Illinois or Tennessee. I will explain how the English Surrey suburbs became the new *centre of gravity* for the art form. This is my ho-hum County's finest achievement. Further, the achievement needs to be appropriately acknowledged and documented. Those are the reasons I felt compelled to compose this book.

————

As I grew older, I followed the development of popular music and became curious as to how Surrey came to play such a significant role in the growth of rock 'n' roll. But let's begin our voyage with brutal honesty, shall we? Surrey isn't the most exciting place in the world. Let's put it this way: it's less opulent than a tourist might wish for. It's tediously *unremarkable*. In places, it can be drab as a doormat. Despite its reputation for being lush and green, the County is filled with cars, overloaded with houses, and bustling with workers. There are no hazards to evade, no barriers to conquer, and no difficulties to confront. There are no dales to descend, no shipyards to sidestep, no mineshafts to skirt, no furnaces to avoid, and no slag heaps to escape. I think it's *because* of these negatives that Surrey has been neglected by history professors in big city institutions. Social historians continue to focus on the growth of popular music in Liverpool, or Manchester, or how it became shaped by furnaces in the West Midlands. Or how it landed on Bristol docks. Surrey's musicians are equally as important as the rest. The fact that my community is in the 'Beautiful South' and known for being 'leafy' doesn't diminish the value of Surrey's music-makers, does it? Social scientists will argue that rock 'n' roll was generated by working class folks, born in poverty, but the most important artists came from reasonably affluent *suburban* backgrounds. Think about this: Surrey was where rock became *nurtured*. If my claims hold true, what caused Surrey to become the dominant force in rock?

While the lives of most significant rock artists/performers were marked by challenges and hardships, a wannabe Surrey musician's life was often the complete *opposite*. Teenagers' lives in Surrey were characterised by an explosive mix of tedium and good fortune.

Fusion has *not* historically existed in my County. In 2021, three quarters of Surrey residents identified as White British, alongside a further 8.9 per cent who reported that they were 'White Other'. The Black or Black British population of Surrey is 1.7%. The Asian or Asian British population of Surrey is 7.7%, and even that population is confined mostly to Woking.

Nothing has occurred in Surrey that *shaped events*. For instance, there was *no* musical integration brought by immigrants (like there was in Liverpool and Bristol.) Nor did any profoundly felt religious traditions keep things vibrant, like they did in the Southern States of America. Kids of Surrey didn't need to avoid mineshafts, metalworks, or shipyards. There were no slums or ghettos from which to take flight.

How did Surrey earn its reputation as a landscape for successful musicians? What was it about the leafy County that inspired musicians in the early days? What factors contributed to the excitement of the Surrey music scene? Those quietly grumbling about such questions might appreciate a reminder of the musicians who emerged from the Surrey rock 'n' roll landscape:

- The County generated progressive rock acts such as Genesis and Camel
- The County produced punk rock acts, like The Stranglers and The Jam
- The County provided succour to The Rolling Stones *and* The Beatles
- The County produced the Nashville Teens, and helped The Yardbirds conquer the world
- The 'Surrey Delta' produced the finest blues musicians of

a generation. Jeff Beck, Eric Clapton, and Jimmy Page lived ten minutes from each other

- The explosion of blues-rock in Surrey sparked a renewed fascination for the genre, to transform into hard rock heavy metal

Often, the ground-breaking projects that Surrey musicians worked-on developed into original sub-genres that would go on to *define* music history.

In this memoir, I will look at some of the most important cultural landmarks. I will also attempt to describe what it was like to live in Surrey during the boom years. Come with me to the 'Beverly Hills' of Britain and see how the County helped influence the history of rock 'n' roll!

4
———

I HAD TO DANCE, HAD TO MOVE
MY FEET

You might be interested to learn I was born amid a global pandemic that originated in China. It was one of the deadliest pandemics in history.

The lethal pestilence reached the United Kingdom a year after it was discovered in South China. I was born in the autumn of *that* same year; at about the time a vaccine was due to be approved.

In the same August, calamitously, my Mother was hit by a car as she negotiated a zebra crossing in the suburban town of Worcester Park. They rushed my Mother to St Helier's Hospital, Carshalton where I was delivered by emergency caesarean section. On the day *after* I was born The Quarrymen played their first gig at The Cavern Club in Liverpool. They were on stage in an interlude between jazz bands; and when John Lennon started to thrash-out Elvis Presley's '*Don't Be Cruel*', the jazz-loving club owner handed him an angry note that read: 'Cut the bloody rock and roll.' That same summer the Blue Moon Boys were flying the charts with their *All Shook Up* —a song written with the million-selling composer Otis Blackwell, a black songwriter from Brooklyn who, by his own admission, had never met the co-writer named Elvis.

My Mother survived her ordeal and made a good physical recovery. Thanks to the wonderful work by the St Helier's hospital staff, I was born a healthy baby. Although, it is worth noting at this stage of my story that we now recognize that Mothers who undergo emergency obstetric interventions should also expect a higher incidence of stress disorder. I now reflect, with honesty, that my Mother was never *properly* stable (mentally, I mean) after the collision at Worcester Park and the emergency caesarean section that produced *me*.

———

I was initially brought up in Morden, Surrey.

For those who don't know the place, Morden, is a modest concrete town, situated just south of the much wealthier and greener neighbourhood known as Wimbledon. The media won't describe Wimbledon as 'leafy' (even though it obviously *is*) because it's in Greater London, but they *will* assume that Morden is leafy because, during the rock 'n' roll years, it was in Surrey. My birth certificate expressly states Carshalton, *Surrey*. This fact presents the first complexity: it's a struggle to accurately identify what Surrey is and how to identify the region I grew up in. This issue will resurface yet again as we contemplate the County's rock 'n' roll fortunes.

St Helier's Hospital in Carshalton was where I was born. Although the area is now part of the London Borough of Sutton, *that* town, plus Cheam, Croydon, Morden, Kingston, and Carshalton were all in Surrey, as were the places I played, where I attended school, where I went shopping, and where we went to see bands. This filled my Father with a curious sense of pride! He made a great show of reminding me, whenever he could, that we dwelt in Surrey. He once overheard me telling a schoolmate, I was sixteen at the time, that I *came from London*. My Dad scolded me in front of my pal. He yelled, 'You come from *Surrey*.' He gave the same worn-out expression, a look of frustrated displeasure, that he *always* gave when he became disappointed. Since I disappointed him *regularly*, it was an expression to which I was accustomed. 'You were raised in Surrey,' he bellowed. 'You were born in Surrey. You ought to be pleased. Why aren't you proud of Surrey?' Dad took two drags from a sparsely hand-rolled cigarette. 'You ought to be proud of coming from Surrey.'

But I was *not* proud of *coming from Surrey*.

I don't know anyone who is proud they come from Surrey. *Truly*. I didn't want people to know the dirty *secret*. Though, I didn't have the gumption to admit such a thing to my Dad. So, after the rollocking, I developed an alternative routine that suggested, to anyone who might enquire, that I came from 'South of London.' I'd provide enquirers with a relaxed smile and a barrow-boy's wink, and perhaps, if they enquired, 'near Streatham?' I would nod. I wouldn't confirm or deny my place of birth because I didn't want to disappoint my Dad.

Why did I feel reticent about *belonging* to Surrey? Well, first off, people from the Metropolitan capital possess *gravitas*. When you tell someone from New York, Paris, Newcastle, Glasgow, or Liverpool that you're a Londoner, they *will* respect you. But the same people will *blank out* if you tell them you're from Surrey. I know this from experience. Most people shake their heads and give withering looks if you tell them you're *from Surrey*. You can almost sense what they are thinking:

'Your Mother attends coffee mornings and takes Valium. Your Father works as a stockbroker and is a prominent Freemason. Every night, your Swedish *au pair* wraps under the duvet with you. You go to art school, which your parents paid for, but all you do is play guitar. You're a real mollycoddled jerk, aren't you?'

Once you tell them you're from Surrey, most folks look upon you with undisguised *hatred*. This is because they *know* you haven't *earned* a place in this cruel world. Because a child of Surrey has everything served on a plate. A child of Surrey is an undeserving little shit. A child of Surrey has everything dished-out. A child of Surrey is born with silver spoons in its spoilt little gob. A child of Surrey never has to graft. A child of Surrey is a jammy, over-indulged, brat.

Regardless of your agreement with this viewpoint, one thing is for sure: nobody feels sorry for someone who grew up in Surrey. Indeed, I've learned that people will hate me just because I was raised in the affluent suburbs. People usually despise me to the point where it takes superhuman strength for them not to bash my excessively cossetted face into the nearest brick wall. When I was sixteen, I made up a lie about where I had been raised because I was too ashamed to acknowledge I was reared in Surrey. I am sorry, Dad. I feel more confident about my upbringing *now*.

———

Why was my Father incredibly proud of me (and my sisters) being born in Surrey? I think it's because my Dad was born within the sound of Bow Bells. He was raised in North-East London. If you are raised within the sound of Bow Bells, according to folk lore, you can *legitimately* call yourself a *Cockney*. My Mother was a Cockney *too*. Mum was born in the shabbiest part of London's East End, though she almost entirely erased this *truth* from her memory. Both of my parents *could* claim to be *real* Londoners, but never claimed such a thing! Why not?

'Where are you from?' people would ask when we were on our annual holiday to Broadstairs.

'Surrey,' my Dad would announce, proudly: 'We're all from Surrey.' He'd repeat this often, and his boast would come with a confident smile.

The canny Thanet people would respond, 'How lovely! How lucky! That's a picturesque part of the world. *Leafy*.' But I knew they were silently scowling and disliking us because of our hidden advantages. The Thanet people subconsciously despised Surrey people. They hated us because we were affluent, pampered, overindulged, and milk-sopped. (We were nothing of the sort, of course, but that's the general attitude when people hear you're from Surrey.) The Thanet people *especially* detested *Surrey kids* because we'd been afforded the type of *privileged* upbringing they couldn't offer their own offspring.

I have to remind myself that people like my Dad had spent much of their life climbing out of the cesspit that London became after the end of the Great War. My Mum and Dad (and my future in-laws too) *bettered* themselves. This *betterment* had taken years of ambition and hard slog. It had probably taken blood and tears *too*. And there is nothing wrong with ambition and toil. They had launched a *new beginning* in Surrey. Therefore, they were justifiably proud of the progress they'd made. I think that's why my Dad was so dismayed when his only son renounced his birthplace. And why my Mum conveniently *forgot* she was raised in London's East End. Dad was infuriated with me because Surrey was a safe homeplace that he and his wife had worked *so hard* to provide.

———

Although it's now tarnished and tattered, the monumental building I was born in stands upon an area that's known, absurdly lyrically, as 'Rose Hill.' Incidentally, the comeback band from Boulder, Colorado has nothing to do with *the* Rose Hill I am about to describe.

If you visit the area now, you'll find it somewhat less Wordsworthian than it might sound on paper. If you stand near the forbidding walls of the hospital, and scrunch your eyelids till they're almost closed, if you peer through your lashes, you might see that the St Helier Hospital (named after Susan Elizabeth Mary Jeune, Baroness St Helier, a London County Council alderman from 1910 to 1927) remains a very impressive structure. It dominates an entire section of the Rose Hill landscape, looming over the immense 'council housing estate' that the hospital was built to serve. (In England we call the type of public homes designed for low-income households 'council housing.' In North America, you might describe the same estates as housing *projects*.)

The St Helier hospital stands as an icon to an audacious period in British social history. Once upon a time, town planners were not afraid of notions such as aspiration and ambition. They started work on the vast St. Helier council housing estate in 1928 — that's the same year that Disney released 'Steamboat Willie' and Ravel's *Boléro* premiered. They finished the building work in 1936 but had planned it in the latter part of the 19th century! To bring us back to the history of rock 'n' roll for a moment, the motivated planners accomplished this colossal undertaking during the years we associate with 'Great Depression' America. In other words, they built an enormous council estate during the same years that swathes of desperate folk fled dust-bowl States to big cities such as Chicago, Detroit, and New York bringing their roots music with them.

The St. Helier's Estate was a housing project built on a truly massive scale. A scale so enormous we can only reminisce about the impressiveness of it these days. I'm sure we'd never have the aptitude or drive to complete (or even contemplate) a work on this unparalleled scale *today*. As an example, let me tell you it took them sixty years to replace a teeny-weeny, prefabricated truss-bridge at Walton-on-Thames, Surrey, a bridge that spans a slim section of the Thames just downstream from where I live. They recently finished *that* bridge. They began thinking about re-building the bridge just after World War Two: that's sixty bloody years. Sixty years to complete a bridge!

The St. Helier's Estate in Surrey accommodated masses-and-masses of people. You must remember that Londoners were still suffering horribly during the same period. Londoners lived in filthy conditions that became *worse* after the bombings in the Great War. By the way, these days you hear little about First World War bomb-ings, but my great-aunt (she lived in Islington, North London) told me that the 'Jerries' bombed her house *twice* during the Great War of 1914-18. She suggested that the Second World War was *easier* because she only got *bombed once!* Most people don't know that Germany's aerial campaign against London became intense when they switched from Zeppelins to heavy bombers (such as the Gotha G.IV.)

But before London's 'clear outs,' triggered by bomb damage in the Great War, people like my Mum and great-aunt lived in the same dreadful conditions that we now think are 'quaint' when we see them in costume dramas on Netflix. Outrageously, nothing had changed for London residents since Dicken's character Artful Dodger picked the pockets of city gents, circa 1828.

One hundred years later, when work first started on the enormous St. Helier housing project, the village of Morden was (like most villages in the County of Surrey) an insignificant rural community surrounded by fields. Presumably, the fields were once moorland but had been husbanded into small, self-sufficient, market gardens. In Staines and in Stanwell (modern-day Spelthorne), we have remnants of the same ancient moorlands. Morden village probably first came about when Celtic tribes moved into the area to build a small defensive enclosure. The name Morden most likely derives from a Brittonic word, *Mawr* (which *actually* meant great or large) and *Dun* (which meant a fort), so the area became 'the fort on the large expanse.' It's hard to imagine how tiny and insignificant this place must have been when you stand with your eyes squeezed shut, by the Co-Op, at the busy Rose Hill roundabout. But back in 1086, Morden was a tiny hamlet, comprising fourteen residences. The population grew very gradually from the Norman conquest, with transformation coming exceedingly slowly. Rural life concentrated around the old church of St Lawrence. The church still stands proud on the main London Road. The public house of this 'village' was The George Inn. In bygone days, fields of fragrant medicinal herbs were grown in the low-lying fields. For instance, there was a sixty-acre lavender farm at Wrythe Lane. There was also a little light industry that clung tightly to the banks of a dabbling river known as the Wandle. You would have found miniature watermills on the banks of the Wandle. These mills pulverized tobacco into snuff. Everything was peaceful. But things were about to change.

5

FORTUNATELY, MAMA; THAT'S FINE

Between 1890 and 1907, the City & South London Railway Company (C&SLR) began building the first deep-level underground 'tube' rail network the world had *ever* seen. This revolutionary railway connected the City of London to the busy neighbourhoods around Stockwell, which lay to the south. This impressive achievement became the first major railway in the world to use 'electric traction.' The ambitious plan was to establish a tunnel *under* the Thames—running a subterranean train-line along two long tubes. Now, remember, this was during the period of 'steam locomotives.' The planners could not use steam engines in confined spaces, underground, inside sealed tubes (because of noxious fumes)—so the C&SLR engineers came-up with a brand-new type of traction. They reasoned, logically, they should position motors *outside* of tunnels, established in the fresh air. The fresh-air motors would then offer power to *drag* trains, and haul them through tunnels, under the river. It was a simple idea, efficient and effective.

In 1926, the C&SLR line was developed from Clapham Common (in the south of London) to the lavender-farming district of Surrey. They proposed that Morden station would become the Southern-most terminus of what they described as the 'Morden to Edgware line.' This railway line became better known as the 'Northern Line' in

1937. Once the Morden line extension opened, in September 1926, the London County Council (the planning authority for London) thought about how they might develop the lands near this, their Southernmost Terminus. The lands they eyed included the lavender fields that I mentioned earlier, which were situated around the 'village' of Morden.

Since the early 17th century, the St. Helier estate's location had a history of long-term charitable endeavours. Henry Smith, a prosperous Londoner who died in 1627, donated a substantial portion of the money he'd made from salting to parishes in Surrey and London. We believe that Smith was born in Wandsworth because he's buried there. He donated £500 to buy land in Carshalton in 1617, with the proceeds of his charitable endeavours going to Wandsworth's underprivileged. Another bequest of £100 was made by a different donor, Mrs. Elizabeth Blackwell. Approximately 116 acres of these philanthropic grounds were documented in 1814, together with buildings, barns, and outhouses. These Wandsworth *Poor Lands* lay on either side of Wrythe Lane at the southern part of the St. Helier footprint. Christopher Muschamp, who passed away in 1660 and is interred at All Saints, Carshalton, was another local benefactor. He left £200 to buy land, and the yearly rent raised from this gift was used to pay for apprenticeships for two underprivileged children who were born in the parish. Pastureland was also bought from farmer Henry Byne, in Cannon Sheephouse Lane, which is now known as Green Wrythe Lane. Like the adjoining Sutton Common, most of this area remained semi-rural right up until the early 20th century. The St Helier estate was built between 1928 and 1936 and designed as a garden city, with landscaping by architect Edward Prentice Mawson who also designed Stanley Park in Blackpool (1922–26). In remembrance of the area's historic ownership by Westminster Abbey, the roads on the estate are named in alphabetical order after Monasteries and Abbeys starting in the north-west with Aberconway Road and ending with Woburn Road in the south-east.

The London County Council planners did *not* limit their ingenuity or ambition. By 1938 (in just twelve years) they built over 9,000 houses on the former lavender fields! The new buildings accommodated an influx of over 40,000 new residents who came from the poorest parts of London. This estate was to become the second largest housing development in the world. (The biggest *ever* estate was the Becontree Estate in Dagenham.) The St Helier estate was an impressive project. An awesome achievement. This was when the word *awesome* actually meant something.

The new St. Helier Estate grew at a bewildering speed. Eighteen purpose-built schools were incorporated into the plans, plus seven new churches. They erected two gigantic pubs. And even a state-of-the-art 2,000-seater movie theatre (The Gaumont.) They constructed sixty shops to serve the people they knew would settle here. The development was so ambitious that the builders (C.J. Wills and Sons) worked-out that the cheapest and easiest way to move all the building materials around the site was to create their own private railway. St. Helier residents still commemorate their purpose-built railway. My neighbours knew the railway, affectionately, as the 'St. Helier Express.'

A corresponding experience, perhaps not on the same immense scale as the St Helier project, but similar in other respects, impacted the entire county of Surrey. Large expanses of what were once sparsely populated rustic lands abruptly became inundated with London folk from the poorest *slum* boroughs. These folk were escapees from the place that William Cobbett once described *as the Great Wen*. It was an invasion. An outright invasion. Nothing could stop the exodus from the Wen and into fledgling suburbia.

Before railway trains arrived (late as always) into my home county, visitors travelled through, out, and *across* Surrey using dangerous, bumpy, and doubtless extremely expensive, turnpike roads. Stage-coach routes sliced across the County. And there's a consequence of this 'slicing' that I shall confront more than once in this book. But, anyhow, it's important to note at this stage that these coaches *rarely* stopped. Why would they? They'd only just left the Great Wen, so their first stop would likely be four-or-five hours into a long trip, and that means their first stop would be way *beyond* the borders of Surrey. That is *unless* coach passengers were robbed along the way, (and often they were! Highwaymen hunted for prey on the fringes of the Capital). In such circumstances, the coaches might have to make an emergency halt at some bleak Surrey inn for a warming pint of ale (brewed on Surrey Hills) while the passengers waited for a parish constable. Stagecoach robbery was *very* real and *quite common*. We know that highwaymen were busy in places like Banstead Downs, Burgh Heath, and the heathlands at Hounslow, and on Staines Moor. It has been suggested that Guildford and Esher were favourite lay-overs for these types of temporary, post-robbery halts. If the worst happened and the coach got robbed, passengers might have to loll on a bug-ridden bed for the night. Sometimes, after a hold-up, visitors would stay a week for a magistrate's hearing. But seldom did any week turn into a fortnight. Nobody stayed long in the county of Surrey. Why? Because Surrey was a place to travel across, to pass over, or to get through *quickly*. Coach travellers were driving towards better, more exciting, and more comfortable destinations. Most travellers aimed for the ports of Portsmouth or Southampton, or further on, maybe to Exeter and the far South-West. In coaching days, nobody (in their right mind) wanted to wait in Surrey! It wasn't a place to stay *within*. Surrey was a place to stay *without*; an area to travel *across*.

But once railways arrived, the exodus from the capital city slums to the villages of Surrey became *unstoppable*. Surrey became transformed from a place a person would rush *through and across*, to a place where a person would like to settle down and rear a family.

Rapid, reliable transportation meant that masses of London workers would travel daily from fresh new homes to places of employment in the sooty Wen. Everyone saw the benefits of the arrangement. The people of cloggy, smoggy London yearned for clean air and healthy living. Plus, land in Surrey was cheap for developers. Hence, it made sense to exploit the wide-open and often neglected open spaces of Surrey. Workers just needed to hop onto a reliable train to get to work because the villages in Surrey were only an hour from the city. This was the suburban dream come true.

'Commuting' as a notion first became possible because of the

Surrey expansion; and our St Helier development led the way. It's true that large-scale suburban development came about in the United States at about this time *too*; but the world's *first* genuine 'Commuter Belt' was established in Surrey, England. Our existing towns, Guildford, Farnham, and Croydon, began to expand at a startling pace. While 'new towns' such as Woking and Redhill mushroomed alongside newly laid railway tracks. Suburbia was grown in the Surrey flask, much like the flourishing crystal gardens we created in our school science projects. Note: the ever-enlarging yeast-cake of Greater London swallowed up the Surrey towns of Croydon and Kingston in 1965. Greater London also gulped-up Purley, Sutton, and Morden the *same* year.

6

THE PRESSURE WON'T GO DOWN

You may wonder, if you live overseas, how big the County of Surrey *actually* is. The hard facts show that Surrey is a landlocked 'authority' with no coastline and occupies an area of around 648 sq. miles (or 1,679 sq. km). That's about the same size as Columbia County, New York, or a little larger than Yuba County, California.

How much did the suburban County grow (in terms of population) since the development of the huge St. Helier Estate, and the other estates, and after the introduction of the railways?

Well, anyone who has ever used the M25 motorway will know it becomes especially busy when you reach the Surrey section. (If you've never visited the County of Surrey, or indeed England, I ought to explain that the M25 is a rotating system of permanent coagulation that encircles the smoke of the Wen.)

There's a good reason why things *get busy* as you enter the 'Surrey section' of the London orbital, and it's *this*: you are driving into the most densely populated urban area of Europe. The Office of National Statistics declared, in a report issued in 2011, that the thirty-one urban sub-units of Surrey (which is part of the 'Greater London Built-up Area') form, when taken together, the largest centre of population in Europe. The population of London's Larger Urban Zone (that's the area that includes all the green and leafy sub-units of Surrey with all the brown bits that Greater London 'stole' from the County in 1965) totals around 11.9 million people. You might compare this figure with the total population of Greater Los Angeles, which is the second most populous city in the United States (after New York City) and is famed for its own suburbia. The population of Los Angeles is about 3.8 million people.

Surrey swelled and overflowed once the St. Helier estate had been fully completed and Northern Line trains began to roll into the southern terminus. The population blossomed, and Surrey society went through a series of great adjustments. I came into being just as one of these great societal adjustments began. Like I already explained, I was born at the start of rock 'n' roll. This means I am a post-Second World War baby, so I was born to a Mother who was persuaded, by government, *to stay at home* and produce offspring to replenish the human stock lost during two calamitous wars. I was born at the end of the Northern Line. I lived my early years in Morden, on the gigantic St Helier estate. We lived practically on top of the giant Southern Terminus buildings. From our back-fence, in Bordesley Road, we'd hear the tube trains shunting in the rail yard. It sounded as if the carriages jerked right up to our back door. I heard the electrical buzz of the 'underground' trains all night long.

———

Back in 1950s Morden, we puzzled about exactly *where* we lived. Who did we belong to? Most of the estate's parents originated in London's East End, so most adults considered themselves Londoners. Indeed, most men still worked in London. But were we Surrey residents? Or were we Londoners? Actually, we felt like limbo-dwellers. For example, Sutton Creameries delivered our milk. Our coal-gas was piped-into the house by the Croydon Gas Company. Our electricity meter was read by the County of London Electric Supply Company (CLE-SCO.) We were told, at school (a school run by the Surrey County Council but that issued textbooks stamped Sutton Borough) that the Sutton & District Water Company (SDWC) supplied our water. I recall we went on a school visit to 'our local' water plant, in Sutton.

My parents paid council rent to London County Council. So, did we live in Surrey or *didn't* we? It's a question we Surrey dwellers *still* ask. Is Surrey part of London? Or is London part of Surrey? For example, why is the Surrey County Cricket Club (the Surrey C.C.C.) situated in Lambeth, at the Oval? Why is the City of Southwark (once a fort run by the 'men of Surrey') part of London? Why is it *not* part of Surrey? Why did the same place, Southwark, become the first area to describe its residents *Londoners*? I don't expect to answer such questions in this book, there are complicated histories involved, so I'll leave you to make up your own mind because we need to get back to the history of rock 'n' roll.

———

The adopted son of our neighbour on the St Helier estate (the son of my 'Auntie' Winnie, who became a major figure in my life) owned a lozenge-shaped Ford Anglia motor car. The car was the same creamy-green as the gunk you see on the edges of village ponds. It was a kind of gloopy sprouting green. I swear this was the only car in the entire Morden/Merton area. The only other mechanical transport we'd *ever* see were the early morning electric milk float or, once a week, the dustman's van. Even the bread-man had a dray-horse back then!

David, 'Auntie' Winnie's 'son,' was the proud owner of this leek-green Ford Anglia. He was a Teddy Boy. There was always a chubby-cheeked, grime-stained, mutton-*choppiness* about David. He possessed oily hair that dripped onto grubby shirt collars, he possessed thickly bruised arms that swelled beefily from his pits, and he possessed chunky legs that were more meat than muscle. David wore a grimace across a sweaty, reddish, face. To me, just a tot at the time, David resembled a happy toad. He reeked of sticky labour and meat juices. And that's because he worked as a butcher's apprentice in nearby Colliers Wood.

'He's got a genuine job. He's got a car. He's *even* got a girlfriend,' Auntie Winnie told everyone. She made this boast in a startled way, as if David's success astonished her every-bit-as-much as it amazed everyone else on our estate. I'm fairly sure everyone in Carshalton was truly astounded that 'her David' had *somehow* made something of himself.

———

I'd better explain what a Teddy Boy is, to those who don't know.

The 'Ted' phenomena took off after the London fashion houses operated a 'Never Mind the Quality, Feel the Width' policy after the demobilization of troops at the end of WW2. During the war-years the rag-trade had been severely upset, first by a shortage of fabrics and thereafter due to the austerity measures that continued right through to 1949. By 1950 the rag trade found themselves having to unload a batch of relaxed-looking *zoot suits*: of the type popularized by jazz musicians such as Cab Calloway. These suits were *supposed* to have gone to demob soldiers. At the start, the fashion houses offered these American-looking suits to British servicemen who had returned home after conflict. But most Brit servicemen rejected the 'look' of the Chicago-style 'mob' (not de-mob!) suits, opting instead for a more traditional English style of smartness. (I guess most British servicemen thought the zoot-suits looked spivvy and had black market connotations.) Therefore, the rag-trade became overwhelmed with a pile of crappy suits that nobody (in their right mind) wanted. They sold tons of these zoot suits to High Street Menswear shops, at bargain-basement prices. Fortunately, for everyone involved, this was just as the young people of the suburbs discovered independent purchasing power. Also, this was when the first post-war youth gangs were being loosely formed.

Of course, young people wanted to look flashy and needed to boast a unique style, so chose the 'Edwardian look' they found in High Street stores, i.e. the zoot suits their Fathers had rejected on demob. The youth 'look' included oversized drape jackets, velvet lapels, and padded shoulders. Jackets were worn with high-waisted 'drainpipe' trousers, and baggy Billy Eckstine-style loose-collared shirts. Ultra-thin bolo ties and brothel creeper shoes completed *the look*. The young men who dressed in this style were quickly identified as 'Teddy Boys' by British Press (supposedly because the elegance of their clothes was influenced by the fashion period 1900-1909, thus defined as 'Edwardian.')

These zoot-suited 'Teds' hung-out together (like young people do) and enjoyed intimidating older folk (nothing changes.) Mostly, though, Teds hung-around in coffee shops or idled on street corners. They listened to trad jazz on jukeboxes (a pre-war American invention that never appeared in Britain until *after* V.J. day) and they took their girls to dances. And, although Teds were jazz enthusiasts, the roots rock sounds that Elvis, Bill Haley, and Eddie Cochran had introduced were starting to gain popularity. Since these sounds were jazz-leaning, they were acceptable to the new tribe.

Sadly, it was not long before 'Teds' gained notoriety. Some Teddy Boys participated in violent confrontations and even implicated in race riots. Although, to be fair, most Teddy Boys were music lovers with fashion-sense, and with brass in their pockets.

———

So, David, 'Auntie' Winnie's adopted son, with his algae-coloured Ford Anglia and his mutton-chops, was one such Teddy Boy. He had a mousey girlfriend named Dianne. She accompanied David *everywhere*. I do not think I ever saw her smile. I never heard her speak, either. Dianne sat by David's side, adopting an air of Trappist silence. I remember she blinked... quite a lot, actually. And Dianne possessed remarkably lank hair. Flaps of dull hair fell onto the collars of her hand-crocheted cardigan. I thought her hair resembled slippery fish tails. Dianne crossed her legs, drew her knees in tight, pulled her elbows to herself, and, in this way, she attracted *less* attention. Dianne assumed little space. This was because in the Ted world girls were decorative *accessories*.

Every so often, David would take me and Dianne 'for a drive.' It's hard to imagine this now, but in the rock 'n' roll days, people went 'for a drive' as form of light entertainment. In the 1950s and early '60s people considered driving a *pastime*, much like running a kite or rolling a skateboard down a hill.

For example, the best part of Christmas holidays was when my

Grandfather (who was a licensed London hackney carriage driver) came to our house in his taxi. After much pressing, he'd announce the exciting words my sister and I longed to hear: 'Let's go for a drive.' We'd clap our hands and feel quite giddy with the thrill of the prospect. Then we'd drive through the Surrey Hills in Grandad's cab. My Nan would be all-wrapped-up in a red tartan blanket, because it was forever frosty in those days. We'd drive to the top of Box Hill. Then trundle into Dorking. It was magnificent and *extremely exciting*. One such Christmas we passed an incident near Box Hill. A motorist had swerved, perhaps on ice, and his little tin car, I think it was a Morris, had collided, head-on, with a tree. A man was trapped inside the car. The engine steamed. In the road lay a woman. Blood gushed from her wounds. The blood reminded me of the tomato paste my Mother put into beef stew. My Grandad said, indifferently and openly, 'Looks like she's dead.' My sister and I gawked at the scene as we passed. Other drivers stopped to help but my Grandfather continued motoring without drama and comment. I now see why he continued, but for years I was unable to figure-out his base attitude. Grandad had continued driving because he didn't want us to see the horror! Back in those days, people didn't make *a fuss of things*. To me, it seemed uniquely sad that a woman had perished on a road at Christmastime just because she'd chosen to go 'for a drive.' But my sister said, '*When* someone passes away is irrelevant. It doesn't matter that it is Christmas. All days are the same in death.' My sister remains, to this day, a very philosophic person.

Anyway, I was reassured that David, the Teddy Boy, would never be as adventurous as my Grandad or indeed the woman who had tomato paste leaking from her head. Luckily for the occupants of *his* green Ford Anglia, David recognized it would *never* make it to the bottom of Box Hill, let alone the top! So, there'd be no chance we'd hit a tree and become tomato puree. David's 'drive' was essentially a mechanized version of a walk around the block. Yet even an outing of such modest proportions was a thing to be cherished. You must remember that going 'for a drive' in the late 50's /early 1960s was an amazing treat! So, Dianne and I looked forward to any 'outing' in his green slime Anglia. We'd rumble past the laundry in Abbotsbury

Road (the Ford made lots of barks, bellows, and rumbles. Pedestrians looked around in genuine panic.) We never quite reached the 'maximum speed of sixty' that David boasted his car would achieve. We'd rumble around Rosehill roundabout and buzz into Central Road. We'd croak and fart our way up to St. Lawrence's church. This was where my parents were married, and where I had been baptised. We would clack along the London Road. Reaching the 'White Bridge' we'd whiz past the Crown Pub, where Kenny Ball and his Jazzmen played a regular slot. Then we'd roll alongside Morden Hall Park and back into the St Helier estate where we'd jolt past the neat allotments spliced into tight spaces between long rows of terraced houses. (One enterprising allotment holder grew a neat line of hops.) We'd thunder, cough, and belch our way back into Bordesley Road, via Buckfast. Thinking back on it, this 'drive' was a journey that *should have* taken fifteen minutes to complete. One way or another, I don't know how he did it, but David made the around-the-block road trips last an entire afternoon.

Sometimes, on some drives, we'd stop at St Lawrence's Church. There, we'd remove ourselves from the cramped confines of the Ford to 'stretch our legs.' This was an important part of any motoring trip in the rock 'n' roll years. One went somewhere (it didn't matter where) to *stretch one's legs.* Cars were horribly uncomfortable in the 'good old days.' At St Lawrence's, Dianne would pull her cardigan tighter than usual around those hunched shoulders. She'd blink into the breeze. David would check his engine oil. He'd always end-up with a long smear of axle-grease along one seam of his trousers.

Periodically, and certainly on every journey, David would pull over precariously. He'd screech to an urgent halt. This would occur every half mile or so. Or every fifteen minutes, whichever came first. These unannounced stops were to *check* or *replace* something that had gone *terribly wrong.* David would slip under the floor of the car to check if the exhaust pipe (held fast with cocoa tins) still dangled. Or he might have to push a headlamp bulb back into place. Or fix the radiator with the spool of gardening twine he carried in his glove box. Once he pulled into the kerb to say *hello* to a Teddy Boy acquaintance. On that occasion I remember thinking that all his friends had the same ruddy complexion. They all had similar muscular arms and wide-mouthed, toady grins. I imagined they were *all* butcher's shop apprentices. But, sure, they were *all* Teddy Boys.

———

On one memorable occasion, David diverted from his usual route to take Dianne and I along a road that was aside from our typical around-the-block course. The lead singer of his favourite band lived in a house on our estate and David *wanted us* to view the place. I knew his favourite band were The Mourners.

David slowed, as if we had mysteriously moved into Beverly Hills aboard one of those tourist buses that take sightseers to the grand homesteads of Hollywood stars. Dianne and I gazed through the dirty car window, hoping to catch a glimpse of this fabulous abode. I expected to see Greta Garbo pruning roses. Or Clark Gable picking runner beans. However, I was disappointed. The house we stopped to view looked exactly the same as *any house* on our street. Perhaps I should have expected this, because *everyone* on the St Helier estate lived in identical ticky-tack homes. Yet, having said that, 'The Mourners' residence *did* possess magic. Why? Because it was the home of an artist. A performer. This is where British rock 'n' roll was born.

David told us that 'The Mourners' played a variety of exciting music in local Carshalton pubs. He identified this sound as *Skiffle*. When David told us about Skiffle, his toad-like face became animated, his beefy hands turned expressive, and he dribbled. Clearly, Skiffle had a vitalizing effect on him. Skiffle was the home-made sound of the suburbs. Skiffle shook the establishment. And, although we didn't know it at the time, suburban Skiffle kick-started a rock revolution. Here, at an ordinary home on an unglamorous estate, in a seedier part of the County, the kernels of pop culture germinated. Here, and in other comparable unremarkable homes, British rock was being nurtured.

7

RUN, CAT, RUN!

The 'Bermondsey Boy' named Thomas Hicks (later and much better known as Tommy Steele) was born in 'real' London. *Real* London, like my Dad.

I should also mention, in order to meet the resolutions set out for this book, that Tommy Steele spent a significant portion of his life in Montrose House, Petersham Village—more specifically, at the so-called 'Tommy Steele corner' of Petersham Road, near the entrance to Richmond Park. During the rock 'n' roll era, Petersham was part of the County of Surrey. (Richmond-upon-Thames and the adjoining districts lost their Surrey connection in 1965, but it's fair to say the inhabitants of the plush semi-royal town have never enthusiastically embraced the London Government Act. I'm sure the opulent residents still believe they reside in a West-Surrey *enclave*. What is more, if *anywhere* is truly leafy it's Richmond-upon-Thames yet, technically, since 1965, it's not even *in* Surrey!

In 1956 Tommy Steele's single titled 'Rock with the Caveman' reached number 13 in the UK Singles Chart.

His album 'The Tommy Steele Story' was the first album by any UK-based act to reach No. 1 in Britain. It was released the same year I was born. Thus, it's another reason I can claim to be a rock 'n' roll baby. Just to remind you, this was the same year that Elvis released

'*All Shook Up*' and '*Jailhouse Rock*.' It was the very start of the Golden years.

———

In 1958 Steele met Elvis.

Years later, Tommy would disclose information about their special ultra-secret meeting.

Let me try to explain what happened because, apparently, the meeting was held in the style of a cloak-and-dagger John le Carré *style* novel. Tommy Steele later disclosed (through Bill Kenwright, the famous theatre producer, and close personal friend) that he had a clandestine meeting with Elvis — in *London* — and had shown the '*Hound Dog*' around London.

If this story is true (and some say it isn't, but we'll get into that) I think it's likely that Steele took Elvis to the birthplace of British rock 'n' roll — the famous '2 i's' coffee bar in Soho (London) in Old Compton Street. (The bar was named after two earlier owners who had the surname *Irani*.) The reason I'm convinced this part of the legend is authentic is because it was *here* that young Michael Hayes (a.k.a. Mickie Most) worked as a singing waiter. We will encounter Mickie later in this book. Mickie worked with Colin Hicks (the younger brother of Tommy Steele), so why wouldn't they have visited the 2 i's? It seems obvious they *did*.

By the way, it was at the 2 i's that Steele first encountered the Shadows, and Cliff Richard (who we shall turn to in more depth, presently). Steele's brother, Colin, and Mickie Hayes (Most) worked alongside Peter Grant who functioned as a bouncer-cum-doorman. Grant would one day become the manager for Led Zeppelin. Anyone who recalls Grant's size, weight, and temperament will agree he acted the part of a competent chucker-outer. Acton town lad Adam Faith hung around this bar *as well*. As did Blackjack bandleader Rory Blackwell, the John Barry Seven singer Vince Eager, the Six-Five Special performer Wee Willie Harris, and Shepherd's Bush renowned rock 'n' roll drummer Carlo Little, who would later play with an early version of the Rolling Stones and was a founding member of

Screaming Lord Sutch's Savages. In fact, lots of luminaries started the most lucrative rock careers in this famous, though cramped, venue.

A year after the birth of rock 'n' roll, in 1958, the '2 i's' coffee bar had a minuscule 18-inch-high stage in the basement, with standing-room-only and a sticky-floor. Music lovers crammed into the ridiculously small space to see the newest and most exciting acts of the day. The acts they saw were mostly jazz and Skiffle combos.

Elvis and Tommy Steele most likely peeked through the murky windows as they passed the place. If they dared enter the 2 i's (I don't think they *did* because they'd have been too recognisable and other witnesses would have since come forward to recall the event) but even if they *did* go inside, it's unlikely they'd have found space to hang around. Music fans were shoehorned in!

But I like to imagine their discussion between Steele and the King went something like this:

King: 'Hey, Uh huh... Who is that lanky, feminine looking singer with the curled lip?'

Bermondsey Boy: 'That's a geezer named Harry Webb — he has a band called the Drifters. He will one day be known as Cliff Richard.'

King: 'Catchy name for a band, the Drifters. Ohh yeah! But he should get it trade-marked. Or somebody will steal it. Uh-huh! That Harry though, he looks too slick for his own good, holy mama! Look at his oily black hair. And those gyrating hips. Why would anyone do that? He needs to calm hisself down.'

Bermondsey Boy: 'Yeah, but one day he will be a big star. Not as big as you, maybe. But nearly! Then he will fade from view.'

King: 'Who is that overweight guy in the corner? I just make him out through the glass. I think I recognise his podgy face. Do you see him? I'm pointing at the guy with sunken eyes. That cat seems like a gross version of *me*. He's certainly way out of condition. Uh huh...'

Bermondsey Boy: 'That is you, idiot! It's a distorted image of yourself you've seen reflected in the khazi door-mirror. It's disturbing though — ain't it?

King: 'Khazi?'

Bermondsey Boy: 'Yeah! I think you lot call it a *can*...'

King: 'Whatever, man, this is frankly upsetting. Let's get outta this place...'

'Yeah, we should split before Grant sees us.'

I ought to point out that it's highly unlikely this scenario took place. And it most definitely *didn't* happen the way I described it! The people of Northern Scotland would be extremely outraged if it *had* happened that way, so I feel I ought to overemphasise my next point: according to Scottish rock 'n' roll fans, Elvis *never visited London*. He only stepped once onto British soil and that was during a stopover at Prestwick Airport, in 1960, *en route* to his American Army camp in Germany.

Therefore, the entire '2 i's' coffee bar incident is fictitious. (Or is it?)

8

HEY, YOU GUYS, WHO'S THAT OUTSIDE?

At about the same time that Elvis and Steele were skulking around Soho looking into grubby windows and making disparaging comments about Cliff (maybe they were, maybe they were *not*) — a young musician tried to make a reasonable living playing trumpet with an unimpressive band not far from my home in Carshalton.

This young trumpeter practised every evening. And took his unexceptional band around Surrey pubs and coffee bars at the weekends. (This guy's day job was a retail clerk at Moss Bros —which is a notable gentleman's outfitters.) The type of music this guy played to his Surrey neighbours had its origins in early 'jug bands' that were formed across the Southern States of America before the Dust Bowl years. Jug bands, so named because one of the artists played a 'jug'— literally a kitchen jug— pushed against the musician's lips to make a trombone-like sound—were the first truly *democratic* sounds. Being a member of a jug band required no money. Being a member of a jug band required no talent. Being a member of a jug band required no knowledge of music or technical know-how. You'd learn your playing skills as you went along. Basically, *anyone* could play in a jug band. And anyone *did* play in a jug band. And jug bands played *any* place that would take them. Some of the most popular music was created by juggers and stompers, who served as inspiration to a new generation of aspiring but untrained musicians with similar homemade instruments and impromptu habits. The sound the new generation produced would be known as *Skiffle*.

Back in the 1920's, the amateur musicians in Skiffle combos performed with their Mum's washboards, kazoos, tin-whistles, and jugs. Tea-chests were turned upside down and thumped. Broom-handles were strung with gut to become bass instruments. Garden hoses or tin funnels were used as horns. Kitchen pots were clattered as percussion. If a musician could shake, rattle, or roll something (*anything* would do) then the utensil would become a musical instrument. It was do-it-yourself music. And was creative, recreational, and of course, totally *free*.

———

I need to tell you that Skiffle, as a recognisable genre, might have sunk without trace if it were not for two particularly important characters. The first of these characters was an American jazz clarinettist named Jimmy O'Bryant. We'll deal with him first. But the second character was a Scotsman who worked and played in London. He's important to our story because he bump-started Rocking Surrey, so his legacy is important. But let's begin with the American.

Jimmy O'Bryant played in a group way back in 1920-21 with Jelly Roll Morton and W. C. Handy. You have probably heard of Jelly Roll Morton: he was a New Orleans ragtime jazz pianist. He kinda pioneered the genre of blues music that we now call boogie-woogie. The genre had a considerable influence on rhythm and blues, and early rock 'n' roll. So, in some circles Jelly Roll, real name Ferdinand LaMothe, is regarded by the rock 'n' roll fraternity as their primogenitor. Incidentally, the word *boogie* most likely originates from the Mandingo word *booga* (which means 'to beat'— as in the *beat of a drum*.) W. C. Handy was known as the *Father of the Blues*.

Back to Jimmy O'Bryant: in 1925 Jimmy and his band went into a studio in Chicago to record a session. There was perhaps nothing particularly amazing or magical about this session, except, you see, the apparatus we would recognise as an electromagnetic microphone had only *just* been invented and O'Bryant's outfit was about to use it – so this was a giant step into unknown territory for these musicians. For us, this was to be one of the most super-monumental moments in rock history. But to O'Bryant's outfit it was probably scary shit! Electromagnetic microphone technology was considered so red-hot *futuristic* that it was terrifying! And that's why nobody had attempted to use the technology (commercially) before. It was momentous when Jimmy O'Bryant entered the scene to give it a shot.

You might wish to consider the following to gain a general picture of how things operated in a Chicago recording studio before 1925:

- there were no acoustics (to speak of)
- the studio was simply a rented back room
- the studio was not isolated from traffic noise or other disturbances
- the recordings went direct-to-disc
- the musicians had to huddle around a large acoustic horn
- this acoustic horn was like a phonographic horn, only larger

You should imagine the famous HMV symbol (His Master's Voice) to get an idea of what it must have been like to cluster around that huge brass horn. You might recall that the HMV symbol has a dog (the Bristol-born dog's name was Nipper, in case you didn't know, and the dog lived in Kingston-upon-Thames, Surrey and was buried in a small park in Clarence Street). Anyway, in the world-famous logo, painted by Londoner Francis Barraud in 1898, the puppy is shown looking into the bowl of a Victor Talking Machine Company brass horn. Now, in your mind, if you replace puppy dog Nipper with a whole bunch of groovy musicians gazing into the same size horn, you get an idea of what the device in the studio must have looked like.

So, to summarise, this event happened in a back room with a big phonograph-looking thing at the centre of things, with elementary electric bits-and-bobs strewn here and there. Up until 1925 there were no microphones, no amplifiers, no mixing desks, no speakers, no isolation booth, and *certainly* no multitrack recording devices. Music was recorded *direct to disc.*

Therefore, typically, Jimmy O'Bryant would collect his musicians around the horn in the centre of the room, and they would play *into* it *as a group.* And I mean, *all at once.* How everyone got around the 'listening horn' is a mystery. Although it's obvious that some things did *not* work out. For instance, you couldn't get a piano close against the horn. Or, if you somehow managed it, everyone would have to stand on the lid to direct their sounds into the bowl. Also, you couldn't have more than two or maximum three singers. Obviously, the recording of an entire orchestra was completely out of the question. Some instruments were notoriously hard to 'get down.' Trombones were difficult, for example, because the slide had to be extended into the bowl, or the trombonist would upset everyone by constantly smashing his slide into a pal's necks.

String instruments were notoriously difficult to record before 1925. It was found that whiny thin stringy sounds could not be captured well over the 'brilliant' sounds that burst from brass. So, if a violin had to be used in a piece, the studio masters insisted that violinists played an ingenious contraption, which looked like a Steampunk version of concert fiddle. This odd-looking gizmo was known as a horn-violin, and amplified sound through a metal resonator (rather than *via* the customary wooden soundbox). It passed its sounds through a metal horn on the side and into the 'recording' horn.

Fortunately, these 'phonofiddles' and other strange instruments had been created by pioneers in music at about the same time as the advent of recorded music. (The Stroviol — the trade name of the most famous horned-violin — was patented in 1899, which is about 20 years after Thomas Edison 'perfected' his commercial phonograph.)

Back to O'Bryant's famous stint in Chicago. I assume the recording session went as follows:

Jimmy O'Bryant: 'Holy freakin' sheeet! What is this piece of crap?' (He is seen pointing at the most recent invention — the earliest microphone —and Jimmy is perplexed.)

Studio Engineer: 'Now, take it easy Jim-Bo. This here is what the boffins call a mike-row-fone.'

Jimmy O'Bryant: 'What the? Where's the freakin' horn? Ain't we 'sposed to play into the horn?'

Studio Engineer: Take it easy, like I said, this new mike-row-fone replaces the big horn we typically use. Your voice and clarinet will still be heard on the disc. You just need to sing and play into this new doohickey.'

Jimmy O'Bryant: 'I will not use any freakin mike-row-wassits. That fangled oojiboo looks mighty dangerous to me! Anyways, where's all those wires going at?'

Studio Engineer: 'They go here. If you do not use the mike-row-fone your sound will not be heard on the recording.'

Jimmy O'Bryant: Yeah! Thanks anyway, but I'll take my chances *without* one. I will yell real loud into the horn— like I always do. I prefer the good old ways.'

Studio Engineer: 'If you do not use the mike-row-fone (and can we please start calling it a Mother -freakin' MIKE from now on, for Pete's sake) then your voice will not come out on the recording we'll be fixing. How many times I gotta tell you, Jimmy?'

Jimmy O'Bryant: 'Okey dokey smokey! Keep your hair on! I will use the darned thing... but I don't like it.'

Studio engineer: 'DO NOT get too close to it! It takes a hundred volts to get that thing to work. There is a huge current running through those wires. It will probably kill you if you so much as touch the thing. So just stand in front of it — then do your best to sing and play into the *thingo*.'

Jimmy O'Bryant: 'But I normally bop around when I sing... I

need to be able to keep moving while I perform. How can I stay put? How can I stand still and sing into this bitch? This is all messed up daddy-oh! I prefer the big horn.'

Studio Engineer: 'Yes, I know you do, Jimmy. But times they are a-changin'. You'll be just fine. Stand yo'self six inches from the MIKE and keep your eyes closed. Everything will be hunky plunky.'

On top of all that business, there was *another* recent development that Jimbo had to get his head around. You see, up until 1925 the record size/speed known as the 78rpm had not been standardized! This meant that records could be 'spun' at whatever speed *you* wanted them to be 'spun' at. I'll explain that in a moment. But at this stage I just want you to know that Jimmy's new record was going to be the first *ever* disc that would be cut at a consistent and standardized speed. And the speed that was chosen was 78rpm. Consequently, O'Bryant didn't *just* sing into the *first* voice microphone... he also cut the first 'industry standard' record!

Before Jimmy O'Bryant stepped into that primitive Chicago recording studio to make rock 'n' roll history – disc buyers, in other words, ordinary people like you and I, purchased records that could— and in fact, they would *need to be* — played at different speeds. Perhaps I should explain *this* curious fact to younger readers: because those born in the compact disc, MP3, and streaming era will not know about *record speeds*. Older readers are permitted to skip this section if they wish — or use it for revision purposes. But here we go: back in the golden days of rock 'n' roll vinyl records came in three 'sizes.' We had 45's (they were 7-inches across — though you could get bigger) and they spun on a record-player turntable at 45 revolutions per minute. (45 RPM.) All records had grooves in them. A needle was required to 'pick up' the vibrations from the track and transfer the sound to the phonographic horn that was like the one we've just been speaking about, but *this* phonographic horn was for *output* and not input. Later, the recorded sounds would be transferred to the *loud-speakers* (but only once they'd been invented.) Most singles ran at 45 RPM, but we also had long players – these spun at 33 ⅓ revolutions per minute (don't ask me why, I'm not *that much* of a geek). Long players were (mostly) twelve inches across (though not always.) Eventually, all 'albums' would be recorded as long-playing 33 ⅓ RPM discs. But you could also purchase a 7-inch disc and play it at 33 ⅓ RPM. Such discs would contain a few more tracks (say, two or three) so became known across the industry as extended plays (or players) thus the abbreviation E.P. Elvis (RCA) issued 28 of these extended-play EPs between 1956 and 1967. It's a little-known fact that E.P.s were his *premium* sellers.

My Surrey pals and I had access to old-style 78 RPM records– these were the discs that spun at 78 revolutions per minute, and we usually bought them at jumble sales (bring-and-buy.) Me and my pals ignored these discs (as sound recordings) because the music they contained was boring (it pre-dated rock 'n' roll.) But, since 78's were fabricated out of the most breakable substance known to all mankind (shellac) we used them as makeshift *Frisbees* or, better still, as targets for air-gun practice. I recall that 78 RPM shellac discs made a very satisfactory shattering sound when hit by a whizzing pellet from a gat-gun. Our bedroom record players still managed 78's — if we ever wanted them to do such a thing (which we didn't) and I remember that we could 'change the speeds' on our turntable decks well into the 1970's.

This is how it worked: We'd check the speed of the disc (it was usually written on the centre, 'label'). We'd place our record onto the platter (which is the central 'round part' of a turntable.) We'd flick a switch to select the correct speed (78, 45 or 33⅓ revs per minute.) Then we'd place the needle onto the edge of the record and play away. We'd made a conscious effort to check and change the speed for each fresh disc. Oh, and every now and then we'd use a comb-sized black velvet brush to collect-up all the fluff, because fluff made the needle act peculiarly: that fluff collected onto vinyl from out of the atmosphere and became accumulated by static.

Almost always, while functioning as a DJ in the early 1970s, me and my pals would play at least one song at the *wrong* tempo. The paying audience would laugh a lot at this mistake, they'd clap their hands and yell expletive-strewn witticisms. However, occasionally, playing a number at an incorrect speed could provoke an extremely dangerous reaction. Imagine if a Teddy Boy requested a *special song* for his sweetheart and you, the idiot DJ, ruined his chance of wall-humping his 'gal' by playing *Someone Else's Baby* (by Adam Faith) at 78RPM thus making Faith sound like Pinky (the red pig) out of Pinky & Perky. It'd be a mistake that could cost the DJ a good kicking, when loading-up the van. As seasoned DJ's we'd handle record speed blunders with effective and quick-thinking patter that would flatter the gal and congratulate the guy on his sartorial elegance! If this didn't work, we'd wait until his mates had taken him home before we loaded the van.

But, anyway, let's head back to 1925 and ask the older generation to re-join us, (they've probably been having a nap, so give them a nudge) because we've now finished our taster-class on record speeds.

If you were lucky, back in the mid 20's, and you possessed a record player (few folks did) and you managed to find a decent disc to play on the platter (even *more* unlikely) you'd have to fiddle around adjusting the speed to get the playback *just right*. And that's because every disc was recorded at a *different* speed! It's a good job I was not a DJ back in the twenties because I imagine I would have earned a solid gold kicking *every night*.

In the 1920's, prior to Jimmy O'Bryant's historic recording, this kind of thing was considered 'normal'. But the record industry admitted it was a ridiculous situation. And, frankly, it was. The record industry agreed that there should be just one size/speed of record. They settled on 78 revolutions per minute on a 12-inch disc. And this arrangement seemed just right.

So, when Jimmy went into the studio on that momentous day, his recording process was at the forefront of science. He recorded onto a newly standardized, globally recognised format – 78 rpm. And used the first electronic recording mike.

Although fortune was not *altogether* smiling on Jimmy O'Bryant (the record sunk without trace – and poor Jimmy died three years later) – but he *did* possess the unerring good sense and truly immense foresight to name his rag-tag washboard 'n' jug companions the 'Chicago Skifflers.' So, thanks to Jimmy, and these new innovations, the word 'Skiffle' entered our musical lexicon.

9

YOU CANNOT SHAKE ME, DADDY-O

After Jimmy O'Bryant, the second most important character in the history of Skiffle was not born in Arkansas, Illinois, or Kentucky. He was not *even* born in America. The next most important figure in Skiffle was born in Glasgow, Scotland. But the guy was educated in East Ham, London. Consequently, we can allow him temporary membership in our story of Rocking Surrey.

According to the Guinness Book of British Hit Singles this man – known across the world as the 'King of Skiffle' – was 'Britain's most successful and influential recording artist before The Beatles.' His name was Tony. But the world would know him as Lonnie Donegan.

Lonnie Donegan started on his lengthy career by playing banjo in a traditional jazz band led by the legendary trombonist Chris Barber. (Barber would eventually become an influential founding-father of British rhythm and blues – as we shall discover later on.) It was said that Barber had learned about young Donegan's talent on the banjo through gossip. Barber, relying solely on this rumour and an intuitive feeling, invited Donegan for an audition that would alter both their lives *forever*. The catch is that Donegan had never tried his hand at the instrument before! Remember, the person leading this make-or-break audition had received training from Alexis Korner at the Guild-hall School of Music. But Donegan couldn't honestly say he'd ever fingerpicked the cut-gut, let alone claw-hammered a hornpipe out in front of experts. Somebody bearing less self-assurance and braggadocio would have been simply terrified by the prospect of such an audition. Not Donegan, though! How he got away with it is beyond comprehension. But he managed to win them over, *somehow*. Donegan handled the most stressful audition of his professional career with a smile on his face and an arsenal of confidence. It was this boldness that would later bring him renown, respect, and fortune. And let's not overlook the fact that Chris Barber was a shrewd operator. He likely saw right through the brag and swagger to identify the audience appeal of the young man's winning smile and positive attitude. In other words, it was Donegan's charismatic attitude, his over-eager bubbly personality, rather than his terrible fingerpicking, which helped him land the spot. Donegan consequently earned himself a crucial position in the Chris Barber organisation.

———

Tony Donegan's stint with the Chris Barber organisation was cut short when he was called-up for national service, in 1949. But he managed to turn *even that* hiccup to advantage. Donegan's military experience compelled him to live and work in close contact with American troops. And the proximity provided Donegan with access to some of the most exciting sounds he'd ever heard, *via* the American Forces Network radio. So, by the time he returned to British 'Civvy Street' in 1952, Donegan's head was stuffed with musical ideas and artistic inspiration; he felt driven by the sounds he'd heard on American radio.

Subsequently, upon his return to the fold, and exploiting his time with Chris Barber to his advantage, the freshly inspired Donegan earned a place touring the British Isles, opening for the American rhythm and blues hero, Lonnie Johnson.

Lonnie Johnson was born at the tail-end of the 19th century in New Orleans, Louisiana and was raised in a family of musicians. He had studied violin, piano, and guitar. In his works like '*Racketeers*'

Blues,' 'Hard Times Ain't Gone Nowhere,' and 'Fine Booze and Heavy Dues,' Lonnie Johnson had successfully portrayed the societal issues that metropolitan African Americans faced every day. He experienced this type of life *himself*, a victim of the Great Depression, he had moved to Chicago after touring with the Bessie Smith band.

After World War II, Lonnie Johnson made the transition to rhythm 'n' blues, and on the back of a string of R&B hits that were recorded for King records (Cincinnati) he came over to England to tour, cleverly calculating that by adding an English 'name' to his line-up he'd probably increase the chances of success for any future tours. Tony Donegan was chosen as his supporting artist.

After the tour, Donegan chose to adopt Johnson's first name, as an homage, because the Depression Era musician, who was by then in his mid-50s and towards the latter end of a lengthy musical career, had been such an inspirational influence.

So, after Johnson returned to America, the newly self-christened *Lonnie* Donegan set out to entertain the people of old London with a variety of blues songs that had been motivated, largely, by African American struggles on the other side of the wide, wide ocean. Along with a hand-picked washboard player, a tea chest bassist, and spanking his own shabby Spanish guitar, Donegan performed the genre of music that had been recorded by performers such as Lead Belly and Woody Guthrie.

After a few noteworthy covers and numerous live performances, Donegan received record deal offers from Decca, EMI, and later, Pye. He even went on tour in America. Taking *their music* back to where it had originated!

When Lonnie Donegan returned to the UK (in 1956) he began working on his first album, to be titled the 'Lonnie Donegan Showcase.' It achieved remarkable success. As a result of his album's accomplishment, eager amateurs around the nation began to be involved in what the newspapers called 'the Skiffle craze.' Everyone wanted to start their own Skiffle outfit. All teen boys wanted to copy what Lonnie Donegan had so brilliantly pulled-off. Youngsters up-and-down the country believed that *anyone* could break into the music industry if an old boy with a worn-out washboard and a very rudimentary musical ability could succeed. For every average British suburban youngster, Donegan made musical escape seem attainable.

Skiffle was the first musical craze that British culture experienced. And Skiffle was jam-packed with D.I.Y. amusement. And for this reason, there was a lot of interest in the genre. Plus, it was dance music. That means that when you played it, no matter how good you were, girls in tight skirts would come over to check you out. Skiffle was appealing. Skiffle had good vibe. Skiffle was seductive. Most significantly, Skiffle proved to be intuitive, thus becoming vital for all those budding artists out in the 'real world' who wanted to become pop stars but didn't have the money or, indeed, the talent; (everyone knew that Donegan bluffed his way into the game.) Skiffle instruments were dirt cheap (or free). If you couldn't afford a clapped-out guitar and a rusty harmonica you could make-do with Mother's cooking pans and lids. No double bass? String-up a broom handle and attach it to a cardboard box. No trumpet? Use a plastic kazoo. No drums? Tap granny's washboard. That's why skiffle became the first teen fad.

In 1958 there were at least 50,000 amateur Skiffle bands in Britain. And that's probably an under-estimate. Here's a list of a few artists who started their musical careers playing Skiffle: the aforesaid Alexis Korner, Ronnie Wood, Alex Harvey, Mick Jagger, Roger Daltrey, Jimmy Page, Ritchie Blackmore, Robin Trower, Barry Gibb, and David Gilmour. The list goes *on and on*. Without Skiffle there would have been *no* suburban rock music. I cannot emphasize this point enough. Without Skiffle there would have been *no British music scene*. You might have heard of a 1956 Skiffle outfit called 'The Quarrymen' (named after the Quarry Bank School.) The Quarrymen were formed by *another* failed banjo-player, though *this* failed banjo-player was John Lennon. Local musicians Paul McCartney and George Harrison joined *his* Quarrymen Skiffle outfit. Yes, that's how important Skiffle would be in the history of rock 'n' roll.

10

A ROCKIN' BAND, I HAVE TO CONFESS

At about this time, in Hadley Road, Mitcham (close to my hometown) one of these new Skiffle bands (an ensemble named 'The Mourners') was founded.

Therefore, we must get ourselves back to the around-the-block drive in Carshalton and I apologise for taking a long*ish* detour — I know it took us across decades and *via* record speeds —but hopefully it has been worth it.

You might remember that David had driven us to a lead-singer's house in his creamy-green Ford Anglia. And you might also remember I was in the back of the car. And you might remember this had taken place in Carshalton. Well, I recall gazing through the mucky glass of the green car, as I tried to catch a glimpse of the famous man.

'Can you see him?' David had asked.

'No, but I can see the front curtains.'

'Are they moving?' David asked.

'Nope.'

Dianne shook her head.

'Maybe he's out,' suggested David.

The Mourners played their gigs in old church halls and grubby Scout huts around the Carshalton area. They made rare excursions into Wallington and Colliers Wood. But Carshalton was their main stomping ground.

'Perhaps The Mourners headed over to Wallington,' David told us.

———

A young trumpet player named Thomas Gray had started *this* fledgling group with a younger brother, the drummer named Pete. I later discovered it was *his house* we had driven-up to in David's mucus-coloured car. Thomas and Pete Gray had previously played with a promising guitarist named Robert Davis in a Boy Scout band. Robert Davis was very heavily influenced by the ultra-successful Skiffle combo known as 'The Vipers Skiffle Group.'

During the skiffle era of the mid to late 1950s, The Vipers Skiffle Group, later known as The Vipers, was a top British band and the one to emulate. The Vipers project had a major impact on the careers of television host Wally Whyton, the music producer George Martin (who would later be called the 'fifth' Beatle), and members of the rockabilly guitar-band The Shadows.

The Vipers Skiffle Group had origins in London in 1956 when Whyton, Johnny Martyn (who was the coffee bar manager and founding member of the Original Soho Skiffle Group), and pal, a baritone-voiced wire salesperson named Jean van den Bosch, started jamming as a trio of singer-guitarists. Freddy Lloyd replaced Bosch in 1958. At the coffee bar, they jammed with the songwriting jazz musician Mike Pratt (he played the part of detective Jeff Randall out of Randall and Hopkirk (Deceased), and singer Tommy Hicks, later to be known as Tommy Steele. By the way, Lionel Bart, the composer of Tommy Steele's hit '*Rock with the Caveman*' and more notably, the creator of the musical Oliver! was a close friend of Pratt, so also connected to the 2i's. coffee-bar skiffle scene. He'd go on to write some of their music. An audition with the freshly promoted 'head' of Parlophone Records' George Martin (Martin saw them playing at the 2i's) in September 1956 landed the Vipers Skiffle Group with a valuable recording contract.

The Vipers Skiffle Group's second single, '*Don't You Rock Me Daddy-O*' produced by George Martin, reached number 10 in the UK Singles Chart in 1957. Whyton was credited with writing the number, but in truth the song was an adjustment of a folk standard known as '*Sail Away Ladies*' which was recorded in the 1920s by Uncle Dave Macon, the son of a Tennessee Confederate soldier.

In 1957, the Vipers released their version of the Liverpool folk-song *Maggie May*, the first pop song to be banned by the BBC. Of course, the BBC ban gave the band (and their song) a tremendous push up the charts and into the public eye.

The Vipers Skiffle Group and Lonnie Donegan were rivals on different labels. Donegan had bigger hits but copied Whyton's style. However, the Vipers' version of Cumberland Gap, a 19th century Appalachian folk song, made the UK Top 10 and out-performed the Donegan version. If you don't know the song, check-out the modern-day rendition by David Rawlings. It is exceptional! The band's final charting hit "*Streamline Train*" followed their success with Cumberland Gap.

The Vipers Skiffle Group continued to record, and for a time anyway, were Britain's biggest stage attraction, second only to Donegan in terms of Skiffle-based success. Whyton and Johnny Martyn made an album for the U.S. market titled 'The Original Soho Skiffle Group', that purported to be a showcase for traditional folk and blues, and with sleeve notes written by the Wall Street Journal musicologist Nat Hentoff. But the Skiffle craze was about to fade, and by 1958 the Vipers had dropped their 'Skiffle Group' designation.

As (simply) The Vipers, the line-up had included the Geordie banjo-player Hank Marvin (who'd named himself after rockabilly star Marvin Rainwater), fellow Geordie-boy guitarist and songwriter Bruce Welch who, although born in Sussex, was raised by an Auntie on Tyneside and attended the same school as Hank (Rutherford Grammar), the North London bassist Jet Harris, and the London

(Hampstead) drummer Tony Meehan, who'd been working success-fully in a cabaret band in Al Burnett's Stork Club. These musicians would go on to form The Shadows and would someday collaborate with Cliff Richard. The Vipers disintegrated when their recording contract ran out, in 1960. Whyton moved on to a successful radio and television presenting career.

So, back to my home patch of Carshalton then: Rob Davis had successfully launched a Vipers-style band and had begun to punt his sounds around the Morden and Mitcham area. His Vipers-style act was the main rival to The Mourners. By 1960, the *actual* 'Vipers Skiffle Group' morphed into what we now recognise as the world-famous 'Shadows' who began playing instrumental guitar-based surf sounds at the 2 i's. Hearing this news, young Rob Davies was quick to follow and started to play similar *surf sounds* with his Vipers-style (*now* Shadows-style) band. Davies, always ready and willing to follow a trend, re-named his copycat band; not surprisingly choosing 'The Apaches' to cash-in the guitar-band's most famous song.

Rob Davies' Apaches had a *very* good drummer named Dave Mount, and mentioning Mount brings me neatly & conveniently back to explain a little more about Thomas Gray, the trumpet player with the Surrey Skiffle outfit known as 'The Mourners'. This group, slightly less successful than Rob Davies' Apaches, played the Carshalton area, offering traditional jazz (when required) or Skiffle (when it wasn't). For a neat party trick, Thomas Gray would put his trumpet aside and do a fairly good impersonation of Elvis on the microphone. The punters loved these Elvis impressions. 'The Mourn-ers' were a labour of love for Gray. He knew, in his heart-of-hearts, that his band *weren't going anywhere*. But Gray loved to perform. Music was his first passion.

Actually, when he'd left school, Gray sought a career in journal-ism. He even managed to get an attractive job with the cinema adver-tising agency Pearl & Dean. If you say the words 'Pearl & Dean' to anyone born in the 1950's they will answer by singing 'Da-da-da-da-da DAH-da-dah.' If you are a younger reader, this will mean *nothing*. But don't get freaked out if you try it on an old-timer: say Pearl & Dean and smile when they sing back da-da-da- DAH-da-dah You'll need to recall that during the golden age of rock 'n' roll, the *only* colour commercials we ever saw were *at the movies*. And Pearl and Dean ran colour adverts between features. A thrilling fanfare of noises would introduce the gorgeous commercials (right before the main film.) Their fanfare was: 'Da-da-da-da-da DAH-da-dah,' and the words 'Brought to you by Pearl & Dean' were writ large on the giant screen. It sounds pathetic, but that's the kind of thing that excited us back in the rock 'n' roll days.

Anyway, back to trumpeter Thomas Gray, who had landed a job with Pearl & Dean, well, music began to take over his life. He felt he couldn't do the Pearl & Dean job the justice it deserved so he quit the desirable position and moved to a more humdrum situation – working as a clerk at the gentleman's formal-wear outfitters, Moss Bros. The outfitter offered better salary and less exertion. Gray figured the enhanced pay would support his music and straightfor-ward work would mean he'd be able to concentrate his talents on his band.

In 1961, during the period when the Apache's Rob Davies was working with his drummer's Dad at a structural engineers in Croydon (making his way from office boy to wages clerk) – his band, the 'Apaches', became successful on the Surrey circuit–they even started to earn a good reputation on the wider surf and Skiffle scene.

But, although the 'Shadows' cover-band image was working for them *at first*, it eventually lost its flavour (on the bedpost!) Conse-quently, the band began to fall apart. Rob and Dave Mount continued playing, first in 'The Barracudas' then later in a group named the 'Remainder'. And when the 'Remainder' required a new bass player, in stepped a guy named Ray Stiles, whose Father worked with Rob at the structural engineers.

While all this was going on, Thomas Gray's 'Mourners' were playing more-and-more rock 'n' roll to Carshalton audiences. And Gray's ever-popular Elvis vocal impersonations started to become the *main part* of the show. The audience loved that rock 'n' roll.

One day, in an emergency, the 'Mourners' needed a lead guitarist at short-notice. Gray invited his old mate Rob Davis to help out. Don't forget that, for years, these bands had been rivals on the Carshalton

Surrey and South London circuit. But now, *finally*, they joined together. And the combo made sense.

'The Mourners' with Rob Davis on guitar and (their) drummer Dave Mount – (he replaced Pete) renamed themselves as 'M.U.D.' which is the acronym for Merton Urban District (the local authority for Morden and Carshalton.) With the start of MUD, Thomas began calling himself 'Les' Gray. They played their first gig as MUD in 1968 at London's Marquee Club (run from '58-1962 as a jazz and Skiffle establishment located in the Marquee Ballroom which was, basically, the basement of the Academy Cinema in Oxford Street). MUD soon became a regular attraction at the Marquee. Incidentally, the Marquee was established by an ambitious Lancashire-born accountant named Harold Pendleton who loved jazz so much that he became the secretary of the National Jazz Federation. Pendleton is said to have encouraged Barber's banjo playing Lonnie Donegan to record Lead Belly's *'Rock Island Line'* thereby motivating the Skiffle craze. Pendleton (with his pal, the jazz trombonist Chris Barber) originated the National Jazz Festival, in 1961, held in Richmond Athletic Grounds (London Scottish) in Surrey. We'll take a look at this festival later and Pendelton's involvement a bit later.

Rob Davis was already showing signs of promise as a songwriter. (I *guarantee* you will recognize some of his songwriting hits and I'll leave you to look them up in your own time) but MUD's first single (for CBS) was written by Davis and cashed-in on the 'Flower Power' trend. If you are a fan of the brilliant rock mockumentary 'Spinal Tap,' you will *instantly* recognise the first MUD song. Basically, it's the Tap song titled '(Listen to the) Flower People.' MUD's song was cynically aimed at the 'flower-power' market that rose after the 'Summer of Love' and the band released it in a futile attempt to cash-in. MUD released two more poorly-selling singles before the Sixties were out.

By 1971, it looked as if the game was over for MUD. They felt frustrated with themselves. They were all washed up. And hadn't even *properly* started. They never seemed to be able to ride the crest of any wave long enough to please an audience. (So much for being surfer-dudes!) These musicians seemed to be two-steps behind all the *other* bands. They were forever playing catch-up! They played trad-jazz when it was past its sell-by-date, they endured with Skiffle when the trend was dead-and-buried, then they bravely offered rockabilly during the psychedelic-pop period. Finally, they'd played hippy-trippy flower power sounds while the Beatles took over the world with Mersey beat. Yes, MUD were Surrey's Cinderella's of popular music.

———

Luckily for us, the prospering song-writing production team comprising of Londoner Nicky Chinn and his Australian pal Mike Chapman (known as 'Chinnichap') were waiting in the wings like two scary, fairy, lairy, godmothers. And Chinnichap were about to sprinkle their brand of pixie dust on MUD and grant them their fairy-tale wishes.

The Chinnichap team had already focussed on a band known as 'The Sweet' and were seeking another similar act to manage. Ultimately, their main purpose was to manipulate the musicians they discovered. They were in search of musicians with similar backgrounds to 'The Sweet' — artists who can be *moulded*. Chinn & Chapman were on the look-out for musicians who had 'been around a bit' and preferred older guys 'n' gals who had 'worked' the circuit. Grown-up musicians were more desirable than whippersnappers because they didn't argue back: they just got on with things. Pus, experienced guys could pick up an instrument and play it. That was a huge benefit. Plus, experienced guys turned up for rehearsals on time and possessed stage confidence. Chinnichap were *only* interested in seasoned pros. In all likelihood, I don't know this for sure, but it's a hunch and maybe it's unfair, but I they sought bands who'd 'given up' on themselves: *has-beens* like MUD. Chinnichap liked to address failure. They enjoyed re-modelling ailing bands into something new –for them, it was like playing with plasticine. And, probably, the most hard-done-musicians were the most fun to re-mould— because they'd do everything and *anything* Chinnichap asked of them. They didn't mind losing their dignity in the process.

'The Sweet' were very much like MUD to begin with. Their origins could be traced back to a little-known British soul band named 'Wainwright's Gentlemen.' In 1964 this small-time band won an area heat in a nationally advertised contest. They even managed to beat Roger Daltrey's skiffle band 'The Detours' in the competition. And although 'Wainwright's Gentlemen' came fifth overall, the competition provided the artists with experience and publicity, so at that stage, they decided to press-on with their musical careers. With drummer Mick Tucker and Hounslow boy Ian Gillan (better known, later, as lead singer for Deep Purple and Black Sabbath) 'Wainwright's Gentlemen' made valiant efforts to succeed.

But when Gillan left 'The Sweet' in May 1965 to join 'Episode Six' (he was briefly replaced by a female vocalist named Ann Cully, by the way!) the Wainwright's Gentlemen project started to get *the wobbles*. It was like an unruly grocery trolley on a steep slope to oblivion. The band eventually careered into a ditch. And broke up in 1968.

From the ashes of Wainwright's Gentlemen only the singer (Connolly) and drummer (Tucker) remained. Subsequently, the two survivors formed a new outfit called 'The Sweetshop.' They pinched the bass guitarist from a local band 'The Army' (Steve Priest) — and started to play the busy South London pub circuit first as 'The Sweetshop' then later rebranded as 'The Sweet'

The Sweet's début single, '*Slow Motion*' (July 1968) failed to chart. And even a shiny deal with Parlophone failed to get them any notice. Their trademark sound combined the rich vocal harmony style of 'The Hollies' with the 1960's bubble-gum imagery of 'The Monkees.' The Sweet were often compared to the kids cartoon band 'The Archies.'

The Sweet (like MUD) were blindly and eccentrically anachronistic. It wasn't until their appearance on the TV show 'Lift Off' playing their bubble-gum number '*Funny Funny*' (from the '*Funny How Sweet Co-Co Can Be*' album, issued 1971) that things really *started* for the band. And it was all down to the remarkable Chinnichap formula.

From 1970 to 1978 Chinnichap's 'Dreamland' record-making

machine churned out nineteen hit records, including five number one singles. They were every bit as effective as anything we have seen since – they were as successful as Stock Aitken & Waterman and *more* influential than Simon Cowell. They were the hit factory of the Seventies.

So, of course, when MUD's Les, Ray, Dave, and Rob were offered a chance to work with the famous Chinnichap team, they eagerly signed a contract. (Mickie Most's RAK records were part of the deal.) MUD was furnished a new *image makeover* (fluorescent drape coats, drainpipe trousers, brothel creepers, and duck's-arse hair-styles) and given a catchy new song to perform, titled '*Crazy*'. The single was released in early 1973 and went to #12 in the UK charts. Both 'Crazy' and their next single '*Hypnosis*' were based on the tango beat. The boys in MUD weren't too keen on the tango beat. But did as they were told. They got on with things. By '73 they found their original rock 'n' roll sound when they issued their third RAK single, '*Dynamite*'. This number reached #4 in the British charts.

1974 saw the release of MUD's biggest hit, '*Tiger Feet*'. The song shot them to the top of the hit parade! Which is where they remained for four weeks. '*Tiger Feet*' became the bestselling record of the year. It was only knocked off the number one slot by fellow RAK artist Suzi Quatro and the Chinnichap written '*Devil Gate Drive*.'

MUD's last number one single, '*Oh Boy*' (written by Buddy Holly's manager Norman Petty) was released in April 1975 – at about the same time that MUD split from the Chinnichap hit-making factory. This decision became the end of the road for MUD. The band free-wheeled for a few years after leaving Chinnichap– living on past glories and fading reputations. The band finally disbanded in 1982. One member of the band went on to achieve greater things, the song-writer Rob Davis. Look him up!

MUD are the very definition of an industrious Surrey based rock 'n' roll outfit. That's why I took extra time to talk about their early career and took you along in my Tardis! I apologise! My aim was to detail the journey of a band that had jazz origins in the early Skiffle era, then experimented with surf sounds, and eventually established a simple but effective rock 'n' roll formula that worked for them. And

MUD never stopped delivering *this* style for the remainder of their careers. Moreover, all members of the band were born in Surrey and came from the working-class council-house background I was raised in. They practised in a hut on Mitcham Common. They stayed loyal to their local area. And a web of family partnerships laced their lives in intricate ways. They went to the *same* schools, joined the *same* youth clubs, and worked with the *same* employers. Their ambitions and talents were never inflated. Their demeanour and unassuming work-ethics matched the ho-hum surroundings of their humble Carshalton beginnings. It's true they extended – as musical artists –*beyond* the home-patch, but MUD never denied their origins. They were proud to be Surrey suburban music makers. The majority of the other artists I will look at in this book will have had similar suburban ties and underpinnings: so, MUD was a suitable place to start.

Sadly, MUD drummer Dave Mount passed-away in mysterious circumstances – his body was taken to St Helier Hospital in Rose Hill on December 2nd, 2006. Vocalist Les Gray moved, with wife Carol, to the Algarve in Portugal in 1992. He died of a heart attack in Lagos in 2004, aged 58.

11

IT AIN'T A GROOVE

Before I close the report on the 1950's Skiffle scene I ought to look in finer detail at Cliff Richard because, along with Tommy Steele and Terry Dene, Cliff was the closest we'd get to crowning a British Elvis! All these artists sprang from the 2i's Skiffle scene but only Cliff made it through to the *other side* to become an enduring rock 'n' roll entertainer. (Steele conquered the West End theatre while Dene abandoned British pop in the wake of a run of bad publicity, in 1964, to become an evangelist.)

Now, I know what you're thinking: *didn't Cliff originate in India? Isn't he from Lucknow?* You're wondering what this has to do with Surrey. But, you see, Harry Webb was born in Lucknow, yes, but his family moved to England when he was eight, and for a while Harry lived in Carshalton, Surrey, just like me and the lads from MUD.

As Cliff admitted, in his autobiography titled 'The Dreamer,' "*Things were hard in Carshalton...*" This comes from a person born on the outskirts of Calcutta! Just take that in for a moment!

Once his Father had obtained a reliable job, Harry Webb's family moved to council housing in the Hertfordshire 'burb of Waltham Cross (then later, to Cheshunt who now 'claim' Cliff as *theirs*.) But, sure, Harry Webb (later to be known as Cliff Richard) attended the Stanley Park Junior School in Carshalton, Surrey.

American readers might be surprised to hear this next bit (because Cliff never *broke* into the States), but the artist dominated the pre-Beatles British music scene of the late 1950s-60s. His '58 hit *Move It* was Britain's first authentically homegrown rock 'n' roll number.

Over an extraordinary career Cliff scored more UK Top 20 hits than any other artist. Indeed, he holds the record, along with Presley, as the only act to make the UK singles charts in all its first six decades (1950s–2000s). He achieved 14 UK #1 singles and is the only singer to have had a #1 UK single in five consecutive decades. Yet Sir Cliff is what we call, in England, a *marmite* brand. (Marmite is a gooey substance, yeast extract in a brown jar, that Brits spread on toast at tea-time. Some loathe the stuff, while others seem obsessed by it.) It's the same with Cliff: he's a marmite brand. You either have enormous affection for *everything* that Cliff represents, or you find you can't endure anther moment of his oleaginous, self-congratulatory, pontificating posture (I think you can guess which camp I fall into!) Nonetheless, whatever your attitude to the marmite brand, Cliff is the quintessential hero of teatime rock 'n' roll. If you're unsure why we Brits both adore and despise him in equal measure, consider his self-idolizing performance in the 1973 British-made film *Take Me High*, then, once you've puked into a sick bucket, think about him *spontaneously* entertaining the crowds on Wimbledon Tennis Final day. Don't you think Sir Cliff personifies the *essence* of solipsistic narcissism that defines whimsical Englishness?

Anyhow, back to the rock 'n' roll years: Harry Webb's Dad bought him a guitar when he was sixteen and like many young lads he strode into the burgeoning Skiffle scene without a *scooby-doo* (Cockney rhyming slang for clue) but with bags of self-confidence. (He later admitted he 'busked' that instrument and held it in photographs to 'look good.')

Harry formed his first Skiffle band, The Quintones, when still at school, 1957. After, he went to sing with the somewhat more successful Dick Teague Skiffle Group.

After Dick Teague, Harry's backing band were The Planets. But in

1958, a guy named Ian Samwell heard Harry Webb performing with his 'Planets' at the 2i's Coffee Bar and seemed much impressed by what he witnessed. So, he asked to join Webb's outfit as their future guitarist. Just after he joined, and probably *because* of his participation, the band was restructured and renamed The Drifters.

Samwell went on to write Cliff's first hit, '*Move It*' (apparently written on a Green Line bus en *route* to a rehearsal). The number was recorded for Columbia Graphophone (sic) Company (it later became E.M.I.) with Cliff on vocals. It has Terry Smart on drums, and Ian Samwell on guitar. Surprising fact: Samwell produced the undeniably 'American sounding' hit *A Horse with No Name,* in 1971. The song was written *with* Dewey Bunnell, who is another Englishman. Dewey went to school in Bushy Park, England (near Richmond, Surrey) with Gerry Beckley, as did their bandmate Dan Peek. We'll be looking into the American camps in Bushy Park (just over the border with Surrey) a little later.

But back to Harry Webb and his (temporary) band project known as the Drifters: a concert promoter named Harry Greatorex offered them a chance of a big show but he didn't like the name 'Drifters' which was probably a relief to *everyone*. The musicians were doubtless aware that Clyde McPhatter's mega-successful doo-wop outfit The Drifters had been named by Atlantic Records boss Ahmet Ertegun, a man you wouldn't want to argue with, *way* back in 1953. *Their* first hit under The Drifters trademark was *Money Honey*, issued the same year.

Greatorex said he'd prefer it if their band project used the lead singer's name, like Bill Haley and his Comets or Buddy Holly and the Crickets. So, Webb, Samwell, and other band members deliberated around a table in a pub and came-up with Cliff which they thought sounded rockier than Harry (although they obviously hadn't heard of 'Old Harry Rocks,' a beauty spot in Dorset. Myth has it that the Devil, in old English folk lore known euphemistically as 'Old Harry,' slept on the stack of rocks, and 'lured' the wicked and vulnerable into his fiery bosom.) In my humble opinion, Harry Rocks would've been a far better stage name, but what do I know? Accordingly, they used

Cliff because it sounded rocky, and they chose 'Richard' because it might remind fans of Little Richard (*actually* named Richard Wayne Penniman... but who knew?)

12

THE KINGDOM OF SURREY

Long before Elvis and long before George III (I mention him because he was the 'first' King of the United Kingdom) there was a King of Surrey. It seems extraordinary, doesn't it, that Surrey (the County) was a kingdom. The Kingdom of Surrey!

My family moved from Carshalton to the suburban village of Cheam. The suburban area of Cheam sits approximately 11 miles south-west of Charing Cross and consists of three distinct parts: North Cheam, Cheam Village and South Cheam. We lived in the *less* 'posh' bit where most aspiring middle-class families moved into: North Cheam.

Cheam Village is-and-was the 'grandest bit' with a village-green character and charming 'Kent-like' timber-framed buildings including the famous Whitehall House, a building that's rumoured to have been used by Queen Elizabeth I to hold impromptu council meetings. Cheam's 'Whitehall' was once the home of the oldest private prep school in the entire country, the much-celebrated Cheam School, founded in 1645. (In 1934 the school moved to its present site at Beenham Court, on the borders of Hampshire but it's always been a Surrey institution.)

Cheam (originally known as 'Cegeham') was once a centre for pottery (known around the world as *Surrey Whiteware*, due to the *silvery* firing clays used in the process and collected nearby.) Cheam was a tiny settlement and, for centuries, it clung to existence, rather than became the kind of fully prosperous village it ought to have been, surrounded, as it was, by fine meadows and rich woodlands.

In the mid-16th century, the outlying areas of Cheam were handed to King Henry VIII. Yes, Henry, the fat King who got through six wives. You may already know that King Henry loved *bling* –and created several awe-inspiring palaces *for himself* on the outskirts of London. One of his bling palaces (the blingiest of all) was Nonsuch.

In 1538 Henry VIII began work on this truly ambitious residence. A church and most of the village of Cuddington had to be destroyed to construct the giant fantasy dwelling. Henry also swiped acres of land from local peasants – to make room for an adjoining Great Park.

Unlike Henry's other palaces – this was built from scratch. It wasn't an old castle given a make-over by a design team brought over from the continent. No, Nonsuch would be built *from plan* and fashioned to out-rival all the other Palaces of Europe. It was set to be the ultimate celebration of power, wealth, and majesty. If you've ever visited Hampton Court and have enjoyed the wonder of *those* Tudor buildings, you can (only) imagine what Nonsuch Palace must have been like. Nonsuch was much bigger, much grander, and more prestigious in every way.

Cheam didn't really begin to exist as 'a place' until Henry's Nonsuch. It was such a vast structure that it required hundreds of servants and labourers to work within the halls and grounds. So, Cheam grew through connection with the palace, and the village gradually spread itself out across the meadows and woodlands, expanding ever wider to service the requirements of Nonsuch.

Nonsuch stayed in royal hands for a few years after Henry VIII's death. But eventually a high-society hooker named Lady Castlemaine (Babs to her friends) got her greedy fingers on the great pile.

The locally born diarist John Evelyn (who lived in Wotton, Surrey, 1620) – described Lady Barbara Castlemaine as the 'curse of the nation.' John Evelyn was, when you come down to it, a seventeenth century gossip-columnist — a bit like his more famous contemporary, Samuel Pepys. These diarists were the celebrity *bloggers* of their period. Evelyn started to get terribly worked up about Lady Castle-maine — reporting about her wild indiscretions in his diaries. He described her wicked extravagances, her undeniably foul temper, and her legendary promiscuity.

Babs came about the Nonsuch property in 1670, through dodgy dealing. King Charles II of England — the restored Merry Monarch (whose Dad, Charles I, was executed at the climax of the English Civil War) paid Babs off by giving her the crumbling edifice as hush money. We never found out what she 'knew' about Charles II to be hushed in this way, but it's a fair bet it was a scandal that could bring down a monarchy.

Babs Castlemaine had the Palace demolished twelve years after getting hold of the place. She had the building materials sold to pay off huge gambling debts. Nothing now remains of this once lavish Palace. The Nonsuch Mansion you can visit these days is a mere folly. Today's building is a Grade 2 listed mock-Tudor Gothic house built in 1802. But if you look carefully, into the porch of the folly, there is one block of stone from the original Tudor Palace. The inscription on the stone reads '1543 Henry VIII in the 35th year of reign'.

To this day, the park at Nonsuch (the pleasant grounds that surrounded the now demolished palace) is an important amenity for the people of Cheam. As kids, we often walked to the park to collect conkers, eat picnics, or see the famous peacocks. For us, it was a reasonable stroll up St Dunstan's Hill. A genuinely nice place to visit (it still is.) Those peacocks fascinated me. Pea-fowl were kept in the grounds of the Mansion – perhaps maintained as a reminder that this place, once-upon-a-time, had regal connections.

———

Although I have no scientific evidence to support my next theory, I nevertheless hypothesise that Surrey society during the rock 'n' roll years was composed of three categories of demographic:

1) the working-class *renters* of council homes who were content with their lot, these tended to produce 'punk' musicians

2) the working-class renters of council homes who were *not* content with their lot. Like my parents, they took-on hefty mortgages and moved away from the estates to become *home-owners*; these families tended to produce the 'art-school' types we'll examine in a while, and,

3) *professional middle classes* i.e., the stockbrokers, bankers, and the semi-titled indigenous 'old money' inhabitants of Surrey, who lived in opulent, sprawling, freehold properties and produced the 'public school' musicians we'll consider in a little while too

––––––

Many of my friends, other family members, and most of our neighbours were part of the *first* demographic; happy, upbeat people, who were comfortable leading 'council-house lives.' I had always been envious of *this* demographic group because they had more spending money than us, they always had fancier stuff, newer televisions, shinier fridges etc., and they had pockets of cash for nights out. Though, it was evident that my parents were destined to belong to the *second* demographic group because they became dissatisfied with 'council-house living' on Carshalton's sprawling St. Helier estate. So, at great detriment to their financial and mental well-being, they moved into their *own property* in the suburbs, at Cheam. It's probable they were subject to parental pressure, i.e., the type of emotional pressure that parents *still* place on offspring when it comes to societal and cultural norms. While my Mother's parents had passed away when she was young, and so she'd 'taken over' the rent of her parent's council home and raised her younger brother in the same house, my Father's parents resided in a handsome *freehold* 'property' on a decorative estate in Hampstead. The much-told family story was that my grandfather, the London cab driver, had been pressurised into purchasing *this* home (real estate) by my grandmother, who was of Romani (traveller) ancestry. My grandmother had felt that if they *genuinely* wanted to become full members of a cultured society, a society that *accepted* them, they'd have to *put down roots* and 'own land.' So, my Nan saved her 'pin money' and secretly put down a large deposit on an empty plot, making the decision a *fait accompli* for my grandfather, who was left with little choice but to accept the situation, invest in the land-property she desired, and work until his dying day to pay the loan off.

As I've already mentioned, my Mother's parents passed away when she was young, and I'm sure that the *only* woman that inspired my Mum (across her entire life, as far as I could tell) was her Mother-in-law, my Nan. My Mum dressed like my Nan. She grew herbs like my Nan. She cultured roses like my Nan. She practiced handicrafts like my Nan. She was abstemious and temperate, like my Nan. She regularly quoted my Nan. She lived frugally, like my Nan. My Mother was frequently compulsive and visionary, like my Nan. Yes, the most inspirational and influential female in my Mother's life, it's fair to say, was my Nan.

So, when my Nan told my parents they *ought to purchase property of their own*, it was the type of pressure they couldn't easily resist.

My parents, however, had another motive for leaving the St. Helier estate in Carshalton. Karolina, my sister, was on her way. And our two-up two-down council house simply wasn't big enough for four.

———

At around the time that the world-famous rock and roll singer Eddie Cochran was killed in a car crash in Wiltshire, England, my sister Karolina was born. My sister was born at St Helier's, in Carshalton. Though, by then, my family had already moved to a larger home in North Cheam.

Eddie Cochran and his fiancée, songwriter Sharon Sheeley, with pop star Gene Vincent, were returning in a private-hire taxicab to Heathrow Airport from a show in Bristol They became involved in a high-speed traffic collision (the cab ran into a concrete lamppost) near Chippenham, in Wiltshire. Vincent shattered his ribs and collar-bone, and further harmed an already frail leg. Sheeley sustained a shattered pelvis. Eddie Cochran, who was flung from the taxi, sustained significant head injuries, and unfortunately died the next day. This was the year the Beatles performed their first concert (under their own name) in Hamburg. Before the Hamburg dates, which were set-up by their unofficial tour-manager and booking agent of the time, Allan Williams, the lads performed as Johnny and the Moondogs, then as the Silver Beetles, when they supported a now (largely) forgotten Liverpool-born (though Streatham based) singer named Johnny Gentle.

Incidentally, and perhaps uncannily, as the Silver Beetles self-appointed manager, Williams had pre-booked Gene Vincent and Eddie Cochran, through the London impresario Larry Parnes, for a Liverpool package-show scheduled for 3rd May, 1960. Of course, fate intervened, so neither Vincent nor Cochrane turned-up to headline the Liverpool date.

(Peculiar fact: David John Harman, later better known as Dave Dee from the beat group Dave Dee, Dozy, Beaky, Mick & Tich was a police cadet with the Wiltshire Constabulary at Chippenham, in 1960. Dave was one of the first officers on scene at Cochran's tragic crash.)

13

SURREY SUBURBAN LIVING

I should point out a few distinctions between Surrey suburban family in the *rock 'n' roll years* and Surrey suburban family life *now*.

Most older readers will be able to recognise the things I set out in a moment, but younger readers might be taken aback by what I have to say. The first truth is that Surrey suburban Mothers didn't 'go to work' in the 1960s. Their 'job' was to take care of the home and raise the kids. They did this *full-time and* were paid by the government to do complete the function (through family allowances topped-up by the bread-winner's salary, i.e. the *man of the house*.) Most mothers performed this role willingly and enthusiastically. For example, my Mum put on a 'housecoat' to begin duties that started before break-fast time, when the boiler needed to be 'fired-up.' Just before Dads came home, suburban Mums would tidy themselves up, take off their housecoats, and prepare dinner for the family. I have chatted with other suburban kids about these memories, and they confirm this was a common experience.

One positive upshot of the suburban 'housewife' arrangement was that, when a child skipped to school or to the sweet shop, *all* the neighbourhood Mums would watch out for them from red-polished porches. You see, Sixties suburbia was a community of young Mums and kids.

Then there was the rule that children should be *seen and not heard*. This was more of a directive than a maxim or catchphrase. Our teachers would tell us to *play quietly*. Silence at the dinner table was an absolute obligation. And if we 'made a sound' when Dad got home, woe betide us!

However, there was also incongruity to Sixties suburban Surrey parenting. It was an incongruity that might appear distorted or even grotesque to the parents of today: the children of the 1960s were not mollycoddled or offered indulgence. Here are some good examples: I once fell from a high tree branch onto concrete. I was told to *pick myself up* and *stop acting the fool*. In the park a dog bit me. I wase told, it *could've been worse*. And then, '*you must have been teasing it*.' When I suffered a bad head cold, my Mum told me to *get over myself*. We were constantly reminded that there was a war on when *they were young*, so sniffles and bruises were considered self-indulgent and dealt with by a harsh cuff to the head. Ear-flicks and arm slaps were part of a child's *everyday* life. Also, a child was *never* asked what they wanted to eat, where they wanted to go, what they wanted to do, or what they wanted to wear. Children *knew their place*. And, if a child ever forgot *their place*, memory would be jogged with a painful whack against bare skin.

———

In our street, almost nobody owned a car, thus everyone walked to where they needed to be, or bicycled (Dad cycled 8 miles to work). Sometimes they took public transport. But, mostly, they *walked*.

I started to walk to school, aged five. I guess the ramble to the school gates took me about twenty minutes. In retrospect, it seems almost inconceivable that a five-year-old youngster was permitted to travel so far by himself. But in the 1960s, Mothers were *not* continually shuttling their children here, there, and everywhere; in Sixties suburbia, Mother's did *not* drive. I mean, they didn't drive at all! This was largely because, even if a family owned a car (which we didn't, very few did), a car was a *man's thing*, so it stayed in a dry garage (where it belonged) until Dad got home to tinker around with it.

Most suburban Mums — or at least all the Mums on my street in Cheam — took what you might describe as an *uninvolved approach* to parenting. I'm guessing this may have a lot to do with the years of sloganeering during the war that encouraged Mums to 'Make Do and Mend' 'Keep Calm and Carry On' and instructed mothers to 'Send Them Out' when referring to the children and men. The official recommendation to Mothers, in paraphrased form, was to "stay calm and make and fix things while sending your men and children outside." If you think I'm labouring the point remember that in England it is typically raining and often depressing to be *outside*... so where were suburban supposed to kids go? If your Mum wouldn't allow you to stay indoors, you'd hope a neighbour might let you in. But even then, you'd have to remain quiet. Here's where your imaginative creativity would come impact. Imagination would kick in! Kids that grew up in the rock 'n' roll years in boring Surrey were often forced to live *inside* their own heads. So, they developed into inward thinkers and conceptualisers. They became practiced at abstract thought. This is when you'd pick-up fingerstyle techniques or learn guitar chords. You might write some songs. This is when you'd take-up up painting and drawing. Or you'd learn how to embroider or cross-stitch. Or, like me, you'd develop an ability to generate and write engaging stories. If it weren't for the *'get over yourself, keep quiet, go outside to play, and stop bloody whining'* attitude of a typical Surrey suburban Mother, I'm willing to bet that half of rock 'n' roll would have withered on the vine!

As a consequence of this 'hands-off' style parenting, and like everyone else I knew, I walked to school. I even walked during the famous 'Big Freeze' of 1962-3 when we all walked to school in our shorts (girls in skirts) with the snow coming over the edges of our wellington boots.

By the age of six, I rode the bus and took a tube to more distant locations. I used public transport *unsupervised*. All my schoolfriends did the same. It wasn't unusual to see a five-year-old sat on the bench seat of a bus, (near the conductor) quietly reading a book. From the age of five *up* we visited the local recreation ground (the 'wreck') without supervision. We rode bikes around the 'block' without supervision and we played football and cricket in the street. These things were common in English suburbia. It's hard to imagine that 'outside' was *not* the horrifyingly dangerous place it is perceived to be *today*, but, instead, a convenient place to send kids if you wanted to 'get rid of them.' *Go play outside* was a common instruction. In the early 1960s, *all* suburban Mothers sent their kids *out to play*.

––––––

Other sayings used on rock 'n' roll era kids included:

Money doesn't grow on trees

This hurts *me* more than it hurts *you* (when administering the cane)

What part of 'no' don't you understand?

When I was your age there was a war on

If your friend jumped off a cliff, would you do the same?

You will laugh on the other side of your face if I catch you doing *that* again

Stop *snivelling* or I'll give you something to *snivel* about

Do it again and I'll knock your block off

Don't come in here with *those* feet

Pick your feet up when walking

Try not to walk on these *floors*

If you do *that* again I will cuff you good and proper

Make any more noise and you'll see the back of my hand

––––––

It's worth considering my thoughts on 1960's Surrey suburban parenting because I think it provides an insight into a young person's cognitive, emotive, and behavioural *state-of-mind*. From the distance I write this memoir (sixty years has passed), it seemed extremely *probable* that if we kids were to *make it* through our rock 'n' roll childhoods, we'd *have to* be super capable, self-assured, self-determining, artistically inspired, and extremely *innovative*.

It wasn't only me who was raised and educated on the fringeland of Surrey during the postwar *'get over yourself, go outside to play, and stop bloody-well whining'* era.

So, too, were: Andy Ellison (John's Children), Andrew Latimer (Camel), Andy Ward (Camel), Billie Davis, Bob Hall (of The Groundhogs), Bruce Foxton (of The Jam), Chas McDevitt (moved from Glasgow to Surrey as a child), Chris Dreja (of the Yardbirds), David Sylvian (of Japan), Darryl Read (attended Parkside Boarding School, East Horsely), Dave Lawson (of Greenslade, he attended Charterhouse School), Denny Cordell (The Moody Blues & Procol Harum producer), Dickie Pride, Ed Tudor-Pole (attended King Edward's School in Witley), Eric Clapton, Gary Brooker (of Procol Harum), Gary Numan (of Tubeway Army who was born and raised in 'modern day' Surrey although purists will argue he came from *Middlesex*), Graham Parker, Hans Zimmer (attended Hurtwood House School in Dorking), Jane Relf (Renaissance), Jean-Jacques Burnel (of The Stranglers, he moved to Guildford aged 12), Jeff Beck, Jimmy Page (he moved to Epsom aged 8), Jimmy Pursey (of Sham 69), Joe Strummer (attended the Freemen's School in Ashtead), Johnny Moped, Keith Relf (Yardbirds), Kirsty MacColl, Kit Hain (of Marshall Hain), Les Gray (of Mud), Les Nemes (of Haircut One Hundred,) Lol Tolhurst (of The Cure), Lynn Ripley (aka 'Twinkle'), Martin Stone (of the Savoy Brown Blues Band), Matthew Fisher (of Procol Harum), Mick Avory (of the Kinks), Mick Jones (of The Clash), Mickey Finn (of T.Rex), Mike Rutherford, Nick Lowe, Nick Mason (attended Frensham Heights School in Farnham), Norman Cook aka Fatboy Slim (attended Reigate Grammar school), Paul Heaton (lived in Chipstead and went to my old school, Nork Park for at least one term), Paul Simonon (the Clash 'London Calling' bassist), Paul Weller, Peter Frampton, Peter Gabriel, Ralph McTell, Rat Scabies, Ray Cooper, Ray Stiles (of Mud), Rick Buckler (of The Jam), Rick Parfitt (of Status Quo), Rob Davis (of Mud), Roger Waters (though he moved out of Surrey to Cambridge during his childhood), Russell Hunter (of The Deviants), Sandy Denny (from the London/Surrey borders), Tom

Allom (the famous Judas Priest sound engineer went to Charterhouse School), Tony Mansfield, Tracey Ullman (she moved to Hackbridge Surrey aged 6), etc. I'm sure there are more!

All these imaginative, expressive, creative personalities spent much of their youth attempting to stay out of trouble, being *seen and not heard*, playing in the street, avoiding a parent's watchful eye, and no doubt ducking a Mother's quick hand and acerbic tongue.

Every suburban kid I knew in the *golden* days harboured an innate desire to *escape*: to escape the monotony and undeniable tedium of suburban life, to escape the insensitivity (often intolerance) of worn-out parents, to escape the cold, detached indifference of suburban post-war *reality*. To escape paint-peeling classrooms. To escape dreariness. To escape the perpetual concrete blandness of Surrey.

I completely understood how young artists felt and what young artists went through in their Surrey rock 'n' roll teen-hoods. And that's because I went through the *same stages* of grey discontentment.

However, there is one principal element that sets *us* Surrey suburbanite youngsters apart from all the other youngsters in Britain. And I mean *all those* who were raised during the rock 'n' roll years in smoking industrial cities: we Surrey kids carry a heavy burden of *shame*. The odour of what I call the *Surrey Guilty Conscience* first appeared in the rock 'n' roll era and has followed us across our lives. The humiliation of having grown up in England's leafiest County has stained us Surrey kids! Do you know how humiliating it is to have grown up in a soft-as-shite Surrey? Coming from Surrey is a lifetime of disgrace. Everyone knows that Surrey offers nothing to be dissatisfied about. Yet Surrey kids are constantly complaining! Why? What have *they* go to complain about? What are their grievances? Children from Surrey attended elite schools. Children from Surrey lived in warm homes. Children from Surrey had wealthy parents who 'gave them everything.' Children from Surrey lived in beautiful surroundings! Children from Surrey are spoilt brats!

———

At North Cheam my Mother enrolled me into Beryl Peter's dance and stage school (a forerunner of Sylvia Young's), and I took ballet, tap, and stage-dance every week, with singing lessons and show rehearsals (or *actual* stage shows) *every* Saturday. I had to be excused from 'regular' school (at Cheam Park Farm) for afternoon performing-arts classes. The Cheam Park Farm teachers grumbled about my leaving school early and created a hostile environment for me. I was very severely tormented by one particular teacher, named Manning. She seemed to 'have it in for me.' My Father griped about having to escort me to various theatres on Saturday mornings (though, during the week, as I already explained, I made my own way to classes.) Dad never fully supported my Mum's vision that I should 'one day' go on the stage! Mum's favourite entertainment was the Black & White Minstrel Show (if you don't know what this is, you ought to look it up, but be prepared for a shock!) My Mother imagined (rather fancifully) that I'd be hired by a travelling minstrel show to perform tap-dance to crowds. Subsequently, she sewed-up a minstrel costume for me to wear and Miss Manning forced me to don the snazzy outfit in front of the whole class (yes, with a 'blacked-up' face) and forced me to dance 'like a minstrel.' The teacher invited my school chums to mock my attempts to entertain. It was a humiliating experience.

———

It wasn't until 1962 that I began to develop a taste for music. Like most families of the period, our family consumed popular music through radio, stage shows, and the occasional visit to the cinema.

This was the year that the Beatles played their first session at EMI's Abbey Road Studios in London (they also fired their drummer Pete Best and replaced him with Ringo Starr, in August.) But the EMI opportunity almost never happened!

At the start of the year, the Beatles and Brian Poole and the Tremeloes (from Dagenham) both auditioned for Decca Records. Decca made it clear they had the option of signing *only one* group. The Beatles were turned down, primarily because they were from Liverpool. This came just weeks after an almost completely disastrous Battle of the Bands gig (December 19th, 1961) in front of an audience of just eighteen audience-members at the Palais Ballroom Aldershot, just across the Surrey border. In all honesty, the Palais was merely a village hall. Joe Meek's London-based outfit Jay and the Jaywalkers did not appear at the event, maybe predicting a fiasco. The poor ticket sales and humiliating low audience turn-out was blamed on the hapless event organiser, a local promoter named Sam Leach; but the overall sentiment of the small crowd that troubled to stay for a few songs before they adjourned to a nearby pub, was that The Beatles were not- really-that-good, and, anyhow, nobody had heard of them (since they originated from Liverpool). Some speculate that following the show, upon their return to Liverpool, the Beatles decided to stay-put in the North-West rather than bother to travel *down south* again. These experiences were undoubtedly devastating setbacks for the band, but also galvanised their drive to 'do it correctly, or *not at all*.'

———

One of my earliest memories of North Cheam was walking to the Saturday morning pictures with my sister, Karolina. Saturday Morning Pictures were held at the Granada cinema. Once we arrived at the theatre, we paid sixpence subscription at the ticket booth. Inside the malodorous smoke-stinky auditorium, we'd be forced to sing the 'club' anthem which was 'The Granadiers' (sic) to the tune of a traditional 17th century marching song. The National Anthem followed, and we'd be required to stand. The theatre manager declined to start the show if misbehaving boys didn't 'stand properly' during the ceremony.

Each week we were entertained by a short serial, plus one or two cartoons, then a main feature. All punctuated by the 'Da-da-da-da-da- Dah-dah-dah' of the Pearl & Dean commercials. You must remember that very few families had television sets at this stage. This was– for many – the *only* visual entertainment to be had. Certainly, it was the only way we'd experience cartoons in colour. Saturday morning pictures were a treat.

My sister was fascinated by Miss Candy's sweet-shop in the foyer. Karolina would stand on her tippy-toes to look into the window and try to catch Miss Candy's eye as she served the wealthy customers who could afford expensive sweets. Miss Candy seemed so glamorous. She had dyed-pink beehive hair (it resembled candy-floss), silk dresses, and wore stockings with lines down the legs. She even possessed a candy-striped car that she parked outside. It was a multi-coloured Morris Minor. It's interesting to note that these days Karolina wears similar clothes and sports candy-pink hair!

Our school class would walk to Cheam Baths once a week. I remember walking to the baths, in single-file, from Cheam Park Farm. It was always bitterly cold in those days (more of that soon.) We would traipse past Cheam's Nuclear Bunker. We felt cold as ice walking to those baths. Even colder coming home. Half wet, and not properly buttoned up, we would arrive in a house that was not heated. There'd be no food till dinner time. And there was no telly or other "entertainment" for us.

By the way, the atomic bunker was near the Queen Vic pub (Chris Barber played at Queen Vic jazz club.) The government decided in their wisdom to site a 'secret' command and communications centre slap-bang in the middle of suburban North Cheam (at Church Hill Road.)

Apparently, the bunker would have been used as the 'seat of government' for all of Southern England if the worse thing happened i.e. an all-out thermonuclear war. It's difficult to imagine this, but I want you to know that in the Fifties and Sixties we fully expected nuclear war to break-out at any moment! We talked about it at school, and our parents told us to *pray*. Presumably, the authorities chose North Cheam for the atom-bomb shelter because they gambled the Soviet Union would never target valuable missiles on a semi-suburban area in Surrey.

———

Our street in North Cheam was full of girls.

When people ask me why I write novels that focus on strong

female characters, I tell them: "I lived in a world filled with strong women."

Like most families of this period, my Father was never much around (too busy) and even when he was physically present he was often emotionally remote. In the 1960s my classmates, my playmates, my relatives, my family, my neighbours, and almost all my teachers, were mostly female. Janet lived next-door-but-one. We were best friends. Janet gave me my first kiss on the lips. I would date this kiss as 1965 because I remember *Michelle* (by the Beatles) being played on the radio.

I still remember how Janet and I first met. I was vaguely aware that a girl in a blue coat lived two doors down from our house in Cheam. I also knew she walked to the same school. One crisp winter morning I caught up with her as she waited diligently by the main road to perform her obligatory 'kerb drill.' She looked askance, as I drew level. She stared at me from the corners of bright eyes. I looked back but said *nothing*. I noticed she had a fringe of oatmeal coloured hair and a very round face. And she wore spectacles.

'What's your name, boy?' she asked.

The question came as such a shock that I temporarily forgot what my answer ought to be. Instead, I felt awkward and made a gurgling sound.

'Very well,' she said 'If you haven't a name, I shall call you *boy*—'

I didn't answer. We crossed the street together.

She said, 'My name is Janet, by the way.'

From that moment we were inseparable. We had lunch together. We sat side-by-side in play-time, and we walked to-and-from school, hand-in-hand. We must have made a very cute pair! We always met-up after school to play in the street. Janet had a younger sister named Heather — and Heather made friends with *my* younger sisters. We were like 'The Famous Five.' We embarked on lots of adventures— usually involving riding bikes around the block.

Also, living down our avenue, were two super-sophisticated sisters named Pauline and Lorraine. Even at age nine, I recognized Pauline (in particular) to be something special. Pauline was chosen to be the May Queen at our school. She was an obvious choice! A boy (my age) told me she was the best-looking girl he'd ever *clapped eyes on*. It's true. Pauline was an angel.

Pauline had long blond hair that tumbled to her waist. She had bright blue eyes. A small flat nose. And peachy skin. She was tall and willowy. Her younger sister, Lorraine, was the same shape — though Lorraine had chocolate-brown hair and darker eyebrows. I was lucky (considerably lucky) because Pauline and Lorraine were good friends of mine. We sat cross-legged on cold pavements and played a game that Pauline had invented, called 'Bead Collection.'

The idea of 'Bead Collection' was that every person in the group was expected to pull-out from their bag a precious mystery object (usually a bead) so everyone else in the group might admire and respond to it. The group had to think-up words to describe the jewel/bead— they should describe how they *felt* about it. They were expected to describe their *response* to the object. For example, Pauline might hold-up a sapphire-coloured bead and the group would be encouraged to describe it: 'This is clear and bright blue. It reminds us of the eyes of a pussy cat ... a poor unloved cat –a cat lost at sea... this makes me feel sad.' I know it sounds drivel *now* but looking back on it — this was my introduction to 'reviewing' and 'criticizing.' Consequently, I owe Pauline a debt of gratitude. I soon found I was quite good at describing things and could communicate an emotional reaction to objects.

The 'beads' in each valuable collection might be badges, charms, plastic drops, or pieces of costume jewellery that were found (by the girls) when rummaging through a Mother's button tins or needle boxes. (It should be remembered that most women had a box of haberdashery, buttons, and ribbons. It was a 'make do and mend' habit they hadn't shaken off from the war-years.)

It didn't matter what the intrinsic value of the chosen 'bead' was — the most important thing was that it had to be individually assessed and evaluated —by the person who took it from the bag (first) and by each member of the group. It was only recently I became to understand how valuable that little game has been to me. Now, when I review something, I just go through the same processes I did back then, as a kid, with Pauline by my side.

Obviously, because I was a boy, the *only* boy, I didn't possess a bead collection. I could only get involved in the appraisal and opinion part of the game. But my sisters loaned me a few beads and Janet gave me a blue pouch to keep them safe. Then I'd participate in the *full game*. And would get closer to Pauline.

We sat under the street-light, on a drain cover, for hours, each person admiring the other's semi-precious objects. Holding pieces of plastic jewellery to the light; turning stones; trying to think of profound things to say about brightly coloured things. I quickly realized that the more abstract the object — the more you can say about it.

I just claimed I was the only boy on the street, but that wasn't strictly true. Another boy lived in our avenue: a rather sad character named Geoffrey. He was the same age I was, in the same class. His parents were a *lot* older than ours. His Mother molly-coddled him. He was her 'only child.' Geoffrey was always dressed up (wearing two balaclavas to school) and always a large, knitted scarf around his head. This was to stop him getting what his Mother described as a 'head cold.' His Mother was forever worried that her precious son would get a 'head cold.' Or get tired. Or get wet. She was always calling him indoors. She tended to call him indoors halfway through the games we played.

Geoffrey rode his blue scooter — on dry days. *We* had pedal bikes. But *his* Mother said a bicycle was *too dangerous* for her Geoffrey: he might go *too far* on the thing. Once, we dared Geoffrey to go around the block on his scooter. He got to one side of the block but got the *collywobbles*. He returned home 'feeling sick.' He *literally* couldn't travel more than 100 meters from home before he became fearful.

Geoffrey was not permitted to have a bead collection, and that's a shame. His Mother disapproved of him sitting on cold pavements to play the game. She said he'd get 'piles and worms' if he sat on an unsanitary floor. So, when we began to play beads, she ushered him indoors.

Geoffrey was much brighter than all the other kids. He resembled 'Walter the Softy,' that's the guy who was always picked on by cartoon bully 'Dennis the Menace'. He had the same shiny black hair. The same sort of round, owlish (Harry Potterish) spectacles, and Geoffrey wore his school uniform *all the time*— even when it was *inappropriate* — for example, at his birthday party. When I mentioned *this* particular issue to my Mother, she said it was because Geoffrey's parents were too poor to afford 'party clothes.' I was suspicious of this excuse, because I had been to Geoffrey's house several times, and his Mum provided fresh food (fruit and nuts), and these were things we could only dream about in our house. Also, there were five in *our* family, but only three in theirs. My Mother 's explanation did not add up. I was convinced Geoffrey's Mother was keeping a barrier between her son and the kids on the block. She (quite rightly, as it turned out) figured her son was brighter than *us lot*. She wanted to be sure he was not 'dragged down' to street level. Today you'd call him a *geek*. He was, basically, a 1960s answer to Sheldon Cooper. Geoffrey was *easily* the best pupil at Cheam Park Farm Junior school, and I mean *by far*. He excelled at *all* his studies. He was a constant delight to teachers. He eventually earned a valuable scholarship to Ewell Castle school, a bus ride away; it's an extremely expensive, *very* exclusive, independent boarding school in Ewell. (It's the school that English actor Oliver Reed attended.) The last time I heard of Geoffrey, he'd become a successful artist and designer.

———

When Janet's parents announced they were leaving Cheam to go and live in Horsham, they organised a leaving party for the whole street. My parents were invited. Our whole family went around to their house to celebrate. Even my Dad went (which was a rarity.)

I made Janet a leaving card. I gave it to her in the hallway. She stared into my face. She didn't look at her card. She said nothing. All the adults were behaving wildly. They were talking loudly, laughing, drinking, and smoking. The Beatles were on the radio, and so Janet and I danced in the hall. My heart really hurt. It felt as if someone had wrenched my innards out and flung them into the fire grate. I felt as if my insides were empty. After the dance she gave me my first kiss. It was a kiss that meant *goodbye*.

I never saw Janet again. I imagine she is something successful *now*. A lawyer or doctor, maybe. I am sure she lives in a big house, with a large family and dogs, somewhere in the wilds of Sussex. I hope so.

———

As I already explained, we'd walk to school in the rock 'n' roll days. Our parents didn't take us to places in the 1960's – we made our journeys *on foot*. *Without* parental supervision. Our fathers were too busy working. Our Mothers were too busy 'house-keeping.' Kids travelled the cheapest way possible: they used shoe-leather. The infant's school was only ten minutes from our house. In those days it was not unusual to see five-year-olds (kitted-out in woollen gloves tied together with knicker elastic, and grey balaclavas, with matching hand-knitted scarves burying frozen faces) walking hand-in-hand to school. With no adults around.

We had just one 'serious road' to contend with on our way to Cheam Park Farm school. The road where I first met my Janet. We were told, very strictly, we must wait at the kerb and complete what was known in those day as 'kerb drill.' We had to do this each time we crossed a 'serious road.' We did the drill religiously. In the rock 'n' roll years we *lived by rules*.

I don't think that I ever saw much traffic, though. The junior school was about twenty minutes further away. A longer walk. We employed a short-cut through the back-passage of private gardens. In 1965 I was given a Moulton mini bicycle (aka the 'bicycle of the future') for Christmas. I would happily spend hours whizzing around Cheam on this contraption. It gave me a profound sense of freedom and opened up new horizons.

———

Travelling distances had always been a problem for residents of Surrey. And for those of us who were raised in the rock 'n' roll years, the restrictions of geography added to our sense of grumpy isolation.

As a child, growing up in North Cheam, my Mother would walk my sister and I *everywhere*. We'd walk to Worcester Park, Cheam Village, Epsom, Ewell, Nonsuch, Morden Park (and at least once a week to Sutton for our main shop), plus Wimbledon *too* – these destinations were considered to be within 'easy walking distance' of North Cheam.

We addressed these walks with the fortitude they deserved. And wore stout shoes. Rarely we'd take a bus to go *'out* somewhere.' I remember we once travelled by bus to Chessington– not to the modern *World of Adventures*, mind, but purely for a 'picnic' of cold egg sandwiches on a bench near a bus stop. Kingston and Croydon were considered 'far enough away' to warrant travel by bus. We had to reach these bustling centres to get our big-ticket items including new Macs (thick raincoats) for the long and cruel winter months.

In 1963, in our avenue in North Cheam, only one household owned a car. This car belonged to a smart young 'professional' woman who lived almost opposite Janet and Heather's home. Her car was a yellow Triumph Herald. It sounds like a cliché, but children could literally play in the street to their hearts content. I remember being ticked off by a policeman (walking the beat). I had been playing cricket in the middle of our road and the beat copper 'fielded' our ball. He called us over and, with a weary look on his face, said, 'Don't play in the street! Don't you know it's dangerous? A car could come and run-you-down any minute! I ought to tell your parents about this (they already knew) and then you'd be *in for it*. Don't let me see you in the street again.' He gave us the ball back.

During that entire stern talking-to, I clearly remember that no cars came down that road. As the officer walked away, shaking his head in despair, there were *still* no cars. We looked toward the horizon. No cars in sight. An hour later, our Mother's called us in for our teas. It was dark. Just after tea I heard a familiar rumble of an engine. I ran to the front window to see the smart lady with the yellow Triumph Herald turn into her front drive. Hers was the only car around.

After the 'last ever' 'Great Smog' of London, during the early parts of December 1962, a wave of very freezing air arrived from Scandinavia during the second week of December. It chilled the Surrey folk to their bones. This was followed by significant snowfall on Boxing Day (26th December) and was quickly succeeded by blizzards.

Nationally, over 95,000 miles of roadway became blocked by snow. Surrey was, perhaps, the worst hit place of all in England. (Scotland had it hardest.) The snowfall seemed more severe in the South than in the North. The villages and towns of Surrey felt more cut-off than ever before.

The villagers of Mugswell (near Reigate Hill) were totally marooned. Drifts were so high that even the snow-plough got stuck in deep snow near Chipstead. Some places, like Pebble Hill, Albury and Abinger remained pretty much isolated from the rest of the County from Christmas up until March.

My memory of the winter of 1962/3 was much the same as everyone else's. We couldn't open our back door (from the kitchen into the back garden) due to an enormous snow-drift that got larger every day. I remember sitting for breakfast, each morning, and attempting to calculate how many inches of snow had fallen overnight. In the end I gave-up because the snow-drift became too deep to see over, from our door. Walking to school was a misery. Our pathetic school uniforms were short grey trousers (for boys) with a grey shirt, green-striped tie, grey woollen jumper, and a dark grey 'raincoat.'

This coat (we called it a Mac) was typically made of a cheap variant of Gabardine. It was a thick cotton-type fabric that Mothers had to 'waterproof' themselves. They did this by wiping the fabric with foul-smelling gum. If you were fortunate, your Mother would perform the holy-rite of water-proofing your Mac *regularly*. My mother was less concerned with household chores than some others, so waterproofing came-around less routinely for my sisters and I! Mum would tell us how *warm* Gabardine was– because heroes (like Ernest Shackleton and George Mallory) had worn the fabric in Arctic conditions. If you want my opinion, the textile was rubbish!

Gabardine may well have been the 'must have' stuff of the rock 'n' roll years – and Shackleton and Mallory may well have worn it with pride (probably over thick furs, I expect) but as an insulating all-weather nature-blocking outer-garment during the winter of 1962/3 it was hopeless. Some kids had special quilted blue-button inserts that were worn *inside* a Gaberdine Mac. My sister had one such insert. I *wasn't* so lucky. But the extra bit of insulation the insert provided didn't seem to work very well, either. My sister said it was a *devil of a job* to button and un-button.

School-girls were no better attired than schoolboys. There were no anoraks or hoodies in the 1960's. No salopettes or leg-warmers. Parkas had not been properly introduced. And there were no cagoules. The world had not even figured out that girls could wear trousers! (Trousers for females were not 'invented' until the French fashion designer André Courrèges introduced the concept of trouser-suits to the world in 1964.) Therefore, all my female school age friends, who made the same journey that I did – had to plod through knee-high snow wearing short grey skirts and thick tights. If these girls were lucky, their Mum's might have given them an extra-long Mac for Christmas (a Mac so big they'd have to 'grow into it.') But at least a lengthy hem might afford them a bit of extra comfort and 'cover' around tiny frozen knees.

Most kids wore huge hand-knitted scarves *too*, (frequently given as Christmas presents by Aunts and Nans.) In 1962/3 *these* gifts were very welcome. Everyone wore thick home-knitted balaclavas too. Fat woollen gloves and cheap Wellington boots completed every school kid's ensemble. I remember that each day the snow went *over* the lips of my Wellies to fall into the *insides* of my boots. By the time I arrived at school I had about a pint and a half of frozen slush gurgling around my toes. Obviously, there were no 'spare socks' available to us in those days –there was nowhere (and no time) to dry them even if we had such luxuries. So, we went through each school day with frozen, sodden feet.

Unsurprisingly, in the miserable winter of 1962-3 we all suffered terribly from *chilblains*. These were a kind of 'mild' version of frost-bite. There was no cure. We suffered in silence. The pain was tolerable, but not kind. The condition produced an interminable itching sensation in your toes. The pain kept us from sleeping. Our toes ballooned-up and turned bright red – *red*, like Rudolph's nose. For years I thought that the famous Reindeer had a chilblain on his nose!

The unkindest, yet supposedly *beneficial*, treatment (it was an old-wives tale) —was that you should *not* (on any account) get your toes warm or near a hot-water bottle or fire, or radiator. Mums all over Surrey would say to kids, 'What have I told you about getting too close to warmth? Keep your toes away from heat. Otherwise, you'll get chilblains.' A child might reply: 'Dad's sitting by the fire –he hasn't got his socks on...' A Mother's answer would likely be: 'Don't answer back! Your Father doesn't have chilblains – therefore, it's safe for him to sit there.' In my mind, that answer didn't make sense.

After a short thaw in the New Year of 1963, things suddenly got considerably *worse*. Habitants of Merstham, for example, endured a thick carpet of snow that covered their entire village like a white duvet – residents were stranded for sixty-six consecutive days. The nights were ridiculously cold too. In Horley, residents measured a record -16 on the night of 23rd January 1963. Rivers began to freeze over, and foxes began to attack livestock, and were behaving like wolves in order to survive. By mid-January, the Thames had completely frozen over so Surrey residents could walk across the river to the 'alien' County of Middlesex. At places like Chertsey, people would skate along the iced river to work. And at Kingston a car was driven across the frozen Thames. All these events marked the beginnings of an exciting year for rock 'n' roll in Surrey.

14

HOW WE CONSUMED OUR MUSIC

Despite discussing record speeds and jukeboxes, it's important to ponder how we 'Boomer' generation experienced music in the 'olden' days. Young readers are incredibly lucky to have music streaming services, YouTube, Amazon, portable audio players, Digital radio, and music video channels.

Let's begin with public performance, since I already mentioned my experience working as a D.J. in the early disco era. What was the preferred way for music enthusiasts to enjoy tunes during the rock 'n' roll era?

When Britain emerged from the war years, *swing* (aka big band jazz) was the prevailing popular music. The sounds had *actually* been around since the late 1920s and early 1930s but gained huge popularity with guys like Glenn Miller and Tommy Dorsey. The swing-era produced stand-out artists like Louis Armstrong, Billie Holiday, and by 1938, Ella Fitzgerald. But the expenses and challenges of World War Two hindered bands from traveling and funding their road trips. For instance, the Stan Kenton Band consisted of five trumpets, five trombones, five saxophones, and a rhythm section. Duke Ellington employed six trumpeteers. While the 'man with horns' Boyd Raeburn went on tour with a full symphony orchestra, which included around fifty musicians. Can you imagine the expense of touring with these big bands? On top of this, progressive musicians were beginning to explore a new sound they called *be-bop* that had asymmetrical phrasing, and complex syncopation, and was for serious listening, *not* for dancing. Jazz inspired artists like Frank Sinatra, Dean Martin, and Nat King Cole were experimenting with lighter, pop-oriented 'swinging' jazz and this was gaining widespread popularity.

The influence of the 'swing' genre in post-war Britain is clearly seen in the chart successes of 1953, successes that included Johnny Dankworth, the Mantovani Orchestra, Ray Anthony and His Orchestra, and Billy Cotton & His Band.

Swinging jazz played by a whole host of smaller swing bands set the backdrop for courting couples across Surrey as they danced in venues like sports pavilions, social clubs, and church halls. The larger ballrooms and more affluent associations could afford the full big-band experience: but, in truth, the *big sound* was becoming a rare luxury in post-war Britain. Soon, almost all bands trimmed-down on size, making touring feasible. My uncle played in trimmed-down jazz outfit, the 'Swinging AJ's' where he performed as a clarinettist. The AJ's played around the Morden and Mitcham area.

———

Before 1952, the popularity of a song was determined by the sales of *sheet music.* The record charts, as we know them in the U.K. began when Percy Dickins of the New Musical Express telephoned twenty music shops and asked them for an inventory of their best-selling *recorded* songs. His list was printed in the NME, as a Top 12, (reflecting a strong English identity and distaste for metrication.) On 14th November 1952, Dickins awarded Al Martino's record 'Here in My Heart' the first-ever number-one position in the new *record* charts. The Italian/American singer's chart-topping hit held the position for 9 weeks, establishing the record for the longest continuous reign at number one in Britain, a feat unmatched until Bryan Adams' 'Everything I Do' in 1991 (16 weeks).

The Stargazers were the first British musical group to top his record charts, with 'Broken Wings,' in 1953. The Stargazers Ensemble who served as backing vocalists for the Ewell, Surrey singer, Petula Clark, on her earliest recordings, including: *You're The Sweetest In The Land*' (1950). Interesting side note: Cliff Adams of the Stargazers wrote the 'Fry's Turkish Delight' jingle you will remember if you're of a certain age!

During the working week, radio was the main source of music for most Surrey residents. The BBC Light Programme (1945-1967) served as a substitute for the wartime General Forces Programme. Running for almost three decades, from 1954 to 1982, was the popular Junior Choice show. Family Favourites (often remembered as Two-Way Family Favourites) was the successor of the wartime radio show Forces Favourites. Andre Kostelanetz and his Orchestra played the show's signature tune "*With a Song in My Heart.*" Another popular record request programme was titled 'Housewives' Choice' that transmitted every morning (1946-67) with the memorable theme tune *In Party Mood*, by Jack Strachey.

Some fortunate suburbanites might have owned a radiogram. It was a costly home contraption, essentially a combination of a radio and gramophone set, usually incorporated into a fancy piece of furniture with a large loudspeaker and sometimes an autochanger. My future Father-in-law owned a radiogram. He'd play six records on the machine at once; the discs were stacked, so they'd play one-after-the-other.

The first British Dansette record player was manufactured in 1952. At least one million machines were traded during the 1950s. The Dansette played 7, 10 and 12-inch discs at 78, 45, 33⅓, and 16 ⅔ rpm discs. In the early 1950s, these machines retailed at around 33 guineas (roughly £800 in today's money), so the machine was beyond the reach of most teenage pockets. Teenagers had to wait until 1962 for record playing technology to become cheap enough (11 guineas) to be affordable.

Transistors (semiconductors) were invented in 1947. But commercial transistor radios were not available until 1954. Before transistor radios, radios and radiograms used vacuum tubes.

Before BBC Radio One was established in 1967, we had 'Pick of the Pops' with Alan Freeman on Sundays, which ran from 1955 to 1972 in more-or-less the same format. Music While You Work ended in 1967 when the BBC Light Programme transformed into BBC Radio 2. It's difficult to imagine a world without independent radio but until the early 1970s, the BBC had a complete monopoly on all radio broadcasting in the UK. There was some competition from the English-language service on Radio Luxembourg who operated the most powerful transmitters in Europe yet, even with this apparatus, their signal was frequently and *deliberately* 'drowned-out' by the BBC. The mid-1960s is now famous for off-shore "pirate" radio stations, and Luxembourg was the first and, probably, the best, of all the pirates.

On the valve radio set in our kitchen, we listened to BBC Home Service, they played:

Wonderful Copenhagen, Danny Kaye
Little White Bull, Tommy Steele
Tulips from Amsterdam, Max Bygraves
I am a Mole and I Live in a Hole, The Southlanders
The Runaway Train, Michael Holliday
Tom Dooley, The Kingston Trio
Donald Where's Your Troosers?, Andy Stewart
The Hippopotamus, Flanders and Swann
There's a Hole in My Bucket, Harry Belafonte & Odetta
Que Sera Sera, Doris Day
Soldier, Soldier, Won't You Marry Me?, various renditions

———

For me, living in suburban Surrey, these radio 'hits' remained entrenched in the rubble & ditches of blackout Britain: they were meant to cheer-up housewives on the home front, or entertain factory workers 'till home-time. For us school kids, these sounds were cringey and *awful*.

———

March 1957 marked the debut of the first Eurovision Song Contest involving Britain. It was also the year when the BBC tried out the Alma Cogan show, featuring the famous *girl with the giggle* who would wear a variety of tight tops. That year Cogan topped the annual NME reader's poll as "Outstanding British Female Singer."

The swing generation stayed connected to big band sounds through Come Dancing (*now* known as Strictly).

Crackerjack! the much-loved children's variety show had been running since 1955 and, remarkably, this relatively mediocre show often surprised younger viewers by introducing some seriously good rock acts, including The Who, Status Quo, The Small Faces, The Bee Gees, Adam Faith, Billy Fury, and Tom Jones. Even now, when you mention the name Peter Glaze to a person 'of a certain age' you'll get the response: It's Friday. It's Five to Five. And it's *Crackerjack!* My Cub Scout pack at Cheam had the honour of presenting a 'guard' for Leslie Crowther of Crackerjack! (1964-1968) when he visited St. Oswald's Church. It was the first time I'd seen a celebrity up-close, and I still possess his autograph. But I don't own a *Crackerjack Pencil*, do you?

———

There seemed to be an endless supply of popular music shows back then, and this is especially surprising when you consider there were only two television channels to choose from. When I think back on it, it makes sense, *though*. Dads were 'out' at work, or spending free time in bars, or at sporting events, or tending to their gardens. Mothers were working nonstop to keep the house tidy. So, TV was a young person's obsession, (and it kept them quiet) just as video games and social media do today. The broadcasters targeted teenagers because they understood that this young audience would develop into the grownup audiences of the future.

The world's longest-running children's TV program, and probably the most famous was Blue Peter, and the show had its debut in 1958. The show featured a few pop acts (such as Brian Poole and The Tremeloes) but is now better remembered for elephant poop, out-of-control Brownie camp-fires, and sticky-back plastic.

My parents' all-time favourite was The Black and White Minstrel Show, which also made its debut in 1958. The Saturday evening prime-time television 'treat' showcased a 45-minute sing-along with both solo and minstrel performances, including country and western songs. People of my generation considered it dreadful, and I'm proud to say I hated it back then, and still do!

Oh Boy! was the first teenage all-music show on British television and aired 1958-1959. It was produced by Jack Good, for Independent Television. Good had previously produced the Six-Five Special for the BBC, which was the first pop music entertainment programme (mostly Skiffle) even if the BBC badly diluted the content *so much* it wasn't really a music show at all and never attracted its intended audience. Nevertheless, Petula Clark, Jim Dale Lonnie Donegan, Wee Willie Harris, Marty Wilde, and Tommy Steele all 'started out on television' on this show. But Oh Boy! was the grown-up adolescent brother of the Six-Five Special. They broadcast their show direct from the Hackney Empire and boasted the likes of Cliff Richard, Billy Fury, Shirley Bassey, and even occasional American stars, such as Brenda Lee and The Inkspots.

In 1959, Juke Box Jury began running. This BBC show followed a format where showbusiness guests formed a weekly panel and evaluated the hit potential of recent record releases. The host was the (most decidedly *uncool*) David Jacobs. The Judges were played snippets of sound on a Rock-Ola jukebox and their decisions earned either a bell for a hit, or a rude-sounding hooter for a miss. DJ Pete Murray always seemed to be a guest on the show, but sometimes the Juke Box Jury attracted *properly* impressive judges, for example, Johnny Mathis, Roy Orbison, and I remember the Man From U.N.C.L.E., David McCallum. Famously, in December 1963, the panel was all four Beatles. In 1964 when the five members of the Rolling Stones formed the panel, (this was the only time in the show's history there was more than four jurors) they quite clearly took-the-piss out of the entire concept.

Drumbeat was a BBC television series that aired on Saturdays from August 1959. It launched the careers of singer Adam Faith and the 'James Bond' composer John Barry and helped boost the singing career of Dusty Springfield, who was then with an outfit called The Lana Sisters.

The variety show Sunday Night at the London Palladium, which first aired in 1960, highlighted ATV's stable of talent that included Cliff Richard and The Shadows. A crowd of twenty million watched their performance! In that particular year, the Eurovision Song Contest was hosted in Britain at the Royal Festival Hall.

Thank Your Lucky Stars, an ABC Weekend show was aired from 1961. High status bands like The Beatles or The Rolling Stones would mime to a handful of numbers.

Top of the Pops, the weekly and best-known pop music show, debuted on BBC in January 1964. The opening acts were Dusty Springfield and The Rolling Stones.

Though, Ready Steady Go! could perhaps be described as the first television rock-orientated show. It was broadcast by ATV from August 1963 to December '66. The show began with the memorable line "The weekend starts here!" and was introduced by The Surfaris' fast-moving number, *Wipe Out*, then later by Manfred Mann's "5-4-3-2-1." (which is probably better remembered.) Keith Fordyce and Cathy McGowan were the show's best-known presenters, but there were others. Fordyce and McGowan were chosen because they embodied the look and behaviour of typical teens! Some of the most successful artists of the rock 'n' roll era appeared on their show, so it retained *oomph* and desirability and is still considered to be the best of this type. Jimi Hendrix made his first television appearance on UK telly on Ready Steady Go!. As did Paul Simon. *And* the Beach Boys. In April 1965, Dusty Springfield created and hosted her own RSG Motown (soul) Special for Ready Steady Go! which included performances by The Supremes, Stevie Wonder, the Miracles, and Martha and the Vandellas. *That* show is still remembered with great affection today.

Blue Peter had competition from another British children's television programme during the rock 'n' roll era and the show's impact cannot be ignored. Magpie (made by Thames Television) ran from July 1968 until June 1980. The rock 'n' roll generation has positive memories of actress Susan Stranks and co-presenter Mick Robertson, and because Magpie focused more on popular culture than on sticky-back plastic and dog grooming, for many young viewers it seemed more relevant and more grownup. In 1974, an adolescent schoolboy favourite, Jenny Hanley, took over from Stranks. By the way, The Spencer Davis Group played the show's cherished *"One For Sorry"* theme tune, which was written by Eddie Hardin—who later became Bo Diddley's sidekick.

15

EPSOM AND BANSTEAD

My wife comes from Nork in Surrey. It's a tiny community built onto the chalk Downs near Epsom. The settlement is surrounded by green fields. On one side is Nork Park. This was originally the gardens and farmland of Nork House – a grand mansion once owned by Colman's *mustard* family. It is now a reasonable public space (the house is long gone) and the park has enthralling views towards London. At the loftiest point —a place called 'Tumble Beacon' — there is an important defensive highpoint. The large knoll (visible from the road) was, in earlier times, a burial mound. Beacons were once an ancient British 'early warning system.' Bonfires were lit on the high hills like this to warn of invasions or catastrophes. They were the original 'relay system' long before radio and telegraph could be used. Firelighters would be alerted by an orange glow on a distant hill, and this would urge them to light a blazing beacon in return. In this way, an alert was signalled around the realm. This telegraph system would have been used for the Spanish Armada, in 1588. It may also have been used during the Viking Age to warn of raiders. Bonfires are still lit on hills to celebrate events such as coronations and jubilees. But the 'Tumble Beacon' (which lends its name to the nearby Beacons School – formerly Nork Park School) was *not* lit for recent jubilees or the coronation.

My wife has lived *all her life* within the County of Surrey. She tells me her upbringing was a period of tedium, interrupted by bouts of boredom. Her family home is too far from towns like Sutton or Kingston to walk to. So, my wife was stuck in Nork, and had no social life to speak of. Her home patch (Drift Bridge) consisted of a pub (for a while the pub had a cinema attached, which was useful) and a petrol station. There were half a dozen shops and a church. It was *too far* from Banstead or Epsom. And even if she took the walk to Epsom or Banstead, the amenities weren't much to write home about.

Epsom had a cinema. It also had a theatre (Ebbisham Hall) and a few other church halls where shows might be put on. My wife's Mother walked to Banstead village once a week, long into her Seventies, to do the family shopping. There was no family car. My wife's Father commuted to London via a long train journey from the tiny Banstead station. The trains from Banstead run to London once an hour, so were jam-packed. It's hard to imagine life without cars. Modern day city dwellers should keep in mind that transport links in Surrey, during the Sixties and Seventies were, at best, rudimentary.

Even *now* in the 21st century, public transport is far from adequate in Surrey. Bus routes are slow and inefficient. There are no underground trains or tramways beyond Morden and Wimbledon. The Croydon Tramlink began operating in 2000. Mainline trains were intended for commuting to London. This means that the lines are connected – *via* major stops – to the City. In other words, they are *not* designed to connect one Surrey borough, village, or town to another! Railways are not at all useful for making journeys *within* the County. If, for example, you want to travel from Banstead to Farnham, you'd best bet is to travel to Clapham Junction in London, then change platform and come *back on yourself.* It would take over 2 hours by train. Yet the journey is only 45-minutes by car!

So, life, for teenagers during the rock 'n' roll period, revolved around homes, playgrounds, streets, church halls, and schools. If you were lucky (like the musicians in MUD) you might have a Scout Hut or a Church Hall available to you, where you might be allowed to practice and perform and join a club. For years I attended an exciting club at St Georges church hall on the St Helier estate in Morden. It was over an hour's bus ride from my home on Epsom Downs. I attended this church-hall club *just* so I could see their weekly folk music concerts. (I understand that St Georges *still* has a thriving youth group running in that same hall.) My wife tells me that by Sunday afternoon, she yearned for the weekend to be *over*, so she could get back to school!

––––––

When I met my wife, I lived at Tattenham Corner on Epsom Downs. My family had moved to Epsom at around the time my (third) sister was born. I've always supposed the move was made to get more space for my parent's expanding family, but in some ways it became a painful move. For a start, my Mother had lifelong friends near Cheam, and the move cut her off from her support group. Then there was the general state of the property we moved into: it was a dilapidated four-bedroom detached house that required lots of renovation, for example it had no central heating, no double-glazing, an outmoded kitchen, and antiquated electric wiring (it still had gas-lamps in some rooms, for example.) And this was during a period when salaries were low, cash was insufficient, and there were more mouths to feed. The other big problem was that the area 'felt' cut-off. Tattenham Corner has very few shops, a lot of rather large houses, and an estate of well-designed council properties on the Downland and Upland Way slopes, and also on the ballooning, if slightly disreputable, estate on the Merland Rise.

The area had one big claim to fame: it's the home of the famous train station where royalty alights (once a year, or certainly *did* until very recently) from the British Royal Train – so the monarch of the day could attend Epsom races (specifically, Derby Day.) The tradition was started with Queen Victoria. She had the train station specially built for her race-day routine. Theoretically, Tattenham Corner is the home of the Epsom Downs Racecourse. In reality, the Downs are exceptionally large and not really *that near* where we lived. The racecourse takes up a fraction of the huge open space. The Derby is a race that is over a mile and a half long. To put this into any kind of perspective, the £23 million Grandstand was at least thirty minutes' walk from our family home; and offered *nothing* to local residents.

Basically, Tattenham Corner is a quiet residential area squeezed between two large estates at Merland Rise and Nork. So, my Mother, without a car, and with no friends or family nearby, found herself stuck inside a sizable property (it was cold and dark) and alone, caring for her baby, my youngest sister.

When I was a young lad I worked at a shop in Upper High Street, Epsom. I'd take the 406a from Merland Rise (a green London Country double-decker) and the bus would trundle me into town. Waiting for the bus might take 20 minutes (we didn't have 'Bus Tracker' apps and the timetable was inevitably missing or faded.) The bus journey took 20 minutes. In all, it took 40-50 minutes *or so* to get to the next town. Rather than waste nearly an hour travelling by bus, as soon as I could afford it, I bought myself a racing bicycle and then I'd pedal down the steep hill and into town. I'd free-wheel all the way. But I struggled back *up* the chalk hills at the end of a working day. I dreaded making my return ride.

If I wanted to buy a new record, Banstead was the place to visit. I could take a 164a bus (a red London Transport Double Decker) from Tattenham Corner. The bus would take me *half the way*. I'd need to get off at the Brighton Road then walk for another 20-30 minutes into Banstead village. This, for us, was the nearest High Street shops to Epsom Downs. Banstead was (and still is) a sleepy place. There are a few restaurants and some reasonable shops, plus a couple of pubs. There was even a Metropolitan Police Station in those days. The coppers must have been the luckiest in the force! They spent all day watering their window boxes and washing their panda cars.

On my way down the hill, on the way to work, I would pass 'Page Motors' at 74-78 High Street Epsom. Rumour spread that this was owned by guitarist Jimmy Page's Father. In fact, the Page Family who owned this garage has nothing to do with Jimmy's branch of *Pages*. Jimmy was born in Heston, Middlesex and his side of the Page Family has roots in Grimsbury, Northhants (now incorporated *into* Banbury Oxfordshire district.)

But the rumour persisted because Jimmy *did* live in Epsom. He attended Pound Lane School. Later, he went onto Danetree School. (This is also where 'Clocks' members Ricketts (bass) and Hilliam (lead guitar) first became friends, circa 1991). Jimmy Page lived with his parents at 34 Miles Road, Epsom (immortalised in 'Miles Road' a song he recorded with his friend Eric Clapton, in 1965.)

Page has been a lifelong believer in luck and kismet. When his family moved into the house in Epsom, it seemed his life was already twisting in strange, predetermined ways. Mysteriously, a guitar had been left in their new house by previous owners. It seemed entirely possible that fate influenced his life story.

Jimmy Page was a slim man with a quiff of shiny Brylcreemed hair. An old photo of him playing with 'The Presidents' (circa 1959) shows him wearing a tidy jacket and crumpled jumper. In the snap he resembles a college lecturer who'd like it if his students thought he was *cool*. Like all his sophisticated friends, Jimmy was enthusiastic about Skiffle. At the age of thirteen (1957) he appeared on Huw Wheldon's talent quest TV programme 'All Your Own'. This was the 'X Factor' of the day. Apparently Huw Wheldon attracted the attention of programme-makers because he'd fronted a fabulously successful national conker competition! Yes, that was the kind of innovative television show they made in the good 'ole days. Furthermore, his new 'X Factor' type show was genuinely revolutionary because it featured real-life children demonstrating real-life talents. And because 'anything could happen' and often, because it was unscripted *it did*, the show became very exciting. The well-liked show launched the careers of several famous musicians, for example the Australian classical guitarist John Williams (who was living in London at the time, studying at the Royal College of Music– between 1956 to 1959.) The show also introduced a pop vocal trio known as 'The King Brothers' (who are remembered fondly for their cover version of Frank Loesser's 'Standing on the Corner.')

And on this, Huw Wheldon's talent show, Jimmy played the song *Mama Don't Allow No Skiffle Around Here* (the song-title was fluffed by Wheldon on the show.) Jimmy played it with a band he'd named the 'J.G. Skiffle Group'. Nothing much came of his telly appearance – but it helped the young man bolster his confidence and continue working as a guitarist. And, indeed, he kept himself remarkably busy – busking and hustling –taking his Hofner President f-hole everywhere he went –constantly networking.

At about this time, in North London, a semi-professional rock 'n' roll act named 'Red-E-Lewis And The Redcaps' were diligently playing their *own* patch. They were clearly a tribute band of 'Gene Vincent And The Blue Caps.' The band was fronted by a singer named William Stubbs aka 'Reddy Lewis' — the band formed in mid-1958. Their first line-up consisted of guitarist Bobby Oats and drummer Jimmy Rook. Interestingly 'The Redcaps' were first discovered at Wandsworth Town Hall. (I say *interestingly* because my future Father-in-law worked at Wandsworth Town Hall – commuting every day from Nork, so I feel a certain kinship for the place.) The busy venue was regularly visited by the prolific songwriter Frederick Heath (later known as Johnny Kidd) and Heath had a Skiffle band known as 'The Frantic Four' (aka 'The Nutters'.) Frederick and the Frantic Four performed at Wandsworth Town Hall several times. In 1960, when 'Freddie Heath and the Nutters' morphed into 'Johnny Kidd and the Pirates' they released a superb pop song titled '*Shakin' All Over.*'

That song, Jonny Kidd's song, hit the top spot in the UK charts and remains internationally, and *very deservedly*, legendary, because *visually* Kidd was one of the most important artists the genre had ever seen. He and his band would 'dress up' in silly pirate costumes. They wore eye-patches, tricorn hats, wielded cutlasses – the complete dressing-up box. Kidd utilised two guitarists in the line-up – not just the tried-and-tested *one*. Importantly, he fronted the band as an ultra-dynamic *lead singer*. Kidd made performance and theatricals part of the rock 'n' roll concert *experience*. Consequently, putting on a colourful 'rock show' became not just acceptable but *fashionable*. Without Kidd we may never have had Queen, Kiss, 'Alice Cooper', 'Marilyn Manson' or 'Cradle of Filth'. Who knows, without Kidd there may have not been a Lady Gaga! Kidd brought theatre into rock!

Sadly, Johnny Kidd died aged just 30 (in 1966) in a road traffic collision on the busy A58 near Radcliffe, in Lancashire. In the car–

along with Kidd –was Pirates' bassist Nick Simper. Simper, who came away from the incident with a broken arm and nasty cuts, later became a founder member of Deep Purple. Simper still regularly plays bass-guitar around Surrey venues– with a band named the 'The Good Old Boys'. I've seen the show many times at the Staines Riverside Club. (He also played with a superb but little-known progressive rock group named Warhorse.)

To reiterate, the first line-up of 'Red-E-Lewis And The Redcaps' included guitarist Bobby Oats and drummer Jimmy Rook. They played a few gigs at the Ebbisham Hall in Epsom – and this is where the young Jimmy Page met the lads. Page, who trusted in karma and good fortune, was unknowingly forming the most significant professional contacts of his career while hanging out with this band. He knew them so well; they allowed him to borrow Bobby's guitar. He played a few licks on the Resonet Grazioso and the band's manager seemed suitably impressed with the Epsom boy's talent. Not long after, following personnel changes within the band, 'The Redcaps' band manager contacted Page and offered him a place as lead guitarist. His schmoozing and hustling paid off.

In 1960, through an intermediary called Ray Mackender, (an advisor to Cliff Richard's Father) the Redcaps were introduced to beat poet Royston Ellis. The poet was looking for a backing band for a forthcoming poetry reading tour he had been hawking around town. He called the project 'Rocketry.' 'The Shadows' were an obvious choice for his touring band, *but* since the amazing success of hit-song '*Apache*' things had got so busy for them they couldn't commit to his 'Rocketry' tour.

Upon the recommendations of Mackender, Ellis chose 'The Redcaps.' The poet made a habit of hooking-up with successful musicians during this period. For example, he'd previously travelled to Liverpool from his home in Pinner, Middlesex to meet up with John Lennon and his art-school buddy, Stuart Sutcliffe. In those days, pop musicians shared an enthusiasm for American Beat poets and Ellis was considered part of the fashionable 'beat scene.' Therefore, he was invited to stay with Lennon (at the Gambier Terrace address) for three weeks. This was around the time of 'Johnny and the Moondogs.'

The Royston Ellis tour proved substantially beneficial for Jimmy Page. Lady luck was *again* involved. For reasons that are even now unknown, all the other 'Redcaps' pulled out of the poetry-tour commitment–leaving Jimmy alone and isolated on stage– playing his guitar for a super-hip crowd. It's unlikely that anyone had ever seen such a magical thing before! The amazing exposure did him no harm at all.

Not long after, 'The Redcaps' hired a new singer named Chris Tidmarsh. Tidmarsh swiftly changed his name to Neil Christian and the band became better known as 'Neil Christian and the Crusaders.' Jimmy Page was offered a position in the newly named band. He toured with 'The Crusaders' over a two-year period. (Side note: *this* band also boasted Herefordshire finger-picking Rockabilly supremo Albert Lee for a short stint.

———

In those days it was not unusual for young people to suffer from very nasty childhood illnesses. It was extremely commonplace to fall terribly sick with whooping cough, measles, mumps, chicken pox, croup, and scarlet fever. Even polio hadn't been properly eradicated. And if you succumbed to scarlet fever – you would be incarcerated in hospital for several weeks. I remember that I got a dose of the measles in 1962. (Although I recall chickenpox was the most uncomfortable illness I endured.) I was laid up with measles for a week– feeling sorry for myself. In those days, a doctor would be called. Doctors performed emergency home visits on kids in the Fifties and Sixties. The Doc took one look, and said, 'Yes, measles.' That was it. No medicines, no tablets, no antibiotics. He just needed be sure that I *wasn't going to die*. Anyway, not on his watch.

It seems amazing, but youngsters really *did* die from childhood diseases back in the rock 'n' roll years. We often heard Mothers talking about kids being "taken poorly" and being rushed to hospital with 'complications.' It was a word we feared. A friend of mine (we used to play cricket on the road in North Cheam) didn't come to school for two days. I went to see him, but his Mother met me at the door. She told me Colin had been "taken poorly" and was in bed. (She wouldn't let me in.) She told me he had glandular fever. The next day he was taken to hospital with 'complications.' The fever mutated into Meningitis. He passed away that same weekend. An N.H.S. programme to vaccinate everyone under the age of 15 against polio and diphtheria started in 1958 and the effort helped to boost the survival rates of young people. But in the 1950s and early Sixties, it was extremely common to fall *terribly ill* during childhood.

So, when Jimmy Page fell *very ill* with mononucleosis during his tour with 'The Crusaders,' his family and his friends were told to hold their breath and prepare for the worst. They likely prayed for his recovery. Even if the disease didn't have scary 'complications,' it still might provide a 'knock-out blow' for a child. These childhood diseases often led to prolonged bouts of fatigue.

During Page's extended period of recovery from the disease, he placed his constant touring on hold and enrolled at Sutton Art College (1962-3). This meant he effectively quit his position with 'The Crusaders.' He probably figured the constant touring schedule with his band was detrimental to long-term health. Page found he suffered from constant bouts of flu-like disorders. Furthermore, he couldn't shake them off. Jimmy realized he would be doing himself a favour if he spent eighteen months convalescing. He felt determined to get his strength back and increase his resilience.

Jimmy was always a hawker. Always busy. Always peddling his skills. So, even when studying at Sutton Art College, he rented himself out as a session guitarist. One day he found himself playing at the famous Marquee club at Wardour Street, in Soho. It was there he met Alexis Korner.

———

Alexis Korner was a mysterious looking fellow.

He sported a frizzy mop of springy hair and possessed an elongated chin. To me, he resembled a *future* Doctor Who.

Korner is often described as the founding Father of British Blues, and it's a fair depiction because Korner was responsible for bringing over big-name blues artists from the States, for example Muddy Waters, Sonny Boy Williamson and Matt Murphy and popularising British-style electric-blues. Korner was born in Paris and was taught guitar and keyboards from an early age. His family fled France to escape looming Nazi persecution. In 1949, Korner joined Chris Barber's Jazz Band. Whilst playing in Barber's band, Korner hooked-up with the talented harmonica player Cyril Davies –they became good friends. They released a record together in 1957. Korner also gigged with 'Ken Colyer's Skiffle Group.' He played mandolin on one of their first recordings (1955.)

In 1961, Korner and Davies formed 'Blues Incorporated' which was conceived to be a loose-knit community of like-minded souls. This blues fellowship included (at various times) Charlie Watts, Jack Bruce, Ginger Baker, Long John Baldry, Graham Bond, Danny Thompson, and Dick Heckstall-Smith. We now recognize this project as one of the world's first super-groups. There has never been a more influential set-up in British rock history than Blues Incorporated! Harp player Davies left the supergroup in late '62. But the 'Incorporated' continued to record and perform, with Korner at the beating heart of the project, right through to 1966. By then the illustrious line-up I listed had all-but flown nest, most of them moving-on to start up their own musical projects. I highly recommend Pete Frame's 'Rock Family Trees' if you want to follow the complicated story of Blues Incorporated, but Page meeting Korner is part of the legend.

———

At the Marquee, possibly through Korner's stewardship, Page met Clapton. He also renewed an old friendship with Jeff Beck. Here were three of the world's greatest guitarists–all from Surrey–at the Marquee. We'll look at this trio of ground-breaking musicians in more detail, shortly, but it's worth adding, at this stage, that through the many networking opportunities gained at the Marquee and via Korner, Page connected with the Decca Records main 'arranger,' a guy named Mike Leander. Even *then*, Leander was a *renowned* music business figure, an established producer and celebrated arranger. He'd worked for the American doo-wop group 'The Drifters' (the *real* Drifters, not Cliff Richard's former band) and also produced for ex-Drifter front-man 'Ben E. King'. Later, in the 1970's, he became even more famous as the executive producer on Andrew Lloyd Webber and Tim Rice's 'Jesus Christ Superstar.' He worked with Paul Raven (now known as the notorious Gary Glitter) on the 'Superstar' project. He became such good friends with Raven that he went on to co-write songs with him. Together, they wrote many of Glitter's most popular numbers including '*Rock and Roll*' (Parts 1 and 2).

At about the time that Page linked-up with him, Leander was working with an artist who called himself Vance Arnold. This singer looked like a mad-professor, with colossal sideburns, and a shock of unruly hair. He'd come from the Northern clubs of Sheffield and had previously been touring with a Skiffle band called 'The Cavaliers' around Yorkshire. Their singer, Arnold, had decided to go to London to 'seek his fortune' with a group he'd named 'The Avengers.'

Vance Arnold had an amazing voice. The grittiest voice anyone had *ever* heard. Everyone 'up North' knew that Arnold was a *very* impressive talent. In 1964 Vance Arnold signed with Decca and recorded a Lennon-penned number '*I'll Cry Instead.*' (The song was later heard on the soundtrack to '*A Hard Day's Night*'). Leander's arrangement of the song was one of the first session-jobs that young guitarist Jimmy Page worked on. Page played guitar on the recording, along with another session guitarist known as 'Big' Jim Sullivan (real name, James Tomkins.)

Cranford, Middlesex based Jim Sullivan was a member of Marty Wilde's 'Wildcats' and gave guitar lessons to the future guitar-super-star Ritchie Blackmore when his family moved to Heston, Middlesex. Legend has it that Sullivan bought his first guitar, a Gibson les Paul, from Sister Rosetta Tharpe, when she visited England. The Wildcats were the opening act in the previously mentioned television series, Oh Boy! and supported Eddie Cochran and Gene Vincent on those UK package tours. Sullivan was, therefore, in great demand as a session guitarist.

After the '*I'll Cry Instead*' job with Jim Sullivan, things started to hot-up for Page; the Leander connection gained him lots more offers of studio work. So prolific were these *two* amazingly talented studio guitarists, by the way, that recording artists would regularly insist their producers got hold of 'Jim' to play on tracks. It wasn't long before Jim Sullivan had to describe himself as 'Big' so prospective clients could differentiate between him and 'Little' Jimmy Page.

Despite huge promotion by the record company, and enthusiastic reviews by the music press, Vance Arnold's single, with Jimmy Page on guitar, *flopped*. Dispirited and dejected, Arnold dropped his 'stage name' and began to perform under his *real* name – a name you'd recognize right away, and perhaps he ought to have used it all along– Joe Cocker. But by then his lucrative Decca contract had been terminated due to dreadful sales. Cocker returned to Yorkshire to take a long sabbatical from the music business. Luckily for us, in 1966, Cocker joined-up with keyboardist Chris Stainton to form a new project called 'The Grease Band' and with this project, he tentatively started back on his musical journey.

———

Surrey has *always* been a suburb of London.

The very first suburb of London was Southwark. Although now quite considered to be a part of Inner London, Southwark was actually the first borough in the County of Surrey, so *ipso facto*, the first suburb. Originally called Suthringa Geweorche (it means fort of the men of Surrey) the area was recorded in the Domesday Book (1086) as Sudweca – which means the same thing. What is more, because the first suburb of Surrey was so near to the seat of power in London, (over-the-river), and so handy for mapping and *taxing* purposes, the villages, hamlets, farms and free-holds of the County were the first places in Britain to be *officially* mapped, named, and assessed for tax. The implications of this are still not fully understood, but it probably means that some of the place-names we find in Surrey seem to have a 'Welsh' ring about them. For example, I remember telling a Londoner I had a girlfriend who lived in 'Mogador' and the

Londoner looked genuinely surprised. 'Do you commute all the way to Wales?' he asked.

This 'Welsh' ring to Surrey place-names is perhaps because Surrey places were *formally* named so early in history by the Normans. The early and authentic names were recorded by those early tax assessors (probably before the Domesday Book was compiled.) Academics call this early Welsh sounding language 'Celto-Latin.' 'Celto-Latin' was the first properly written-down language of the British people.

In Surrey, we get the word *wealh* cropping up in place names. It means 'Welsh Speaking' and is rare to see the phrase written in English place-names (less so in Wales.) Just a little way down Wrythe Lane, a road a lived a minute from – you come to the peaceful community of Wallington. It's one of those 'Welsh' sounding names (it means the place of Welsh speakers.) To the East is Wallington's big ugly sister– Croydon. But to the South is the village of Wood-mansterne (it means 'thorn bush by the boundary of the wood' in that same Welsh-sounding 'Celto-Latin.')

Wallington was one of those areas (like its close neighbour Morden) where lavender had once been grown for commercial purposes. Back then, it was a small, pretty village with two mills and a bridge over the River Wandle (there's that *wealh* again.) Wallington somehow managed to maintain its identity as a small-town community right through to the rock 'n' roll years. (Whereas, I think, Morden lost that 'sense of town' when the St Helier Estate was built.)

Leading from Beddington Park to the area of South Beddington, in Wallington, is Demesne Road. A *demesne* refers to lands that were once held by the Crown. We can safely assume this was once a border area for a huge deer park that spanned across the entire wooded expanse of Surrey, just after the Norman Conquest. It was on the edge of a part of this, Nonsuch Park, that Geoffrey Arnold Beck was born. He lived in Demesne Road, Wallington. (Side note: the prominent English jazz pianist and composer, Neil Ardley lived nearby.)

As a ten-year old boy, Jeff Beck sang in his local church choir. He passed his time by sticking bits-and-pieces together in a valiant attempt to construct his own guitar. It was an ongoing kind of therapeutic 'Blue Peter' project for him. He spent his whole life trying to perfect his home-made instruments. He was also extremely keen on fine art– and this occupied as much of his time as his experimental guitar-work. After leaving school he attended the Wimbledon School of Art, near Merton Park. This is the same college that 'The Snowman' author and illustrator (Raymond Briggs) attended in the late 1950's before he was called-up to perform National Service.

In 1963 Beck joined the Croydon based covers band 'The Rumbles.' He showed great prowess as their lead guitarist, and it quickly became evident he could easily mimic the guitar-parts from the famous 'Gene Vincent' and 'Buddy Holly' numbers he was asked to play. This natural mimicry was a valuable commodity. It meant that he could try his luck as a session musician in the busy London studios. In 1964 Beck appeared as a session guitarist on '*I'm Not Running Away*' a song recorded at Pye by the Manchester-based band 'The Fitz & Startz.' Although it was a one-hit wonder for 'The Fitz & Startz' it marked the beginning of a profitable career for Beck as a session musician.

When we look back at to the experiences of both Beck and Page we see that living close to London –being able to easily commute to central studios– helped them develop formative careers. This was a major advantage of Surrey living. It was not as if you were isolated from the London version of 'Tin Pan Alley' indeed, it was just a short train ride away. But you could easily flee home to the safety and boredom of the suburbs when things got too hot to handle. Or if you needed to lick your wounds and re-gain your strength. Contrast this with the experience of Joe Cocker. He had to give up a secure job in the North (a gas fitter) and gamble *it all* on a risky make-or-break trek to London. The 'flash in a pan' project in London went sour. He returned to his native Yorkshire and may never have ventured out again. But Surrey suburban *chancers* could try over-and-over to get it right!

Reasonable prosperity and a secure family home helped Beck and Page– and others like them– to do more-or-less whatever they wanted. This is *still* the case for Surrey kids. You could be certain that you wouldn't be compelled to work in a factory, go down a mine, or work on the docks if you lived in Surrey. It's likely your Dad had a steady income from a regular commute, which made your life fairly comfortable. Growing up in Surrey, you could survive on 'the bank of Mum and Dad' for years. Both Beck and Page enjoyed this kind of privilege. They had the option to opt for 'art school' life rather than doing hard physical work. In a little while, we will examine the 'art school set' in more detail.

————

Surrey is theoretically an economically deprived County due to its relatively weak soils. Historically, the primary benefit of Surrey was its ability to transport merchants and business travellers to the wealthier and more productive regions of the West of England (and her ports) in a secure and fast manner. Surrey was not seen as a place to establish a permanent residence.

There are only fourteen market towns in Surrey. This excludes the original market town of Southwark, and other 'London borough' towns such as Sutton, Croydon, and Kingston. The list excludes Bletchingley, west of Godstone, a market town that had already shrunk to the size of a village by the 14th century. The list *includes* Staines that is technically in Surrey, but Spelthorne people maintain their town is in Middlesex (and they're justified to think that!) Hence, to lay things out, the County area has 14 market towns yet measures over 642 square miles. Each individual market town of Surrey must 'serve' around 45 square miles.

Chertsey
Dorking
Epsom
Farnham
Godalming
Guildford
Haslemere (Charter Fair)
Horley

Leatherhead
Redhill
Reigate
Staines (Middlesex)
Walton-on-Thames
Weybridge
Woking

———

This relative lack of market towns renders Surrey that empty 'feeling' and helps support the notion that Surrey is isolated, a sense it *still* retains. Compare Surrey with Devon that has an equivalent population: the clotted-cream County has over 45 towns. But perhaps Devon is an unfair comparison given the size of it, so what about neighbouring East Sussex, with a relative size? That largely rural County, with a smaller population, has 17 market towns.

I know I have excluded them in the above list of market towns, but for the purposes of music making and performance venues, there are three *major* conurbations in Surrey. During the rock 'n' roll era, most rock 'n' roll activities gravitated around the 'big three' —

- Croydon (now a London Borough) with a wider population of 384,000
- Kingston upon Thames (now a London Borough) with a population of 175,000.
- Guildford, the largest town in present-day Surrey with a 'wider' population of around 144,000

*current estimates

The other large towns of the County are, in truth, swollen housing estates. Woking is the largest of these bloaters. It's the second largest town in present day Surrey with a population that compares with

Guildford and exceeds it if you include all the out-lying districts. Present day Ewell has a population of 40,000. Farnham has a population of 37,100. Camberley has a population of 30,200 [These figures from the 2001 Census.)

———

In the early part of 1962 – a year before much of Surrey was hidden under a blanket of snow – a strange fellow calling himself Elmo Lewis could be found energetically hustling his skills around the Soho area. He was an accomplished slide-guitarist (and harmonica player). He was a good-looking chap, always smartly dressed, though he sported a remarkable toadstool shaped death-cap hair-style. Elmo Lewis became friends with some exceptionally talented musicians including Alexis Korner. He also became friendly with the future Manfred Mann singer Paul Jones. He dropped his slightly daft Confederate name – and started going by his first middle name and *actual* surname: Brian Jones. He hooked-up with Paul Jones and they started to play regularly with Paul's band, the 'Roosters.'

In January 1963 both Jones's (Paul and Brian) left the 'Roosters'. (A young fellow named Eric Clapton took over Brian's role– as the 'Roosters' new lead guitarist – but that's another story I'll leave for a rainy day.) Brian Jones quickly placed an advert in 'Jazz News' inviting musicians to join a *new* R&B group he was forming. Stu Stewart (raised in Sutton, Surrey) was the first to respond to the advert. Stewart was a burly looking thick-jawed Scotsman, and a talented keyboardist. He was also a self-confessed *jazz-nut*. He didn't actually 'fit in' with the general style or image of the band. Although his days with the band were numbered from the outset, *actually* he'd stay with their project through thick and thin– and for a long while to come.

After Stu Stewart's appointment, the Dartford (Kent) lad Mick Jagger *also* replied to the same ad. Mick brought along a school-chum named Keith Richards – so both could audition *together*. Both got jobs in the *new* band. According to Richards, Brian Jones produced one of the most famous band names in rock 'n' roll history in a moment of blind panic. Whilst on the phone to a venue owner – trying to flannel him into giving this new and completely unheard-of R&B outfit a gig – the voice on the other end of the line asked something like: 'what are you called then?' According to rock 'n' roll legend, a copy of the album 'The Best of Muddy Waters' lay near the telephone that Jones had used. He looked down for inspiration and saw track five. It read '*Rollin' Stone.*' 'We are the Rollin' Stones' he exclaimed. We don't know if he secured the gig, but in *flash* he'd arrived at a name!

The 'Rollin' Stones played their first gig on 12 July 1962 at the Marquee Club in London. The line-up was Jagger, Richards, Jones, and Stewart. Brian Jones also managed to recruit Dick Taylor into a semi-permanent position on bass guitar. (Taylor was actually a considerably talented *lead*-guitarist but pushed 'back to bass' by Jones.) Dick Taylor later formed his own band 'The Pretty Things.'

The Rollin' Stones also found themselves a drummer, a temporary guy named Tony Chapman. Chapman was with the London-based band the 'Cliftons' along with Bill Wyman. Charlie Watts was still playing with Alexis Korner at this time. He was convinced to move to the Stones in the early part of 1963. When Watts joined the line-up, Chapman left the band, flying off to form his own project called 'The Preachers.' He joined forces with the prodigiously talented 14-year-old Bromley singer/guitarist - Peter Frampton.

Not long after the departure of Chapman, his best mate Bill Wyman contacted the group enquiring about the role as permanent bassist. He was grabbed *too*. Like the Beatles, the band then all moved in together. They shared an apartment (described by Richards as 'a beautiful dump') at 102 Edith Grove, Chelsea.

At this stage of their development, it should be noted that Brian Jones was very much the band-leader of the Stones. According to Charlie Watts, he was a man on a 'crusade,' constantly working to get the band more gigs and appearances. Jones was also determined that their band should be billed as an R&B act. The band played blues clubs, jazz clubs, just anywhere they could get a stage. Jones took an 'extra' fiver from the pot - as a reward to himself for his role 'as manager.' This led to resentment within the group and bitter criticism from other members. Soon afterwards, a fellow called Giorgio

Gomelsky – a former Swiss air-force pilot who we will encounter in more detail, shortly– became the group's *de facto* manager.

It should be stipulated at this point that the Stones were largely from Kent. (Bill Wyman was from Lewisham, South London and Jones was born in Cheltenham, Gloucestershire.) So, what was their connection with Surrey? Why did a magical and mysterious Thameside venue become almost a *sacred* birthplace of British Blues?

16

JAZZ BLUESED BY BARBER

Chris Barber was born in the lovely Welwyn Garden City, Hertford-shire, on 17 April 1930.

The boy started learning the violin when he was seven years old at the delightfully old Hanley Castle Grammar School, which became a setting for many novels written by P.G. Wodehouse. (In his books, it became the Market Snodsbury Grammar School.)

At the age of fifteen, the musician began to get seriously inter-ested in jazz. It's worth remembering this was before Miles Davis and John Coltrane (John was just starting out as a clarinettist in a Navy band) but Charlie Parker began making public appearances. This was still the era of Nat King Cole and Glenn Miller and the swing band conductors such as Benny Goodman.

Following the war, Barber went to St. Paul's School in London (the same school that the celebrated 'blogger' Samuel Pepys had attended) and started visiting to bars to watch jazz ensembles. After that, he attended the Guildhall School of Music for three years where he met Alexis Korner.

In order to perform blues and traditional jazz music, Barber founded the New Orleans Jazz Band in 1950. The ensemble consisted of up to eight amateur players, including Korner on guitar and Barber on double bass. And he turned pro two years later.

When cornetist and trumpeter Pat Halcox was unavailable in 1953 for performances in Denmark, trumpeter Ken Colyer assumed the position. Ken had already been playing with the successful Crane River Jazz Band (CRJB) and had even performed in front of Princess Elizabeth at the Royal Festival Hall in London when it opened, 1951. In the British jazz community, Colyer was well regarded; he'd even performed in the world-renowned Bourbon Street bars of New Orleans with George Lewis's ensemble.

As a result, Colyer joined Barber's band, which later adopted the moniker Ken Colyer's Jazzmen due to Collyer's popularity and his undeniable international reputation.

Donegan's performance of 'Rock Island Line' was part of this band's debut recording session in 1954, which resulted in an album titled: *New Orleans Joys*.

'Rock Island Line' became a bigger hit when released as a single under Donegan's name, and as we now know *this* hit kick-started both the British Skiffle boom and Donegan's solo career.

In the late 1950s and early 1960s Barber played a major role in setting up the first UK tours of blues musicians such as Big Bill Broonzy, Sonny Terry, Brownie McGhee, and Muddy Waters. As a fixer and arranger, Chris Barber played a pivotal role in the development of British rock 'n' roll history.

The Rolling Stones, Eric Clapton, Peter Green, and other young musicians were influenced to get interested in the blues by the far-reaching effects of these UK tours put together by Barber. The sounds these Surrey musicians established—drawing from Big Bill Broonzy, Sonny Terry, Brownie McGhee, and Muddy Waters—became the 'British rhythm and blues' explosion, which propelled pop charts throughout the 1960s and advanced the rock 'n' roll subgenres that we now refer to as heavy rock, metal, and prog.

Barber is the man who can legitimately lay claim to being the *Father of British Rock*. Even though he took some incredible chances to advance blues-rock, he never lost his modesty. For instance, he invited blues guitarist John Slaughter to a 'pure' jazz event that featured Acker Bilk, Alex Welsh, and Kenny Ball. Moreover, he collaborated with Rory Gallagher on a jazz-blues album (*Drat That Fratle Rat*, 1972.)

———

After moving to London in 1948, the guy I previously mentioned, Harold Pendleton, a jazz enthusiast from Lancashire, frequented backroom jazz clubs such as The Flamingo, Wardour Street (also known as the Shim Sham Club), the Ealing Jazz Club, Ronnie Scott's in Soho, and The Bull's Head, Barnes and, occasionally, The Establishment in Greek Street (known for its comedy nights, but they also hosted jazz sessions.) It was during one of *these* jazz nights that Pendleton met Chris Barber. By that time, Barber had founded the National Federation of Jazz Organisations of Great Britain (NFJOGB) with Pendleton elected as secretary, likely because of his love of and commitment to *traditional* jazz. Pendleton was the guy who insisted on the organization's name being shortened to the National Jazz Federation (NJF).

The two jazz aficionados started planning gatherings, some of them quite ambitious, to promote British jazz and British musicians. Even though they didn't have a regular location for the concerts they were trying to get up-and-running, their organisation sponsored concerts (200, annually, held in various locations around the Home Counties.)

When Pendleton took over running jazz nights at Oxford Street's Marquee Ballroom in 1958, the two jazz lovers increased the frequency and scope of their events and invited American performers, including the likes of Muddy Waters, to play their club. Despite Pendleton's personal distaste for the genre, at around this time the Marquee started organising rhythm and blues evenings. After he'd seen how popular blues music had become at the Ealing Club, he didn't object when one of his nights featured the up-and-coming youth-outfit, The Rolling Stones.

As the NJF's secretary, Pendleton organised Barber's first National Jazz Festival, held in 1961, after he'd taken an active role in the earlier Beaulieu Jazz Festival, hosted at Lord Montagu's Hampshire estate from 1956 to 1961. Pendleton was probably also inspired by the popularity of Elaine Lorillard's Newport Jazz Festival in Rhode Island. Over time, this major event on the international music calendar expanded to include not only jazz but also blues, rhythm & blues, and rock.

The first National Jazz Festival was held at Richmond Athletic Ground in the peaceful town of Richmond-upon-Thames, still a part of Surrey before 1965. As one might anticipate, British jazz legends Johnny Dankworth and Chris Barber headlined the first event. Additional acts included: the Mike Cotton Jazzmen, the Ronnie Ross Quartet, the Tubby Hayes Quartet, the Alex Welsh band, Ken Colyer's Jazzmen, the Sutton Chicago Jazz Group, and Terry Lightfoot (among others.)

However, by the time of the second festival (held on July 28–29, 1962), the word 'blues' had been conveniently *added* to the title (though, not the event poster!) And even if the headliners were acts like the Chris Barber Jazzband, Ottilie Paterson, Johnny Dankworth, and (this time) Kenny Ball & His Jazzmen... there was a hint— possibly no more than a suggestive *soupcon,* really— of what would come *next* in British music, i.e. the great British blues explosion. As a last-minute addition to the festival, Alexis Korner's Blues Incorporated were invited to play a sideshow gig. Both Barber and Pendleton admitted the rise of interest in Korner's Chicago-style rhythm & blues sounds had been, to use their word, 'startling.'

At the third Richmond Festival (August 10–11, 1963), a new act that had been drawing large crowds to The Station Hotel in Richmond— local boys, the Stones—performed on the club house stage while Acker Bilk performed a mainstream set on the festival's primary stage. Acker Bilk's Paramount Jazz Band set boosted performances by Chris Barber, the Cyril Davis Rhythm and Blues All Stars, the Alex Welsh Band, Humphrey Lyttleton, and many other British jazz luminaries.

Long John Baldrey, who was reportedly among the first British musicians to perform blues vocals in nightclubs, was the other 'surprise' performer at the third festival. For years, Baldry had performed at Eel Pie Island in nearby Twickenham, Middlesex. Baldrey also occasionally shared the stage with the Rolling Stones at the Station Hotel in Richmond. However, it was during his time as a vocalist with Alexis Korner's Blues Incorporated that Harold Pendleton and Chris Barber became aware of him as an emerging star. Baldrey played a prominent role in the highly influential Blues Incorporated album 'R&B from the Marquee' (1962). Baldry also had a significant part to play in the development of the emerging blues-rock genre. He assembled a band that backed The Rolling Stones when they made their stage début in July 1962 at Pendleton's Marquee Club. And Baldry and Paul McCartney grew close following a Liverpool Cavern Club meeting in the early 1960s. Baldry joined the Cyril Davies R&B All Stars in 1963, where Nicky Hopkins was pianist. After Cyril Davies passed away in 1964, Baldry assumed leadership of the outfit, and the band changed its name to Long John Baldry and his Hoochie Coochie Men, with Rod Stewart on co-lead vocals and the former Sunrisers Skiffle Group musician, Geoff Bradford, on guitar. Later, with Julie Driscoll on vocals, and Brian Auger on Hammond organ, the Hoochie Coochie Men transmogrified into the band project named 'Steampacket' (1965.)

Following the dissolution of Steampacket in 1966, Baldry created Bluesology, which included guitarist Caleb Quaye, keyboardist Reg Dwight, and (Soft Machine's) jazz saxophonist Elton Dean. You will be aware, I'm sure, that Dwight eventually changed his name to Elton John (perhaps in honour of Baldry and their sax-player.)

For a brief period, Baldry's Bluesology was led by the Philadelphia-born actress/singer Marsha Hunt, who is best known as the three-line character *Dionne* in the popular rock musical Hair. Marsha was a backing vocalist on Alexis Korner's band Free at Last. The songs 'Marsha's Mood' and 'Brown Sugar' by John Mayall (and later the 'different' and much more famous *'Brown Sugar'* number by the Stones) were reportedly inspired by the superfine-looking Marsha. She married Mike Ratledge of Soft Machine, but also dated Marc Bolan and Mick Jagger at the same time. This was the swinging sixties, after all! (Karis Jagger is the offspring from the relationship with Mick). Marsha also joined the rock & soul group The Ferris Wheel, though Linda Lewis eventually took over Marsha's position.

It's interesting to note that Marsha's picture, taken by Justin de Villeneuve of 'Twiggy' promotion fame, was widely used on the play-bills and posters for the first London production of Hair, (Shaftesbury Theatre). Her amazing 'frizz' became a famous symbol of swinging London in the 1960s and, later, a popular student bedroom poster.

By the time of the fourth National Jazz and Blues Festival, which took place August 7-9, 1964, the Rolling Stones, Gary Farr's T-Bones, Manfred Mann, Georgie Fame and the Blue Flames, The Yardbirds with Clapton, and a renowned jam session featuring Georgie Fame, Jack Bruce, Graham Bond, Ginger Baker, and Mike Vernon were among the many rock-blues titbits offered to festival goers. Although British jazz greats were *still* well-presented, one of the main draws of *this* festival was the Mississippi jazz-blues piano pioneer Mose Allison.

Although Richmond was where the festival started and in many respects was a natural home for the event, local people had never welcomed the unwashed masses to their little patch of leafy Surrey heaven. The festival's final year at Richmond took place in 1965. The vexed issue of fans sleeping rough (especially in Richmond Park) had long been a cause of disagreement. While previous years' the organisers had supplied a spacious marquee for campers to squat in, Pendleton was prevented from setting-up the tent in 1965, forcing many *more* fans to sleep in the woods and green spaced around town. This brought about *the end* of the Richmond festival. Added to that, the quantity of festival-goers had increased year-on-year; in 1964, the audience totalled 27,000; in 1965, it totalled 33,000.

Furthermore, it should come as no surprise that by 1965, the 'scruffier' R&B bands had significantly outnumbered the clean-cut jazz ensembles. The Yardbirds, The Who, The Moody Blues, The Animals, Spencer Davis, and Steam Packet, were among the youthful (and hairy) acts performing on the main stage! Chris Barber played the event, of course, as did Kenny Ball and Ken Colyer, but the jazz days were fading!

The National Jazz and Blues Festivals later became the much more famous (and much larger) Reading Festival. Pendleton retired from his role at the Reading Festival in 1988. Just before that, he sold the Marquee Club. Pendleton died in 2017, aged 93.

Despite his immense success over many years as a *pro* jazz musician, Chris Barber never lost the fervour of a resolute amateur Englishman seeking an outlet he and his friends might have satisfactorily addressed in an allotment hut. This sort of peculiar amateurism sets the English apart from others! It's also true that Barber never wavered in his belief that jazz constituted the most avant-garde and inventive music in all history. But for introducing us to the most important and trailblazing artists of a revolutionary new sound—British rhythm and blues—we owe him an *enormous* debt of thanks.

Chris Barber died on 2 March 2021, aged 90.

Surrey hosted one more Jazz and Blues Festival, though this time at Kempton Park Racecourse, Sunbury-on-Thames, August 1968. Historically, Sunbury had been in Middlesex since before anybody can remember, but in 1965 Sunbury, Kempton and surrounding communities that were initially intended to form part of a newly created County of Greater London, were *instead*, almost as an afterthought, 'transferred' to Surrey. Friday's biggest name at Kempton was Jerry Lee Lewis but The Herd had higher billing. The Saturday evening main stage boasted The Nice, Jeff Beck, and Arthur Brown. Traffic were at Kempton on the Sunday night bill, after Chicken Shack and Spencer Davis. Apparently, unlisted, Glass Menagerie made an appearance before the Fairport Convention set, on the Sunday afternoon.

17

THE ART SCHOOL SET

On a boring weekday afternoon at Tattenham Corner, my sister and I were practicing in the bedroom for an upcoming show, while our Mother was gardening in the back garden. Suddenly, we were startled by a loud and terrifying explosion. The boom had the potential to break the windows, but it didn't. But the whole house shuddered as if we had been hit by an earthquake. While we were unsure of the cause of the explosion, it occurred to us that it might have been a terrorist incident. This was during a turbulent period in Northern Ireland known as the 'troubles,' when the Provisional I.R.A. broke away from the Official I.R.A. and had threatened a bombing campaign in mainland Britain.

In fact, in October 1974, two pubs in Guildford, Surrey were bombed by the Provisional I.R.A.

It was unclear, though, why any Republican sympathiser, worth his salt, would choose to detonate a bomb in the sleepy suburb of Epsom Downs on a weekday afternoon!

The answer wasn't as thrilling as a terrorist incident, but my Father still managed to criticize 'art school types' after the explosion.

It seemed that two long-haired art school 'types' who lived a few doors down were 'experimenting' with explosive chemicals in their backyard. The army, police, fire brigade, and ambulance (not required) arrived, and the art students were taken away for questioning, presumably by Special Branch. However, they returned the next day, unruffled and unharmed, and continued to act just like the typical art school types they had always been, in other words: slouchy and ragged. It seems they 'got away with blowing themselves up.'

My Father commented on the *dishevelled and unkempt individuals*, calling them a *burden on society*, during a conversation at the blue Formica kitchen table over breakfast.

'Who are a burden on society?' I asked. 'Are you talking about those hippies down the road that exploded the bomb?' Dad's remarks made me uncomfortable as, back then, you could have easily described me as a 'dishevelled and unkempt individual' with long, unclean hair, a ratty trench coat, filthy loon trousers, and strings of love beads.

'I'm referring to *all of them*, not just the bombers down the road.' He added. 'They are *all a complete waste of space.*'

'Every one of them?' I enquired, running fingers through my long hair.

'Yeah *every last one*. But specifically, those who are part of the *art school set*. What a joke. Students are already terrible—they laze around all day and get paid to avoid work. But the art school set are the worst. They're continually messing around and wasting our money.'

It's important to note, back then, that students attending college for tuition were 'paid' by grants, which might sound absurd to students of Generations X, Y, and Z! One in seven 18-year-olds were in higher education in 1972. The student grant for a kid from Surrey, a kid who probably came from a prosperous home, might be around £400-500. That's about one hundred quid *per week* spending money (by today's prices and taking inflation into account.) It was *not* a lot, I agree, but it was sufficient to 'get by' on when you are living at home with parents who gave you *everything*.

My theory is that a major factor in the success of the County's rock 'n' roll output was the abundance of art schools in Surrey, which attracted a group of imaginative and carefree people drawn to the concept of free-form creativity and, as I've already explained, were urged during their early childhoods to 'go out and play' by suburban parents. Men like my Father, in spite of their criticisms art-school slackers, brought prosperity and tranquillity to a generation of young people. Men such as Dad shaped our upbringing, and they had left us alone (in our bedrooms or on the street) to be encouraged by inventiveness and experimentation. In short, we were busy doing art when we weren't generating chaos (by blowing stuff up) or looking scruffy in trench coats as we loafed around all day. The *'Pretty Things,'* as David Bowie described *us*, were incomprehensible to the wartime generation. We were unintentionally driving our parents 'insane.'

Guildford School of Art was formed in 1856. The Farnham School of Art was founded in 1866. The Croydon College of Art was set up in 1941. The Kingston School of Art (KSA) broke away from a technical institute, first established in 1899 to become a separate institution. And Wimbledon School of Art began in 1890.

Sidcup School of Art, about ten miles from the Surrey border, amalgamated with the Bromley School of Art (that opened in 1878) and the Beckenham School of Art. Of course, London had at least ten art schools within easy commuting distance from Surrey. I argue that there is no other place in Britain, or perhaps the entire world, where there's such a wide array of options for prospective art school students. Furthermore, these entities *weren't* contemporary; they weren't a 'Sixties' phenomenon. Since the Victorian era, Surrey had been known as an *optimal* environment for the development of emerging artists.

Surrey and South London art schools produced a sizeable number of rock musicians during the rock 'n' roll years. According to Keith Richards, Sidcup Art College was more or less 'a kind of guitar workshop.' It was at *this* guitar workshop-cum-art college that Richards reconnected with an old primary school buddy, Mick Jagger, who'd been taking classes, though also enrolled as a student at the London School of Economics (LSE). It's said the idea of forming the Rolling Stones came to them at Sidcup college. Indeed, the Stones performed at the college Christmas dance on December 12, 1962, with a lineup that consisted of Jagger, Richards, Brian Jones (enrolled at Cheltenham Art College), Ian Stewart (Tiffin School,

Kingston), Ricky Fenson (Sidcup Art College), and Tony Chapman (Sidcup Art College too.) So, the musicians re-paid their dues to the institution that brought them together. The Dartford (Kent) band the Pretty Things, one of Britain's earliest R&B outfits, *also* formed at Sidcup Art College, in 1963. The bassist Dick Taylor left the earliest template of the Rolling Stones to return to Sidcup Art College to complete studies. While there he developed the Pretty Things.

Jeff Beck and Tom McGuinness went to Wimbledon Art School (now known as Wimbledon College of Arts.) Tom played with the Roosters which was Eric Clapton's first band out of school, he was bassist in an early incarnation of Manfred Mann and, in 1969, he formed the very highly respected country-blues outfit, McGuinness Flint with drummer Hughie Flint. In 1970, Ayrshire singer-song-writers Benny Gallagher and Graham Lyle joined the line-up and wrote 'When I'm Dead and Gone' along with another ten numbers for the band.

In 1930, the Kingston School of Art separated from the Kingston Technical Institute (founded in 1899) and during the rock 'n' roll years *this* institution went on to educate, amongst many others, Angie Bowie, Eric Clapton (who did not graduate), and Sandy Denny (who also did not graduate).

Denny, who went on the become a lead singer for 'Fairport Convention' (she was born at Merton Park) also studied at Kingston. At the College of Art, Denny became active in the campus folk club. John Renbourn, a guitarist, and potential member of Pentangle was one of her undergraduate pals and he probably inspired and influenced her progression into folk rock. Denny began touring the folk club circuit as an art student with an American-influenced set that included songs written by Tom Paxton and a smattering of traditional English folk tunes. Legend has it that her debut public performance was at the Barge in Kingston, aka the Kingston Folk Club. The Barge was *exactly that*, a rescued Dutch sailing barge that had been moored on the Thames at Kingston Quay. In 1965 Paul Simon performed at the Barge. Jackson C. Frank was also a guest performer (he was in England recording with Paul Simon.) The source of this material is John Martyn, a New Malden, Surrey native who, these days, is primarily recognised as a 'Scottish' folk performer. Martyn clarified that in April 1967, he performed at the Folk Barge for the first time. Discogs claims the UK budget label *Summit* released a disc titled *Hootenanny At The Barge,* in 1965. The label suggested that the songs were recorded 'live' at the Barge, Kingston, though this does *not* appear likely. Anyhow, the mono disc featured performances by Theo Johnson, Dave Shelley, Janet Greenfield, The Barge Group, and Roger Evans (misprinted Rodger on the disc cover).

Another student of Kingston College of Art was 'Yardbirds' lead singer Keith Relf (born in Richmond). Relf went on to form folk-rockers Renaissance with his sister, Jane Relf. The early line-up of Renaissance included Yardbird's drummer Jim McCarty, and Strawbs / Nashville Teens keyboardist John Hawken, who also played with Spooky Tooth, and a lesser-known outfit known for a while as Third World War. The band had Louis Cennamo on bass guitar.

Sadly, Keith Relf died from electrocution in 1976 while playing an electric guitar in his basement. This, despite organising a new band project called Illusion, which was intended to be a reunion of Renaissance's original line-up which had dissolved when bassist Louis Cennamo left to spend more time with Colosseum. Keith Relf was only thirty-three when he died. He never witnessed the creation of the Illusion project and was laid to rest in Richmond Cemetery.

Another Kingston Art School student was Bert Jansch collaborator John Renbourn who busked around pubs with Mac MacLeod (as the Hurdy Gurdy band) and who worked with Florida's Dorris Henderson.

Richard Drew, also known as the Zacron, was born in Sutton Surrey, and studied painting, drawing, design, and etching with Eric Clapton. He attended Kingston College of Art where he met Jimmy Page. He designed the iconic volvelle (rotating) *Led Zeppelin III* album cover (1970).

Possibly the most influential Kingston Art School (mature) student would be Tony Visconti, who had moved to London from New York in 1968 to work with Georgie Fame, and under the expert tutelage of the Cranleigh School educated record producer (Island) Denny Cordell. Cordell's family had moved to England from

Argentina and raised Denny in Surrey. He attended the same (fee paying public school) as Blue Peter's Christopher Trace. Visconti is well-known among rock fans worldwide thanks to his partnerships with Marc Bolan, David Bowie, and— perhaps, to a lesser extent— Gentle Giant. (Despite being of Scottish-Jewish heritage, the founding brothers of Gentle Giant—originally known as Simon Dupree and the Big Sound—were in fact based in Hampshire, an English county that borders onto Surrey. For a brief period, future pianist Reg Dwight, later to be known as Elton John, was part of the Simon Dupree 'Big Sound' lineup.)

The Epsom Technical Institute and School of Art was constructed through public funding and the efforts of Surrey citizens and Epsom Urban District Council. Lord Rosebery (the 5th Earl of Rosebery) was a significant contributor to the Institute's financing. In the 1930s, the school was transferred to the Surrey County Council under trust to support art and technical education in the district. This is where the two 'Tattenham Corner bombers' that I mentioned earlier were 'educated.'

You might have expected Jimmy Page, who lived in Epsom just a few roads from Epsom School of Art, to have attended *this* school but he enrolled at Sutton Art College while recuperating from a bad case of glandular fever. Whilst at Sutton Art College he met artist David Juniper who went on to create the album sleeve for *Led Zeppelin II* (1969) —which, you might recall, is the celebrated German Air Force 'Flying Circus' tinted photograph that became a favourite bedroom poster.

Fittingly, the talented rock photographer Keith Morris, who was responsible for several iconic pop-art graphic images of Marc Bolan, Led Zeppelin, Van der Graaf Generator, Nick Drake, Janis Joplin (she'd only make one appearance on stage in the UK, at the Royal Albert Hall on 21st April 1969 supported by the pro-rockers Yes), Fairport Convention etc. Morris took the photographs (with Nigel Marlow, a fellow graduate) for the Emerson, Lake & Palmer's 1971 live album '*Pictures at an Exhibition*'. Both these artists attended Guildford School of Art. As did music producer Daniel Miller, who studied at

Guildford Art School 1969-1972 and made huge contributions to the electronic music scene.

Despite being outside the scope of this book, I ought to give recognition to Guildford's A.C.M., *established in 1997*. The Academy of Contemporary Music has been honoured with the Queen's Award for Enterprise in Innovation (Technology) and acknowledged as a world leader in music industry education. Newton Faulkner, Matty Healy (of the 1975), Ben King (the lead guitarist of The Yardbirds), and international artist Ed Sheeran—winner of Grammy, Brit, and Ivor Novello awards—are among the many of Guildford ACM's illustrious alumni. It's good to know that Surrey, even in the 21st century, still provides arts education to the dishevelled and unkempt *burdens on society* (sorry, Dad!)

18

THE GOMELSKY METHOD

If you were a creative novelist planning to write the origin story of Giorgio Gomelsky's musical career, his background would seem contrived. But if you are able to set aside your disbelief and tolerate a little backstory, his narrative is truly remarkable.

Gomelsky was raised in fascist Italy during World War II, though his birthplace was Tbilisi, in Georgia, (formerly Tiflis.)

At the age of ten, Gomelsky stumbled upon jazz, unknowingly defying the German curfew by seeking refuge in a friend's attic. There, in the attic, he discovered a gramophone and a collection of jazz records. Later, as a form of protest against the authoritarian regime, he and his buddies would blast black music from the top windows, down at the nazi stormtroopers below.

The family decided to move to Switzerland in 1944, as it was a much safer country. Gomelsky attended a Benedictine school near Locarno, in Ascona, Switzerland. Once the war ended, he started gathering a huge assortment of records by combining funds with jazz-loving buddies. The Voice of America, sometimes known as VOA, was the United States international non-military radio broadcasting service, founded in 1942 and Gomelsky was introduced to be-bop via the VOA programming.

Then, he went to a groundbreaking international boarding

school established by revolutionary educationalists Paul Geheeb and his wife, Edith Geheeb Cassirer. The renowned institutions, commonly known as *Swiss Schools*, place a strong emphasis on extracurricular activities rather than academic study. Gomelsky attended their Swiss campus. Incidentally, there is *still* a Swiss School in Thorpe, Surrey which Emma Caulfield Ford went to. as did Ascot born Camilla Luddington of Grey's Anatomy fame. Whilst a student at the Swiss School, Gomelsky rode his bicycle all the way to Paris to witness Charlie Parker perform at the Salon de Jazz.

During this period, Gomelsky's Mother, who was a talented millinery designer running a small studio in London, began sending her son Melody Maker. This allowed him to learn English and gain insight into the British jazz scene.

Gomelsky decided to document the emerging UK jazz scene after reading the Melody Maker every week and viewing the 1948 Oscar-nominated film Jammin' the Blues, starring Harry Edison, Red Callender, Lester Young, and many others; the movie influenced his avant-garde creative concepts.

Gomelsky departed for London and quickly befriended Chris Barber, the prominent jazz musician, along with Harold Pendleton from the National Jazz Federation. Gomelsky wanted to capture Johnny Dankworth on film, but Pendleton convinced him to shoot Chris Barber in a *Jammin' the Blues* style short-film, instead.

The final product was captured in just one day and featured four songs, interspersed with studio session footage and audience reactions from the Royal Festival Hall. Given that this was Gomelsky's inaugural professional film, and he was a newcomer to London, it received an astonishingly positive reception. Gomelsky secured funding and filming rights for the forthcoming National Jazz Festival after being invited to assist as a volunteer.

Despite Chris Barber's trad-jazz band launching the Skiffle craze in Britain—propelling Lonnie Donegan to fame with 'Rock Island Line'— it became clear to all involved that Skiffle was falling out of fashion. Therefore, shrewdly, Barber, known for his jazz-inspired sets, began to incorporate blues into his concerts, often featuring his old school pal Alexis Korner on vocals/guitar and Cyril Davies on harmonica.

Notwithstanding Barber's concert sets being restricted to country-blues, Korner was enthusiastic about introducing elements of electric Chicago-style blues, and especially *jams*, into their shows. Therefore, and with this objective in mind, Korner formed his *own* band, known as the Alexis Korner Blues Incorporated, and recruited musicians who shared the same passion for urban blues, such as Dick Heck-stall-Smith, a saxophonist from Shropshire, and Charlie Watts, a drummer from Middlesex.

During *that* period, Gomelsky began to write for Jazz News and became heavily influenced by Korner's expressive style of jammin' blues, to the extent that he became almost missionary in his eager-ness to spread the message. Through Jazz News, he popularized the term B.R.B., British Rhythm and Blues, and authored multiple arti-cles scrutinising and praising Korner's modern blues.

Korner and Davies rented a room above a pub on Wardour Street with the intention of running shows for the emerging blues enthusi-asts. But they also wanted a larger venue to spread 'the holy gospel of the blues,' and so convinced Pendleton to permit them to host a weekly Blues Night at the Marquee (Thursdays.)

Gomelsky got involved and invited both Christine Keeler *and* Mandy Rice-Davies to one such Blues Night, which attracted signifi-cant media attention and helped establish the Marquee as the popular nightspot it became, and the Blues Night a successful weekday event on London's social scene. It also showcased Gomel-sky's expertise in handling P.R. and branding.

Gomelsky aimed to expand the popularity of The Marquee Blues night through *more* electric-blues performances, though Pendleton wasn't as excited, so let the idea slip. Gomelsky's brilliant move, as an alternative to more nights at the Marquee, involved organizing bands and musicians into cooperatives, promoting collaboration to secure bookings, and assisting the bands and artists in managing their *own* business matters, reminiscent of the Jazz Societies' strategy.

Pendleton was understandably displeased with Gomelsky's apparent attempt to threaten his club, his business, and his festival, especially when Gomelsky set-up a rival club night in Soho. But Gomelsky understood that in order to advance the genre, he'd probably need the help of Pendleton and Barber, in the long-term. Though he also believed that to keep the blues genre alive and relevant, it was *vital* to attract teenage listeners, and that meant involving younger musicians.

Gomelsky decided to abandon running Blues Nights in London altogether and, instead, launch a new series of Sunday night blues sessions at the Station Hotel in Richmond, Surrey, a move that seemed almost suicidal in commercial insanity. Why Surrey? Well perhaps I can explain: to begin with, Richmond was not (in those days) in London, so his blues sessions would not infringe upon Pendleton's or Barber's commercial interests. Furthermore, Gomelsky felt confident these nights would appeal to a younger audience who had a passion for blues, thanks to the presence of *so many* art schools in the area, notably the bustling Kingston Art School.

Moreover, in the basement of the ABC Cafe in neighbouring Ealing, there *already* existed a well-established and thriving blues club. The ABC was conveniently located just 20-minutes by bus from Richmond station. Charlie Watts had initially met Brian Jones in April 1962 at Ealing ABC cafe. Mick Jagger, Keith Richards, and Brian Jones were introduced by Alexis Korner at Ealing. The core of the Rolling Stones band project came together *professionally* at Ealing. Jack Bruce, Ginger Baker, Eric Clapton, Graham Bond, Long John Baldry, Rod Stewart, Malcolm Cecil, Dick Taylor, Paul Jones, Dick Heckstall-Smith, Manfred Mann, (then known as the Mann-Hugg Blues Brothers,) and locally born pop sensation James Royal, were among the many performers that appeared regularly at Ealing.

Returning attention back to Richmond, Gomelsky persuaded the Stones—whose repertoire was strained by the demands of performing two 45-minute sets—to make use of a 20-minute *rave-up* version of Bo Diddley's '*Crawdad*' at their show's culmination. The song is taken from the 1960 album *Bo Diddley in the Spotlight* (recorded 1959.) The general idea of the cover song performance was to liven-up the atmosphere at the Station Hotel to send punters home with a spring in their step. According to legend, Gomelsky came up with the moniker 'The Crawdaddy' for his club spontaneously—probably acknowledging the highlight of The Stones' performance was, of course, their Bo Diddley cover.

One of the first acts to play Gomelsky's newly christened Crawdaddy was the Dave Hunt Rhythm & Blues Band, an outfit that boasted Charlie Watts on drums and (for a time, anyway) Ray Davies (Kinks) on guitar. Indeed, the Dave Hunt Rhythm & Blues Band are involved in the Rolling Stones narrative because they became snowed in during the harsh winter of 1962/63, so couldn't get to the venue on time to play their set. As a result, the Rolling Stones were engaged to replace them, and played their first 'full band' session. Purists will argue that the Stones performed at the Crawdaddy during the previous summer, but *that* line-up was without Bill Wyman or Charlie Watts.

The Star public house in Broad Green, Croydon, *also* hosted events organised by the Crawdaddy Club of Richmond. The Yardbirds were the major draw at The Star, although other Richmond Crawdaddy bands also performed at the Croydon 'branch.' For example, having been being 'dared' to come up on stage and sing, Julie Driscoll began her singing career at The Star.

To his astonishment and growing sense of accomplishment, a full-page article on The Crawdaddy was published in The Richmond and Twickenham Times. Gomelsky showed his friend Patrick Doncaster, the music critic for the Daily Mirror, the piece from the Richmond and Twickenham rag. Doncaster felt compelled to visit the club, and, afterwards, wrote a half-page article about blues in Richmond. The article's depraved attitude horrified Ind Coope Breweries, who owned the Station Hotel, and they ordered the club's *immediate* eviction.

However, destiny took over, as it often did in Gomelsky's life, because the National Jazz Festival was being hosted less than half a mile from the Station Hotel, at the Richmond Athletic Association's clubhouse and grounds. So, the Crawdaddy Club relocated, lock stock and barrel, to the Richmond Athletic clubhouse, which was a space beneath the grandstand that offered approximately three times greater capacity than the Station Hotel.

Performers that performed at Gomelsky's Crawdaddy at Richmond Athletic grounds included Rod Stewart, Elton John, Long John Baldry, and Led Zeppelin.

Later, Gomelsky founded Marmalade Records and oversaw the Yardbirds. Besides producing early albums for Jeff Beck, Jimmy Page (both of whom played with the Yardbirds), the psych-pop outfit the Blossom Toes, Rod Stewart, John McLaughlin (Gomelsky produced McLaughlin's 1969 debut *Extrapolation,* engineered by Eddy Offord), and continuous work with Alexis Korner, Graham Bond, and Soft Machine, Gomelsky also signed Julie Driscoll, Brian Auger & the Trinity to his Marmalade label (distributed by Polydor.)

In his efforts to open-up and strengthen collaboration amongst artists, Gomelsky set-up recording sessions between American blues performers and British rock musicians. For instance, he connected Sonny Boy Williamson with Eric Clapton of the Yardbirds, and they played The Star, Croydon.

Giorgio Gomelsky then turned on his feet and left. Like he'd done many times before, across his life. Always turning, always seeking fresh meadows, like a magnificent butterfly. When he arrived in New York City in the mid-1970s, he recognised the feeling of home he'd been seeking his entire life. So, he opened-up shop. Gomelsky died there, too, in January 2001, having helped popularize the early b-boy hip-hop artists of the Big Apple.

19

THE SURREY DELTA

The Mississippi Delta riverfronts are criss-crossed by tar-roads and iron-railways, though the settlements *themselves* are under-developed and the agricultural economy does not fully support jobs and businesses. Yet from this unpromising landscape, the country blues prospered. The story of the blues was delivered by musicians such as teenage guitarist Blind Lemon Jefferson (Texas), the jack-of all-trades bluesman Charley Patton (Mississippi), and the fingerstyle/slide-guitar legend, Blind Willie McTell (Georgia).

If you're wondering what these performers have in common with musicians in Surrey, I'd like to propose that they share more than you might first think. These three guitarists—blues pioneers—endured several drawbacks: they were underemployed, under-stimulated, disenfranchised, misinterpreted by an older generation, and, perhaps most importantly, they were extraordinarily driven by the sounds they experimented with. Doesn't that sound as if I'm describing Jimmy Page, Jeff Beck, and Eric Clapton?

Jimmy Page was born in Heston, Middlesex in January 1944. His family moved to Miles Road, Epsom, when Jimmy was eight. He attended Pound Lane Primary School, and at eleven, Page went to Ewell County Secondary School, West Ewell. The legend is that he discovered his first guitar 'hidden' (i.e. left behind by previous owners) in the house their family moved into, as described earlier.

Jeff Beck was born in Wallington, Surrey, in June 1944. Wallington is about 5 miles from Epsom. Jeff attended Sutton Manor School and then Sutton East County Secondary Modern. Jeff built his own instrument, glueing cigar boxes to a fence post with model aircraft glue.

Eric Clapton was born Ripley, Surrey, in March 1945. Ripley is about 12 miles from Epsom. Clapton grew up believing his Grandmother, Rose, and her second husband, Jack Clapp, were his parents and that his Mother was his older sister. He never met his Father, who was a Canadian soldier who had returned to Canada before he was born. His Mother married another (different) Canadian soldier and moved to Germany, leaving Eric with his loving grandparents. They bought him an inexpensive steel-stringed guitar for his thirteenth birthday, though he didn't get on with the instrument because the strings bit into his fingers. He went to Hollyfield School in Surbiton.

All three of these young men were disenfranchised*, misunderstood, under-employed, under stimulated, and probably *even* half-starved. Most importantly, they were exceptionally motivated and *very* keenly creative.

* The Representation of the People Act of 1969 lowered the voting age from 21 to 18 for elections.

———

In May 1963 a band known as the Metropolitan Blues Quartet performed at Kingston Art School, supporting jazz-giant Cyril Davies. Their line-up included Richmond born vocalist Keith Relf, Epsom Art School student and guitarist Anthony "Top" Topham, Kingston-raised rhythm guitarist Chris Dreja, the Hampton School (just over the river) bassist Paul Samwell-Smith, and his Hampton School-mate, Jim McCarty, on drums.

Topham and secondary school-chum Dreja had been trad-jazz

fans and often visited the Railway Hotel in Norbiton that stood on the junction of Coombe Road and Station Road, (near Kingston). Bands often used the Railway Hotel, including the Metropolitan Blues Quartet, as a rehearsal room. On his pages, Kingston-area bass player Ron Drakeford, of the skiffle-inspired Canal Street Jazzmen, described a scene that is extremely reminiscent of the jazz circuit found south of the Mason-Dixon line. Kingston-upon-Thames was laden with busy jazz-haunts: Sandy's Barn at the Fighting Cocks, in London Road; The Swan in Mill Street (near the Arts College); a venue over Burton's the Tailors, always known as Burton's; and The Grey Horse in the Richmond Road. The town had the Jazz Cellar, the Jazz Barge (the 'folk' club at The Barge has already been considered), and the Commodore Club that was once a boathouse that sat between two rivers. The art school had its own jazz club, known as the Continental. Big-ticket shows were played at the Coronation Hall (aka Coronation Baths or just the Kingston Baths). Their dance floor was a boarded-over swimming pool. Acker Bilk, Kenny Ball, Ken Colyer, Dick Charlesworth, and Alan Elsdon all played 'The Coronation.'

With their base established in Bushy Park, just across the river (literally a bridge from all the clubs), the American Forces brought a large jazz-loving inflow to the Kingston-upon-Thames venues. General Dwight D. Eisenhower coordinated the D-Day landings from the Supreme Headquarters Allied Expeditionary Force (SHAEF) at Camp Griffiss in Bushy Royal Park. Under the code-name Widewing, a collection of makeshift structures northeast of Bushy Park served as the de facto headquarters for the United States Eighth Air Force, which was commanded by General Carl Spaatz and later Ira Eaker. Because of their regular presence at Kingston clubs, the servicemen from these American bases in Bushy—many of whom originated in the Southern states—became a reliable source of rare records for the local population. In Kingston, during the late 40's and early 50's, you could get hold of jazz discs that were rarely seen outside the ports of Liverpool and Bristol (the only other sources of transatlantic connectivity before commonplace commercial airline travel became a *thing*). The regular jazz-hops hosted by the servicemen at their American base-camps *also* educated a Surrey population. The Bushy Park bases were in use for quite some time, (though Eisenhower moved out of Busy Park quite early on, in 1944, to a forward operating base at Southwick House, Hampshire.) Most of the camp's huts were removed by 1963.

During the late 1950s and early 1960s, Kingston's thriving jazz scene had a significant impact on many local performers of the rhythm and blues genre. However, as blues music gained popularity among the younger suburban population, jazz eventually lost its prominence.

The Metropolitan Blues Quartet lineup changed their name to the Yardbirds in September 1963 after performing a few more shows under the Blue-Sounds moniker. It has been suggested that Relf first coined the band name; perhaps having discovered the word in Jack Kerouac's novel *On the Road*, where Kerouac referred to rail-yard hobos sticking around for a train that would take them 'anywhere.' (A consistent theme in blues songs.)

According to Topham, jazz saxophonist Charlie "Yardbird" Parker used it as a friendly moniker and they might have used the name in his honour. But I suspect a less pretentious explanation, it may be more prosaic, and although my suggestion is not infallible, I think it might be this: these wannabe musicians were 'likely' found loitering outside venue back doors, in the brewery back-yards that stood between a stage and the main building of the pub (for example at Kingston's Fighting Cocks). They loitered in such places in the hope of lending a hand to the booked band, helping with anything from lugging gear to tuning guitars to setting up sound to possibly landing a 'guest spot' on stage. As a result, these gregarious, goofing-about, grovelling lads were dubbed the 'back yard birds' (by the working musicians they looked up to) since it was in the back-yards of Surrey's venues they'd frequently be spotted, pushing their luck!

Gomelsky invited the them to be his house band at the Craw-daddy Club shortly after they picked up their new moniker: they were to be known as The Yardbirds Ever the astute business-thinker, Gomelsky reasoned it was good sense to hire youngsters from the local community since they brought a sizable following of gig-goers, mates, groupies, and art-school chums with them to his concerts.

From as early as 1962, seventeen-year-old Eric Clapton was "yard-birding" at pubs and clubs around Surrey. He was frequently spotted hanging around the back doors of the venues, hoping for an opportunity to help with setting up sound, tuning guitars, or conceivably landing a "guest spot" on stage. Along the way, he began playing in a duo with fellow aficionado of roots blues and trad-jazz, the Longford Secondary School pupil Dave Brock. Longford School was in an area of Middlesex, close to Bushy Park on the Surrey border. Brock would later become renowned as Hawkwind's "Doctor Technical" and the driving force behind the first "space rock" band in history.

Anticipating the duo's fizzling demise, Clapton joined his first "real" band, the Roosters, a Surrey R&B group that had been founded by Tom McGuinness. The guitarist had assembled a young cast of musicians that included Ben Palmer on piano, Robin Mason on drums, and Terry Brennan on vocals. Plus, of course, there would be McGuinness and Clapton on guitars. They rehearsed at the Wooden Bridge Hotel in Guildford, or the Prince of Wales in New Malden, but Clapton acknowledged in his memoirs that they "practiced more than they performed." Incidentally, *this* band has often been confused with Del Turner's 'Roosters' who *also* played venues in South-West London. Del Turner's version of The Roosters, a completely *different* outfit, played regular gigs at the Cellar Club, in Kingston upon Thames, hence the confusion. Del Turner's Roosters had Turner on rhythm guitar, Pete Jeffries on lead guitar, Ron Jeffries on bass, and Jim Strachan on drums. They were quite a 'big deal' at the time and even got profiled in Jackie magazine (March 1964.) But, anyway, back to McGuinness's Roosters, because of the group's lack of accomplishment, Clapton and McGuinness left to join the considerably better-known Liverpool band, Casey Jones, and the Engineers. Clapton had his first touring experience with Casey Jones. However, the guitarist left after around seven shows because he became unhappy with their pop-oriented material.

The Liverpool singer Brian Cassar, also known as Casey Jones, had achieved some success with a Latin-pop trio known as Cass & the

Cassanovas (sic). Ultimately, he established the Casanova Club in Liverpool, where John Lennon's band, the "Silver Beetles," performed once Lennon had left Liverpool College of Art. (The early Beatles also performed under the name "The Rainbows" and "Johnny and the Moondogs," but 'Cass' Cassar booked them as the Silver Beetles.)

Pop manager Larry Parnes held auditions in spring 1960 to find a backup band for Duffy Power, who was an emerging singer from Fulham, West London that he was promoting at the time. Cass & the Cassanovas got the position, but the departure of Adrian Barber interrupted their transfer to London. So, Hutchinson, and the band's 'new' bassist Gus Gustavson, departed the Cassanovas and established The Big Three. The Big Three were shipped to Hamburg's Star-Club after Brian Epstein signed them to *his* agency. (Adrian Barber later emigrated to the United States and rose to fame at Atlantic Records as a much-celebrated in-house producer and recording engineer. He worked on the Allman Brothers Band's 1969 debut album.) At various times, Cilla Black and Beryl Marsden were 'backed' by The Big Three.

In 1963, Clapton joined the Yardbirds, possibly knowing his time with Casey Jones and the Engineers was terminating. With his distinctive finger play technique, Clapton quickly rose to prominence as one of the most talked-about guitarists on the R&B scene. When the band replaced the Rolling Stones at the Crawdaddy Club, they developed a sizable cult following with their distinctive covers of early Chess/Checker/Vee-Jay tunes.

One night at the Crawdaddy, Giorgio Gomelsky awarded Clapton the sobriquet "Slow Hand" because he'd take an inordinately long time to fix a broken string during a set. His slowness infuriated the paying audience, who proceeded to slow-hand-clap Clapton in a *typically* English manner, demonstrating their growing discontent.

"For Your Love" was composed by rising talent Graham Gouldman, who also composed hits for Herman's Hermits and the Hollies. It became the Yardbirds' first momentous success, in March 1965. Later, Gouldman and his Mockingbirds bandmate Kevin Godley (drums and vocals) would establish po-rock chart toppers, 10cc.

However, Clapton found the pop-oriented sound of Gouldman's

"For Your Love" too much to bear, and on the day the smash song was released, he departed the Yardbirds.

Clapton recommended Jimmy Page to be the guitarist to succeed him in the Yardbirds, but Page turned down the offer, out of respect for Clapton. Instead, he proposed his old pal, Jeff Beck.

Beck joined the Yardbirds team in March 1965.

20

GRANT FACILITATION

I want to be clear right from the start that the subject of *this* chapter is the famous rock 'n' roll manager, and *not* the student grants my father detested being doled-out to art school students.

The London Charterhouse, a prestigious and ancient school and hospital, acquired a 68-acre site outside Godalming, Surrey in 1864. They built a main school building and three boarding houses at the location.

Throughout its long history, established c. 885 by will of King Alfred the Great, the market town of Godalming has benefitted from a location on the principal route from London to Portsmouth Dock-yard. Additionally, the North Downs provided good grazing for sheep, there were local deposits of Fuller's earth, and the Wey provided a source of water and power for fulling mills. A cottage industry developed in the town during the 17th century, producing woollen, silk, and later cotton garments. The route through Godalming between Kingston upon Thames and Petersfield was turnpiked in 1749 and became a major arterial route for coach traffic and freight. The town sits on the confluence of the River Wey and River Ock, so river navigation was also a key factor in the town's success.

Godalming experienced growth in the mid-19th century due to

the opening of its first railway station in 1849 and the establishment of Charterhouse School in 1872. Godalming is believed to be the first town with both public and private electricity, reflecting its affluence and enlightenment.

With the growth of pupil numbers at Godalming Charterhouse, the school underwent continuous expansion throughout the 20th century. The administration acquired more land to the north and west, expanding the grounds to over 200 acres (81 ha). They also consecrated a new school chapel in 1927, which was designed by Sir Giles Gilbert Scott, who is perhaps best known for designing the red telephone box. For a long time, Charterhouse originally accepted boys only. The school began accepting girls in sixth form in 1971. Charterhouse is one of the most expensive HMC (Conference) boardings school in the UK. It won't be long before we discover that Charterhouse had a number of rock 'n' roll era musicians among its student population. However, the first *Carthusian* I want to investigate is a sheet-metal factory worker from South Norwood, near Croydon, Surrey. Following his time at the metal-works, Peter Grant found employment as a stagehand at the Croydon Empire Theatre until 1953, when he was enlisted for National Service.

Being of impressively large build and possessing a level of forth-right self-confidence that is still rare in the rough-and-tumble world of rock 'n' roll, it was obvious he'd make a top-notch club bouncer, so once he returned to 'civvie street' from Service, Grant secured employment as a bouncer (security doorman) at London's 2i's Coffee Bar, the haunt of Cliff Richard, Adam Faith, Tommy Steele, et al.

Standing at 6 feet 2 inches and having dabbled in wrestling, he was definitely *not* a person you'd want to tussle with. Indeed, film studios hired him as a bit part actor, a stuntman, and body double. He appeared in action films such as J. Lee Thompson's *Guns of Navarone* (1961), where he played a commando and he frequently functioned as Robert Morley's body-double. (If you can imagine, in your mind's eye, Robert Morley, you ought to be able to imagine the girth and weight of Grant!)

This exemplifies the contradictory nature of Surrey life, doesn't it? Despite graduating from an esteemed private school that *literally* serves the sons of state leaders and royalty, a young man who originated from a modest suburban background works as a sheet metal worker and lands a job as a nigh-time bouncer at a club. The environment of Surrey is a mixture of irregularity and beauty, of failure and triumph. Peter Grant is a perfect example of Surrey's contrasts, the combination of privilege and struggle.

In 1960, Don Arden, a musician and talent agent from Manchester, signed Gene Vincent, the famous American rock 'n' roller in order to 'develop' his career in the U.K. This signing kickstarted Arden's journey into pop. Arden had also helped launch Elkie Brooks' career. She had been working as a vocalist for Humphrey Lyttelton's band before Arden 'handed' her. Brooks later sung with blues-rock group Dada before putting together Vinegar Joe. Oh, and in case you hadn't 'connected the dots,' Sharon Osbourne is Don Arden's daughter, aka Mrs. Ozzy.

During the mid-1960s, and seeing money-making opportunities in it, Arden shifted his focus to managing *beat groups*. Before launching The Nashville Teens, a genuinely *pure* Surrey product (that we will consider shortly) Arden managed tours for numerous 'big name' American artists whose labels were hoping to gain notoriety 'over here' in Europe. Among the famous musicians he promoted were Chuck Berry, Little Richard, Bo Diddley, the Everly Brothers, Brian Hyland, and his own 'talent,' Gene Vincent.

Arden, ever the brittle and shrewd business entrepreneur, realised that importing such names from the United States and pushing them through Britain's run-down theatres, town halls, and motion picture theatres, and getting them, *and* the press packs to 'behave' themselves would take a substantial amount of 'muscle'; but it would have to be the kind of muscle that could think *for itself,* would never give into temptation, would never back down, would never accept the word *no,* and *would* definitely block a door and prevent people from entering if he didn't like the look of them! The 'larger-than-life' 2i's bouncer, Peter Grant, was the obvious choice to run these shows for him, so, Arden signed him up!

Arden presented 'caravan of stars' style packaged variety shows for these American rock 'n' roll acts. For example, Chuck Berry, who was on parole from the Chicago courts when he came to Britain to work for Arden, would open a show with Carl Perkins as main support act, while The Animals, The Nashville Teens, Kingsize Taylor & The Dominos, and The Swinging Blue Jeans were also added to the 'packages' to draw-in younger suburban audiences.

The Rolling Stones' favourite Soho club, Beat City, London's Hammersmith Odeon, and the Finsbury Park Astoria were among venues that visited by Arden's package in the south. But his shows toured *extensively* in the north, most likely because Arden understood the geography and demographics, though it's worth noting that Berry performed at the Croydon ABC on May 21, 1964.

Bo Diddley was 'packed' with the Everly Brothers, Julie Grant, The Flintstones (who also backed Little Richard) and this band boasted Terry Marshall (on tenor sax) who was the son of Hanwell, West London-based Jim Marshall, the same guy that supplied gear for Ritchie Blackmore, Big Jim Sullivan, and Pete Townshend. Jim Marshall founded Marshall Amplification. (When this group recorded with Joe Meek, they were known as The Stonehenge Men.) Mickie Most was also on *this* 'package.' Most had known Grant since his days at the 2i's Coffee Bar and they'd become future business partners, but in the late 1950's to mid '60's Mickie Most had toured with his own backing group, singing Eddie Cochran, Gene Pitney, and Buddy Holly numbers. But the most teen-sensational act on the Bo Diddley package was the Rolling Stones! By all accounts, at the Guildford Odeon show, Brian Jones played Elmore James numbers (backstage) with Bo Diddley.

Brian Hyland, of *Itsy-Bitsy Teenie Weenie Yellow Polka Dot Bikini* and *Sealed with a Kiss fame*, was packaged with Little Eva (*The Loco-Motion.*)

Australian pop-act manager Robert Stigwood also put on package tours during the early 1960's. Stigwood managed the actor-turned-singer John Leyton who, as we shall discover, played a significant, though unexpected, role in the career trajectory of the Beatles, but for now we are still looking at Peter Grant.

As we have learned, Simon Napier-Bell co-produced the Yardbirds' first studio album, Roger the Engineer and he had had overseen the smooth-*ish* entry of Jimmy Page into the band, but in 1966, and seeing how he had so efficiently operated Ardens big-names package shows, Napier-Bell asked Peter Grant to take over management of the Yardbirds, who were constantly touring colleges and clubs and yet, somehow, struggling to make any headway.

Grant took over management of the band, and his confident dealings with promoters and his commanding presence at venues led to the Yardbirds' landing themselves a tour that actually *made them money*. To keep costs low, ensure prompt payment for his musicians, and maintain artistic freedom, Grant toured widely *with* his group of performers. In contrast to previous managers, Grant participated in a hands-on approach to management that was unprecedented in the industry. He frequently visited the locations where his band would be performing and deciding arrangements and offering 'unrefusable' suggestions to venue managers!

The Yardbirds as a band project folded in 1968, despite Peter Grant's terrific management style. Jimmy Page was the last man 'standing' so he formed a new group with Robert Plant on vocals, John Bonham on drums, John Paul Jones on bass, and himself on lead guitar to honour a contract, that had been set-up by Grant, to tour Europe (as The New Yardbirds.) The Yardbirds' permission to use Page's name expired after the tour, and Chris Dreja served Page with a 'cease and desist' order stopping the outfit from using the designation. As a result, the group decided to rename their project: Led Zeppelin. There is an unconfirmed theory regarding how the band got *this* name, and it has to do with The Who. According to the well-worn narrative, Moon, and bassist John Entwistle predicted that a 'supergroup' with Page and Beck in it (sic) would fail terribly, lose popularity, and go down with the general public like a 'lead balloon.'

The group dropped the 'a' in *lead* at the suggestion of Peter Grant, because he knew the media would pronounce it "leed." It's unclear why the word balloon was supplanted by 'zeppelin,' but the replacement was a brilliant example of commercial promotion working hand-in-hand with artistic interpretation. With these two subtle changes—I have my suspicions Peter Grant made *both*—they created the unique promotional architecture of restraint and lustiness that Heavy Metal would come to stand for in the years that followed and Led Zeppelin would come to *epitomise*. Note: They were publicly billed as Led Zeppelin for the first time when they played The Great Hall, at The University of Surrey, in October 1968 (the Surrey campus was *still* at Battersea in '68.)

Grant was successful in getting Atlantic Records to offer the band a humongous five-year advance contract of \$1.25 million (by my calculation at today's rate.) At that stage, this was the biggest deal a new band had *ever* been awarded. This deal gives you a taste of Grant's pushiness and efficacy as an artist-manager!

———

Not only was Dusty Springfield, who was born in Ealing, a true radio star and occasionally presented the Ready Steady Go! pop show, she was *already* a friend of John Paul Jones.

Dusty had recently signed with Atlantic Records and was recording her first Tennessee album at the American Sound Studio in Memphis. There is a rumour that executives at Atlantic signed Led Zeppelin with Dusty's approval, and without ever meeting the musicians. That's how they got the deal! On a wing, a prayer, and a glamorous wink from Dusty!

Grant's idea of advocating rock acts as *serious* artists was revolutionary in the world of rock 'n' roll. This attitude didn't just help propel Led Zeppelin into the stratosphere, it also benefited all the *other* bands that came after. Grant was certain that in order to maximise financial potential and creative *significance*, rock bands should focus their creative resources on producing albums rather than 'pop' singles. He insisted that his rock musicians were serious, dark, and heavyweight, whereas 'pop' entertainers were frivolous, effervescent, and lightweight... singles were ideal for pop artists, but were *detrimental* to the rock 'image' he was endeavouring to manufacture. Additionally, Grant believed that live performances held greater implication and authority than television, and with that in mind, he maintained that anyone who wished to see Led Zeppelin must attend their shows and see the live act for themselves.

Grant's intuitive understanding of larger audiences, developed during his time with Arden's package tours, and contributed to Led Zeppelin's unique success in the U.S. Led Zeppelin held the vast majority of their concerts in America under Grant's direction, resulting in *enormous* earnings for the band. It was his understanding of the American touring scene that propelled Led Zeppelin to the vanguard of a burgeoning American heavy-rock market.

Furthermore, Grant insisted that his band received the lion's share of ticket sales instead of sharing earnings with booking agents and promoters. Grant's prior experience of managing difficult individuals like Gene Vincent and Jerry Lee Lewis gave him a solid foundation when it came to handling the obvious chaos that accompanied a Led Zeppelin tour.

In subsequent years, Grant took up management for *other* bands that were signed to Swan Song (a label which *he* helped set-up.) These included Stone the Crows, Bad Company, and Maggie Bell. Perhaps one of his (rare) mistakes was to decline a large offer to oversee Queen, in 1975.

Peter Grant died in 1995. He was just sixty. A hard life of rock 'n' roll ups-and-downs had worn him out!

21

THE FINEST SURREY BAND?

The Cruisers, a Weybridge / Addlestone rock combo that featured Mick Dunford on guitar, John Hawken on piano, Pete Shannon on bass, and Dave Maine on drums, and with Terry Crowe on vocals, developed into a new band project in 1962, during the British beat boom. They sought a new vocalist and gained two-for-one in the process; Arthur Sharp (aka Art) who worked in the "Aerco" record store in Woking, and had been gigging with the Variation Six Skiffle Group, and Ray (Ramon) Phillips who joined the line-up from the Phoenix City Band. They formed what could probably be considered the first successful 'Boy Band' in the UK, comprising two attractive and talented lead singers. Their Everly Brothers looks, and the Everly's song "*Nashville Blues*" served as inspiration for the band's new identity: The Nashville Teens.

Like the Beatles, the Teens served their rock 'n' roll 'apprenticeship' in The Storyville Clubs of Cologne and Frankfurt, and in The Star Club in Hamburg. They gained recognition for having supported Jerry Lee Lewis on his historic album "*Jerry Lee Lewis Live In Hamburg*." Their first two recordings, "Big Bad Blues" (with Carl Perkins), and "Long, Tall Sally" (with Jerry Lee Lewis), provide a decent indication of their skills and ability. Yes, these boys from Surrey were taken *very* seriously. They performed with other emerging acts in Germany, including the Spencer Davis Group. But the travel and working hours were challenging. After nonstop performances through the night, the boys had to sometimes drive a full day, before putting on another show.

It was at one of those shows, after a long journey, that Mickie Most spotted them (at that stage he was performing his own act with a backing band). Most agreed to take them on, and they were willing to give him a shot, because they'd become exhausted.

———

Over in the 'real' Nashville, Tennessee, 4,000 miles from Surrey, a North Carolina born singer-songwriter named John D. Loudermilk wrote country-pop hits for artists such as the Everly Brothers, Johnny Tillotson, Chet Atkins, Paul Revere & the Raiders, Johnny Cash, and more. In fact, Loudermilk was one of the most prolific songwriters of his generation (born 1934.) George Hamilton IV's recording of "*Abielene*" is among Loudermilk's best-known and most popular compositions. He also composed "*I Wanna Live*" for Glen Campbell, "*(He's My) Dreamboat*" for Connie Francis, and "*Turn Me On*," which although published in 1961 and recorded by Mark Dinning (of Teen Angel fame) became better known *much* later, when it was covered by Norah Jones.

Loudermilk was most proud of 'Tobacco Road,' a 1959 country-blues song that told a semi-autobiographical account of his *own* poor upbringing in North Carolina. Although Loudermilk recorded and sang the song himself, it was not a tremendous hit for him. Loudermilk saved the tune "for a rainy day."

———

During the 'beat boom' (the teen-trend that gripped Britain, then America, roughly between 1961-67), the Newcastle-upon-Tyne rhythm-and-blues combo The Animals, led by Jarrow-boy Alan Price on organ and vocals, relocated to London.

Mickie Most, who gained recognition for his work on "*The House of the Rising Sun*," a unique song The Animals had been performing while on tour with Chuck Berry, also produced their first commercial hit, "*Baby Let me Take You Home*." Though, of course, their rendition of *House of the Rising Sun* became a tremendous trans-Atlantic hit for them, and its popularity *even* startled Bob Dylan who helped popularize the traditional song.

On the back of his success with *Rising Sun*, Most was looking around for a similar song for his Surrey band, The Teens, the band project he had taken-on in Germany. He happened upon Loudermilk's forgotten song, "*Tobacco Road*." Most gave the song the same hard-edged, pop vibe he'd brought to The Animals' smash-hit *Rising Sun* (both songs were released in June '64.) So, the Nashville Teens recorded Mickie Most's production of "*Tobacco Road*" and it became another transatlantic pop hit for Most, and a career-high for the Surrey band, peaking at number 6 in the UK and number 14 in the U.S. singles charts.

With the success of "*Tobacco Road*," the Nashville Teens rock 'n' roll credentials were obvious, and they further cemented their position in the British pop hierarchy by supporting additional top-ranking American stars on their package tours to Britain. However, The Teens lacked a standout member (or members) of their group that the record-buying public, especially adolescent girl fans, could 'dig' i.e. get *into*. To illustrate what I mean, watch their superb music video for "*Tobacco Road*" (I recommend that you do, anyway!) then contrast *their* slick appearance of with that of comparable videos from The Animals. Compare the Nashville Teen *looks* with that of the cheeky rapscallion Alan Price, or the scrappy battle-hardened Eric Burdon. The Teens had no scruffiness. No bad *attitude*. They had *no* street appeal. And this was a period when possessing a roguish and subversive anti-adult disposition meant *everything*. The Nashville Teens were just too fulsomely silky-smooth for their own good!

Things deteriorated for the Teens right after. Without employment authorization, they found themselves detained in New York over Christmas, 1964. Along with several other UK acts, they'd embarked on the British Invasion Tour; but Mickie Most had mishandled their work permits. A falling-out with Most resulted from *this* oversight and then the failure of their next number, "*Find My Way Back Home*," which was a song the band had insisted upon, but which Most absolutely despised, perhaps thinking it was a public slur. Once they found their way, '*Back Home*,' the band started booking into smaller venues, and were overlooked by many of the type of 'big name' artists they would have supported *before*.

Barrie Jenkins left the group in 1966 to join the Animals. Roger Groome filled in as drummer for a while. John Hawken went via the Yardbirds to Renaissance, Vinegar Joe, and the Strawbs. The Nashville Teens project unravelled.

In 1969, Lenny Butcher replaced Roger Groome, and the band went through several guitarist changes before settling on Len Tuckey and Roger Deane. Their last recording of the period was a cover of the Fats Domino number, "*Lawdy Miss Clawdy*," 1973.

Ramon is the remaining founder member of original Nashville Teens. Together with The British Invasion All-Stars, which featured Jim McCarty of The Yardbirds and a few members of The Downliners Sect, Ramon released an amazing CD titled '*Regression*' in 1990. He plays with Englebert Humperdink's one-time bass guitarist, Colin Pattenden, Simon Spratley on keys, the Jackie Lynton Band guitarist Ken Osborn, and the 'Teens' longest-serving drummer, Adrian 'Spud' Metcalfe. I had the good fortune to witness Ramon's lineup perform at the Staines Riverside Club prior to its arson attack, and I have to say they were extremely loud, incredibly thrilling, and exceptionally skilled. I'm glad I got to see them. During their half-time break Ramon came over and we chatted about the 'good old days.' Side note: The Mickie Most / Nashville Teens version of "*Tobacco Road*" was cited by composers Nicky Chinn and Mike Chapman as an inspiration Sweet's "*Block Buster!*" by The Sweet.

22

MOD ANTI/MOD OLDHAM

At around Easter time, 1964, whilst living in North Cheam, I went for a walk with my sister up Stonecott Hill, turning right at Gleeson's, over Pyl Brook (a tributary of the river Beverley), beyond the Baptist Church, to visit a secret sweet shop we'd never been to before. The sweet shop was run by people my parents described as 'Foreigners.' It had a lingering, spicy smell that was new to me. Inside the store were countless jars of boiled sweets and huge trays of pocket-money delights such as penny chews, frother bars, and gob-stoppers. My sister's favourite were 'Sherbet Pips.' These were purchased over the counter and weighed out and served in little paper bags. Sherbet Pips were like Tom Thumb drops, only they were light pink and purple, smothered in a delicious sprinkling of sherbet. I liked Sherbet Pips *too*, mainly because you got a lot for your pennies, but they got sticky in the paper bag. As an alternative, I grabbed a whole lot of ha'penny chews.

Outside the shop, we happily filled our cheeks with sticky treats. It was *then* we heard a buzzing commotion coming from a distance, up on the hill. The North Cheam weekend shoppers gazed into the horizon too, intrigued by the unusual disturbance. Approaching from Morden and Wimbledon seemed to be, what looked like to me anyway, a huge plague of buzzing locusts. As my sister and I watched in astonishment, a line of countless motor scooters headed towards Cheam, riding in the direction of West Sussex. It was like watching a row of slightly wobbly knights wearing acorn-green armour, riding into battle. As the protracted line of mods buzzed past, I made-out the smiles on the faces of the pillion passengers and the flicking 'tiger' tails tied to a hundred gleaming handlebars. The brilliant mirrors and over-the-top lights dazzled us. The spectacle was so bizarre and so *extremely* extravagant that my sister said it was like *watching an alien invasion.*

The coffee bars of London in the 1950's and early 60's were places where young bohemians spent time together. They stayed open until the wee hours, long after pubs closed (licensing laws meant that public houses closed at 11 p.m. but coffee bars were permitted to stay open without a licence.) These coffee bars were fitted with jukeboxes. Traditionally, bourgeois 'art school' Mods would hang around their preferred coffee bar, hoping to put a choice record on the platter.

The Mods, short for 'Modernist,' were a loosely knit group of terribly misunderstood youngsters who sprang from the smoky beatnik café scene of the 1940s and continued to flourish through the traditional jazz years and into the subsequent skiffle era. When combined, they created an underground subculture that was uniquely *British.*

At first these Mods listened to jazz. But, over time, they began to explore the blues, then went on to discover the raw power of British rhythm & blues and, a little later, Northern Soul. In 1964, the coffee houses of London were crowded places; they brought kids from the suburbs into the heart of London. But once the coffee bars appeared in the *suburbs*, or in some of the most economically depressed areas of South London, they started to attract the worst kind of rude-boy trouble-maker, the type of Mod we historically associate with the subculture.

Perhaps even worse than this image change, there was also growing over-commercialisation of the fad. The Mods were targeted by big business. Fat cats saw rich harvests in teen fashions. Like other gimmicky crazes (hippies and punks, for example) the Mods were about to be exploited by shrewd (capitalist) marketeers, advertisers, and enterprisers. Where once the right-thinking Mod would customize his own suit, or help a friend find 'just the right shoes' at a jumble-sale, or he'd frequent his mate's barber's shop, by 1964 the movement had turned stylized, stale, and ultra-commercial. Television shows like Friday evening's 'Ready Steady Go!' began to influence young spectators. High Street outfitters racked-up 'Mod Gear.' Newspapers such as The Mail carried photographs of up-and-coming Mod celebrities.

Nevertheless, the Mod era was an exciting time to be a teenager in Surrey. Evenings were spent hanging around dives in town, listening to beloved bands or admiring gleaming machines. Weekends would be spent tootling to Brighton, sometimes even as far as the Isle of Wight. It seemed as if *everyone* had a Lambretta. And *everyone* shopped for a Burton two-tone suit.

The Mods gathered in places like the Kingston Baths (where the best rhythm & blues were played) or got together at the Orchid Pub in Purley, or over at Wimbledon Palais. At Tolworth, close to the newly built monstrosity named 'Tolworth Tower' (on the A3) was one of the best music venues in Surrey – the Toby Jug. Their cave-dark room held about 300 Mods who came to see artists like The Yardbirds, John Mayall, American blues pianist 'Champion Jack Dupree', 'Sounds of Blue' (the pre-cursor to 'Chicken Shack') and others.

Other Mod venues in the area included the Coronation Hall in Kingston (now a Wetherspoon pub, go visit it to see some nostalgic photos from the Mod period), the Kingston Poly, Ewell Tech, the 'Three Fishes' (technically 'The Royal Charter'), and 'over the river' into Middlesex (across the bridge) at 'Eel Pie Island.'

The Mods contributed to the definition of the 1960s as 'Swinging' and brought-about the beginnings of our society's intolerance and rejection (perhaps *fear,* too) of youth culture that continues *to this day.* In reality, though, these lower-income kids, obsessed with *couture,* were more likely to read fashion publications, watch art films, or spend time at the hairdresser than cause fights in backstreet boozers. These arty individuals would converse long into the night about existentialism, or went about looking immaculately groomed and coiffed, and would congregate anyplace that had a jukebox. During the early

1960's the Mods became a force for good – because they were art lovers, deep thinkers, and *fashionistas*. In those days, the Mods were *very far* from our modern perception of parka-garbed yobbos, obsessed with violence and scooters, the type of character seen in *Quadrophenia*.

In 1962, one of these Mods, a very handsome young man with tinted glasses, and with a mop of rebellious golden hair on an intelligent head, was smooth-talking his way around the bustling cafés of Soho. He grabbed the chance of a job in an up-and-coming Carnaby Street store, working for the self-styled 'King Of Carnaby Street' himself— John Stephen. Through *this* connection, the Mod met another famous name — Mary Quant, the 'inventor' of the miniskirt. The Mod began to hustle for Quant *too*. He was a natural charmer, a sweet-talker, and a brilliant schmoozer. He was a go-getter and an unruffled huckster.

This well-dressed, well-educated Mod had been brought-up in Oxfordshire, the son of a Dutch-born United States Army Air Forces pilot named Andrew Loog. (His Father died when his B-17 bomber was shot down over the English Channel, exactly nine months before the baby boy was born.) His Australian Mother was a nurse stationed in England (her maiden name was Oldham.)

Taking his name from both parents and calling himself Andrew Loog Oldham, this young fellow connected with the English singer-songwriter and record producer Joe Meek. He became Meek's publicist. Meek is best remembered for his 'Tornados' 'Telstar' hit in 1962.

————

Joe Meek, who'd completed his national service in the Royal Air Force, founded an independent record label called 'Triumph Records' when he returned to civvie street. He also founded an independent production company known as 'RGM Sound' and in 1961, and he operated it from a run-down flat above a shop, in Holloway Road, Islington.

Meek's first 'Holloway Road' success was '*Johnny Remember Me.*' It was recorded by actor and celebrity, Johnny Leyton who we shall consider shortly. Robert Stigwood heavily promoted the disc. The brief partnership between Meek, Stigwood, and Oldham would likely transform the face of British recorded music *forever*. The legacy of their cooperative agreement meant an individual (any individual) could release a recording from their *own* independent 'cottage' label and bring the hand-crafted product to market: manufactured, distributed, and released– using the supporting network of a Major label.

It was a mutually beneficial relationship because it helped Major Labels scout-out and secure new talent without incurring financial risk (or risk to reputation.) It also meant that pro-active entrepreneurs and *their* artists could affect the taste and attitudes of the 'big players' in subtle ways. Today there are only three Major labels remaining: (the 'Big Three.') But in the rock 'n' roll era there were at least 3,500 large independent record labels. Many of these functioned as sub-labels for Majors or, at least, in discrete hush-hush arrangements. (Hundreds more independent labels were formed during the punk years, but all folded.)

After collaborating with Joe Meek, Loog Oldham worked on the publicity for Bob Dylan's first visit to Britain. Dylan had travelled to the U.K. to appear in a beatnik drama titled *'The Madhouse on Castle Street'* written by Jack London, for the BBC. At the end of the play, Dylan performed two songs on national television. This outrageous bare-faced publicity (Oldham earned a fiver for the hook-up that he'd arranged between Dylan's manager Albert Grossman and the Beeb) meant Dylan surreptitiously crept into the homes of British fans.

It would be two more years before Dylan became a household name – but this early, and very valuable publicity– helped him make the ascent. Oldham arranged a few gigs around town for Dylan, notably at The Troubadour Folk Club in Old Brompton Road. During *this* visit Dylan hooked-up (to play modern folk) with the English folk singer Martin Carthy, who had a residency at The Troub. Carthy has been linked to British folk movement for over sixty years and has played with all the greats: Steeleye Span, members of Fairport Convention, and The Albion Band. But the most important service he performed for the world-wide folk movement, and the service for which we are very much indebted, was to inspire Dylan at The Troubadour.

––––––

Andrew Loog Oldham worked for Brian Epstein and the Beatles during the snowy months of 1963 while '*Please Please Me*' was rising in the charts. In April of that year, just after the thaw, a friend advised Oldham to take a trip down to Richmond, Surrey, to see a new band that had been performing a residency on Sunday nights. Oldham excitedly made the trip to Surrey to see what all the fuss was about. He immediately saw the potential of this *new* group. It was the embryonic 'Rollin' Stones.' Through his experience working with Epstein, Oldham realized that the Stones could be launched as London's *answer to The Beatles*. It was a pitch that could not fail.

Oldham had lofty expectations for the Stones. To begin, he did not like the name they'd given themselves: 'the Rollin' Stones' — he thought it looked amateurish and guessed it would appear awkward on a record sleeve — so he had it changed. From Oldham's involvement onwards, the band would be known as the 'Rolling Stones' with the 'g' appended. But Oldham also removed the burly keyboard player, Stewart, from the Stone's line-up because he didn't think the guy *looked right*; he didn't think Stewart fitted the band's visual aesthetic. Plus, Oldham didn't like bands with more than four members. (At this point he 'put up' with Brian Jones, but only just.)

Decca Records, which had passed-up signing the Beatles, didn't want to make the same mistake again, so they hurriedly gave the 'Rolling Stones' a recording contract with *very* agreeable terms. But Oldham was too young to sign the contract. At the age of 19, the Mod was the youngest member of the organisation. He had to get his Mum to counter-sign for him.

The biggest change Oldham made to the band was to position them as the 'bad boys' of pop. To this end, he ensured they always looked *moody* in press photos; he allowed them, actually he *encouraged* them, to go about town in dishevelled clothes and looking *ungroomed* and unhealthy, which was the exact-opposite of the

Modernist way. Whether this was deliberate is unknown, but it seems clear that Oldham disrupted the Mod subculture, of which he had been an integral part. Perhaps he did it because he realised the Mod fad was turning flaccid, becoming accepted by mainstream society, so, therefore, being a 'Mod' was no longer a trendy alternative for teens. Oldham accurately predicted that pop art and psychedelia would be *the next big thing*. Thus, he reinforced the *part*-fabrication that the Rolling Stones were anti-cultural yobbos who dabbled in recreational drugs (not entirely fictional), and he suggested they disregarded social norms, and were questionable role models for the good kids of suburbia. (Which is why the kids of Surrey went mad for them!) As Terry Jones *nearly* said (in his role as Brian's Mother in Monty Python's *Life Of Brian*) they looked like *very naughty boys*.

Oldham was also conscious that there was money to be made in song-writing. He was surprised and disappointed that the Stones didn't write their own material at the time he took over. Allegedly, and this might be apocryphal, but I like the image so I don't mind repeating it, Oldham *literally* locked Jagger and Richards into cupboard under the stairs and told them they couldn't emerge until they'd written a song. When the boys finally produced their first really good song. '*Tell Me*' (their first attempts were soppy and pathetic) it was less inspired by the blues and more inspired by beat-flavoured pop. But what the hell? It was better than paying Lennon & McCartney *more* royalties. Side note: The Stones' second single '*I Wanna Be Your Man*' had been a Lennon–McCartney-penned song. Legend has it that the Mersey boys scribbled it onto rough paper in front of Jagger and Richards, almost rubbing their noses in it! The number was released as a single in November 1963 and became the first song to be performed on BBC's new show, Top of The Pops.

23

THE BEATLES COME TO SURREY

In March 1963, after the long-struggle of the coldest winter on record, a breathtaking double-header show — featuring singers Chris Montez and Tommy Roe — was being advertised on bill-boards around Croydon. Californian vocalist Chris Montez – who had experienced plenty of success with his '*Let's Dance*' single (four weeks in the UK charts) was going to be performing on stage (at the ABC Cinema in Croydon) with Tommy Roe (now best remembered now for his single '*Dizzy*' -1969) but who – at that stage – had a single titled '*Sheila*' (it sounded a bit like '*Peggy Sue*') rising high in the British charts.

The main support for these American rock 'n' roll stars was the London pop-trio 'The Viscounts' (these days remembered for '*Who Put the Bomp In The Bomp, Bomp, Bomp*', released in 1961.) The Viscounts band member Gordon Mills wrote some songs for 'Johnny Kidd & The Pirates' at about this time – but perhaps he's perhaps best known for writing '*It's Not Unusual*' which is the song that launched the career of Tom Jones. (He resembled Jones and, although born in India, was raised in the Rhonda Valley.)

Mills eventually became the manager of Tom Jones and also Engelbert Humperdinck. In the 1970's Mills went on to become a talented producer – working with the Waterford-born singer-songwriter Gilbert O'Sullivan, amongst others. (His daughter *Clair* became the subject of the famous song written by O'Sullivan in 1972.)

Managing to secure a warm-up slot (underneath 'The Viscounts') at this hugely anticipated gig in Croydon was a little-known band from Liverpool: They were called The Beatles. They'd recently released two singles '*Love Me Do*' and '*Please, Please Me*' and were starting to gain a *modicum* of attention. Legend has it that when the Beatles heard all the girls screaming outside the ABC Cinema in Croydon they *actually* believed all the hullabaloo was *for them*. In fact, the girl-craziness was for Chris Montez.

The people of Surrey were not ready for The Beatles.

In fact, some Surrey folk wilfully and very stubbornly went on ignoring the band for years. This was partly because they were from 'Up North' and also, partly, because they had long-hair.

It's worth remembering that this was a year after the fabled 'Decca Audition.' The record label rejected the Beatles at a try-out in their London studios. After the audition, Decca record-execs said: 'Guitar groups are on the way out.'

The Beatles may have been 'big up North' and used to playing packed houses in Merseyside, but success was denied them in the Wen. And this was *also* not long after their dismal non-achievement at Aldershot. They had failed to generate *any* audience at a pitiful Palais Ballroom battle-of-the-bands gig, held in the army-town in 1961. Weeks after this dismal effort, Brian Epstein took over from Sam Leach as the group's manager. At lease *he* promised a more hopeful future.

The ABC Cinema (situated in Broad Green, Croydon and demolished in 2005) was where Chris Montez and Tommy Roe were to be playing. But it was not the only music venue in Croydon. The Fairfield Hall was a much larger venue. And the Fairfield Hall was far more important.

Fairfield Hall stands on the site of a field that was used for a fair (thus Fairfield) for over five and a half centuries. During the Second Word War (1940) a damaged Messerschmitt ME109 was displayed on the Fair Field as a fundraiser for the local spitfire fund. The German fighter plane had been shot down over Surrey and it was lent by the Air Ministry to help raise cash for a spitfire that would, one day, bear the Croydon coat of arms. Over 26,000 people paid to see the plane. It was a highly successful fundraising idea.

Fairfield Hall was opened by The Queen Mother in 1962. The architects chosen for this important project were Robert Atkinson and Partners (more famous for their fancy art deco style designs.) On this occasion, however, they managed to produce drawings that were remarkably similar to the designs for the Royal Festival Hall (situated on the Southbank in London - and built ten years earlier.)

The designers ignored the lessons learnt from the Royal Festival Hall project – (the main lesson being that reinforced concrete was acoustically *inappropriate* as a construction material for a concert venue) and pressed ahead with the works anyhow. They seemed oblivious to the fact that the Royal Festival Hall had recently called in an expert on acoustics (Leo Beranek) who concluded nothing could be done to improve the structure that would make it useful as a concert venue.

The Fairfield building was three halls in one structure: The Concert Hall, the Ashcroft Theatre and The Arnhem Gallery. We locals have always referred to this building (quite correctly) as the 'Fairfield Halls' (we added the extra 'S') because it's a combined building with three spaces. The concrete edifice has been a cold and unwelcoming host to scores of internationally famous musicians since the day it opened.

At around this time, the famous Liverpool impresario Brian Epstein had been sending his roster of artists on 'package tours' just like Arden had done. His fourth 'Mersey Beat Showcase' package, starring artists from the Epstein 'management stable' was due to take place at the Fairfield Hall in Croydon, Surrey, in April 1963.

The Fairfield Hall line-up included 'The Beatles, plus 'Gerry and the Pacemakers', and 'Billy J Kramer' and 'The Big Three.' None of these acts had enjoyed major chart success at the time of this package show. Accordingly, it was expedient to choose the far famous and reliable John Leyton ('*Johnny Remember Me*') as the headline act for this *crucial* Croydon show. However, luckily for the history of music, Leyton reported sick on the night. His appearance was cancelled. This left the Beatles at the 'top the bill.' It was a triumph. Epstein correctly reckoned on this. He knew that if the Beatles were to enjoy any success 'down South' at all – they absolutely *had* to crack the huge populations of the London suburbs. The Fab Four appeared again at Croydon's Fairfield Hall, later the same year, on September 7th. The second visit was a sell-out headline show.

24
___

WHEN MY DAD MET RINGO

My Father was a Metropolitan police officer, serving at Tooting police station for almost his entire service. During the 1960s he rode a 'Noddy Bike' around the South London borough. The 'Noddy' bike was a Velocette LE motorcycle. These motorbikes were quite heavy and stupid looking. But the officers loved them. The Noddy could get to places quickly and efficiently. They'd sneak up alleyways and rush across open spaces, often getting to places that other officers couldn't reach. And each bike was equipped with a 'wireless' that despatched radio calls direct from Scotland Yard, so Noddy riders got the 'cream' of the emergency calls.

My Dad was also one of the first officers to drive a 'Panda' car in London. His panda was the colourful Morris Minor. He has also got to drive the Tooting wireless car 'Whiskey-3' when a 'Class 1 or class 2' wasn't available to drive it (my Dad was only a 'Class 3' driver.) He'd also take out the station van 'Whiskey Delta-2' on a Saturday evening.

When we lived at Morden, he'd bicycle to work. When we moved to North Cheam, he got himself his own 'pop-pop' Velocette motorcycle, and he wobbled to work on it. He'd leave home in full 'Noddy' uniform, wearing those 'zebra' stripes (his duty-band, worn on the left forearm, to signify he was 'on duty' while riding to work.) I remember watching him tootle up the road to parade for 'Late Turn' (his tour of duty started at 2 p.m.). I'd silently pray he'd stay safe and come home to us.

One Sunday, during June 1963, my Father came down from the upstairs bedroom in high spirits. He sat down at our blue Formica table-top and started to eat his breakfast, porridge followed by thickly buttered toast, washed down with tea, even though it was gone one o'clock. Dad always had his breakfast at lunch-time, because, like most shift-workers, he had to fit in his mealtimes around 'Lates' and 'Nights.' But at *this* mealtime he had something on his mind, so gathered the whole family around to explain what he'd done over the weekend.

Apparently, on the night before, the Beatles had played a show at the great Cecil Masey designed Granada Cinema, in Tooting. It was the 14th date of their British tour. A sizeable crowd had gathered outside the cinema. And it was so conspicuous and *so* frenzied that the boys from Liverpool feared for their safety and were forced to scurry out of the back door of the cinema and make a stealthy and elaborately planned escape. This was via the station van (sometimes called the 'black mariah') that had been strategically positioned near the fire escapes at the rear of the cinema and was driven by my Dad.

The Beatles' own official limousine functioned as bait near the main doors. This had the effect of convincing the crowd and waiting paparazzi that the boys would leave the venue at this point. Mean looking bouncers and management types supported this ruse by gathering around the car in an agitated state. Most of the fans gravitate towards the focal point in the hope of getting a rare glimpse of long-haired Liverpool lads, almost certainly hoping to claw bits off them. But the band hurried through the rear fire exits, and piled into the back of Dad's police van before it dashed off. All the group members jumped into his van via the swinging doors at the back. Dad thinks that Paul pulled the door closed. All except *Ringo*. He kept his cool and calmy took a front seat alongside the policeman. Alongside my Dad.

We watched in awe as my Father told his story. We started to ask several questions at once. What was Ringo like? What did he say?

Was he handsome? What was he wearing? Did he give you anything? Did he provide any words of wisdom?

My Father told us that Ringo was genuinely nice. Apparently, the band were temporarily staying in Trevelyan Road, on my Dad's patch. Dad was instructed to deliver them safely to their guest house, where they slipped from his van and in through a side door of the hotel. Dad told us that all the musicians were polite, and all said, 'Good night' and thanked him.

When asked about the concert, my Dad seemed genuinely more impressed with Roy Orbison (who supported the Beatles at these shows.) He said Orbison – as a performer – was *far* stronger and more exciting than The Beatles. Like most adults 'down south' he wasn't enamoured by their long hair and Mersey accents. But Dad was impressed by the two drum sets used by Orbison's band and mentioned it several times over.

———

On 21 June 1963, The Beatles made their only live appearance in Guildford. They played the Odeon Cinema (located on the corner of Epsom Road and Jenner Road.) It had seating for 1,623 people in the stalls and circle. (The place was demolished in 2002 to make room for shops and apartments.) An advertisement of the time testifies that the Beatles headlined the show – but played with a support bundle of seven acts as part of the 'Jimmy Crawford Package Show.' They played two performances – at 6:15pm and at 8:30pm. Musicians worked hard in those days! Part of the 'Jimmy Crawford Package' was Lance Fortune who was booked to replace Eddie Cochrane on his ill-fated Gene Vincent tour of 1960.

25

SURREY'S ROCK ROYALTY

It was in 1963 that the Beatles made a permanent move from Liverpool to London, and from the Wen to Surrey.

After nearly three hundred gigs played at the Cavern Club, the Fab Four played their final show at the iconic Liverpool venue in August 1963. They up-rooted and moved to the Capital. And that's because *that's* where the action was during the Swinging Sixties!

The band stayed for a while at the President Hotel, in Russell Square, Bloomsbury. After this, they moved (together) into a cramped fourth floor flat at 57 Green Street, Mayfair. This was the only period in Beatles history when *all four* members lived together. The arrangement was far from perfect – baby Julian (Lennon) was born in April 1963 – so it must have been an uncomfortable squeeze. After just two months of living in this confined space, both George and Ringo moved out. By the mid 1960's John, George and Ringo had *all* moved into Surrey's 'stockbroker belt' – sometimes known as the 'Beverly Hills of Britain.' The only Beatle left in London was Paul.

In 1964 the Beatles accountant, Dr. Walter Strach, came up with an amazing idea for the disposal of approximately £2 million that was sloshing about in Beatles current account and was causing sleepless nights for the bean-counters. He had already had some earnest meetings with Brian Epstein about finding appropriate tax shelters for this loose cash - and one of the best ideas was to invest in some real estate. He urged the Beatles to purchase some great big properties in Surrey. The idea was that the boys could all live together (the dream was that they would be next door neighbours on the same estate) where they could live in a rich oasis of safety, security, and prosperity. Large homes in the stockbroker belt would clearly be long-term investments — and it would also mean that the musicians were never more than an hour away from the recording studios in London.

So, on that sage advice, in July 1964 George Harrison purchased 'Kinfauns' in Claremont Drive, Esher, Surrey. Situated on the Claremont Estate, the property cost him £20,000. The house was snake thin, angular, and disjointed. With lots of dark corners and obscure edges. In many ways it was the perfect choice for the 'dark horse' of the band. It seems George viewed the whole house purchasing matter *a chore*. Chronicles of the time suggested he probably bought the first house he saw ... just to please Walter Strach and get the job over with. That may be true – but it was an appropriate property, nevertheless. It was the perfect hippie retreat. The one-storey dwelling closely abutted the walls of the much grander Claremont House. The house was rather slender, with bow windows at the front, and green meadows on the sides. It had a row of standard rose trees leading up to a fairly insignificant front door. It could have been mistaken for an unremarkable old-folks bungalow— the type of property you might see around Staines even now. But for George the bungalow became an idyllic love nest. He lived in the hand-painted one-storey hippy shack until 1970. Then purchased the far more imposing Friar Park, in Henley-on-Thames.

Although born in Taunton, Somerset, the model Pattie Boyd moved with her family to Guildford, Surrey in 1947. She attended Hazeldean School in Putney for a while, and when she left school, she found work as a shampoo girl at the famous Elizabeth Arden salon in London. While working there, she was spotted by a fashion magazine and lured into the glamorous world of fashion. Boyd began modelling in 1962 and was photographed by Sixties snappers David Bailey and Terence Donovan. Through this exposure, she managed to be cast as a schoolgirl in the 1964 Beatles film: 'A Hard Day's Night.' At this stage she was romantically involved with *another* fashion photographer named Eric Swayne. Because of this relationship, she declined a date with George who had been eyeing her up on the set, all the while. But a few days into filming, and after she had broken up with Swayne, Pattie Boyd returned to the set and George gathered the courage to ask her out on a date. She accepted. Their first date was to 'The Garrick Club' in London and was supervised by Beatles manager Brian Epstein. He *wasn't* a trusting man.

In the early months of 1965 Boyd moved into the snake-like bungalow at 'Kinfauns' with George. The couple were engaged on Christmas Day, 1965. They were married on 21 January 1966. In an unpromising ceremony at a dull registry office in Ashley Road, Epsom. Paul McCartney was the best man. Right away, they settled into a blissful suburban existence, thriving in the labyrinthine house, to create a hippie camp which soon became the magnetic hospitality centre for arts, music, and creativity in Surrey.

Kinfauns was a sprawling 1950's deluxe bungalow on a lush plot and surrounded by a tall brick wall. A pool was installed in the back. Kinfauns was presumably the home that the Beatles gathered at *most*, as it was only a short distance from the homes of John Lennon (Kenwood) and Ringo Starr (Sunny Heights), both in St George's Hill. Among the many visitors to Kinfauns were Yoko Ono, Eric Clapton, Jackie Lomax, Brian Jones, and Suki Potier. Mick Jagger and Marianne Faithful once popped around, but nobody was in! Paul McCartney recorded a demo version of 'Junk' at Kinfauns. At the bungalow, they recorded *Mean Mr. Mustard* and *Dear Prudence* as demos.

It's likely that Bobby Whitlock, Billy Preston, Bobby Keys, Dave Mason, Gary Brooker, and Ginger Baker visited Kinfauns (they worked together on the *All Things Must Pass* project in 1970. From 1973 and onwards, Harrison recorded most of his projects at Friar Park, in Henley-on-Thames.) It's been claimed that Derek and the Dominos was first muted at Kinfauns, as a venture after Blind Faith sort-of tailed-off during the late summer of '69.

Delaney Bramlett and Bonnie Bramlett were also visitors to

Kinfauns. Upon hearing pre-released mixes of the album to be titled '*The Original Delaney & Bonnie & Friends (Accept No Substitute)*' in 1969, Harrison offered the American rock-soul duo a contract with the Beatles' Apple label—which Delaney & Bonnie signed despite prior contractual commitments to Elektra.

In mid-1969, Eric Clapton brought Delaney, Bonnie, and Friends on *his* tour as the opening act for Blind Faith. Clapton became close companions with Delaney, Bonnie, and their band, and suggested he preferred *their* music to that of Blind Faith's! Impressed by their live performances, he'd often appear on stage with the duo and continued to record and tour with them following Blind Faith's breakup. Clapton facilitated a fresh record deal for Delaney and Bonnie through his then-U.S. sub-label, Atco (Atlantic) Records. He also played alongside Harrison, Dave Mason, and others on Delaney and Bonnie's third album, the live On Tour with Eric Clapton (Atco). This would be their most successful album.

Sgt Norman Pilcher of the Drugs Squad targeted George and Pattie Harrison's Kinfauns bungalow on the day of Paul McCartney's wedding (to Linda Eastman) March, 1969. He chose that specific date because he knew they'd be out, and his men could search the place unheeded! The squad brought-along a drugs sniffer-dog named Yogi. Harrison thought this was in poor taste. Pilcher had *already* busted Mick Jagger, Eric Clapton, and John Lennon, though he seemed to be principally focused on The Rolling Stones' Brian Jones, for some reason. Anyway, at Kinfauns they found a lump of hashish, making the raid a minor success. These days you'd get a warning for this but back in the late 60's Harrison received a fine as a penalty. But the conviction didn't help with the musician's international touring commitments.

John Lennon purchased Kenwood House on the St. George's Hill estate, Weybridge, Surrey just a few days before George bought his bungalow. It was a far more imposing property than George's. The mock-Tudor home was built in 1913 and stood in lavishly landscaped grounds. The house had 22 rooms. It was said that John did not like the property – he remarked, at the time, it was a *stop-gap home*, but had the place extensively refurbished, *anyway*. Improvements included a new swimming pool.

The Small Faces / Faces drummer Kenney Jones has made Hurtwood Park in Ewhurst his home for several years. During the 1970s, Maurice Gibb of the Bee Gees owned a house called The Firs, in Esher.

Elton John, Tom Jones, Cliff Richard, the songwriter/music manager Gordon Mills, and Englebert Humperdinck were *all* residents of the St George's Hill community of Weybridge, Surrey. It truly was (and the area *still is*) the Beverly Hills of Britain.

26

_____

OVER THE GARDEN WALL

Having explored Charterhouse School in Godalming and learned about rock manager Peter Grant's beginnings, we ought to return to their Italianate courtyards and landscaped lawns to examine the origins of *another* internationally acclaimed rock act and ponder the circumstances of this school's most privileged students.

Let us begin with an aspiring guitarist named Anthony Phillips, born in Chiswick, West-London and influenced by The Shadows. He teamed up with Rivers Jobe, a schoolboy bass-player, to form a group called Anon. He'd been acquainted with Jobe since early days at a prep-school which served as a 'feeder' school for prestigious institutions like Charterhouse.

At the 'big school' in Godalming, Phillips and Jobe put the band together. Anon's original line-up included Rivers Jobe on bass, Richard Macphail on vocals, Phillips on lead guitar, and Rob Tyrrell on drums.

Eventually, a guy named Mike Rutherford joined them, on rhythm guitar. This is a name that might ring a bell with readers. Though Rutherford was forced to leave the set-up by his house master, to be replaced by another schoolboy, named Mike Colman. Anon's main style of music was British R&B, with a strong focus on John Mayall numbers.

The extent to which *actual* history influenced the screenplay for 'School of Rock' is unknown, but it's reasonable to suppose that the story I'm about to convey had some bearing on Mike White's comedy film of 2003. So, here's how Charterhouse became a real-life Surrey based 'School of Rock.'

Charterhouse School disapproved of all music, except classical. Accordingly, parents and teachers put pressure on the members of Anon, demanding they decrease their 'rebellious' pursuits, particularly during school hours. Parents felt that their child playing rock at the priciest school in Surrey was a waste of dough; teachers took issue with the young musicians' longer hairstyles and, obviously, absolutely loathed their loud music and thought they'd be better off applying themselves academically.

Anyway, the adult pressure grew too much for Macphail, and he capitulated and left the fledgeling band. Meanwhile, Rutherford had his guitar confiscated by his form master, but they couldn't stifle his singing voice! How would 'the man' confiscate his vocal cords? Rutherford continued as the band's vocalist and, after several disagreements with staff, managed to retrieve his guitar too.

Meanwhile, over at a different 'house' at Charterhouse (if you read Harry Potter books you'll be familiar with the concept of 'houses' in posh private schools), teenagers Peter Gabriel and Tony Banks had formed an alternative band. Their project, known as 'Garden Wall,' originated during their first year at the school when Banks and Gabriel despised the place and were desperate to find a way to alleviate the misery: music offered an escape. The band project was a 'look' over the 'wall' into freedom. Gabriel's origins can be traced back to Cobham, one of the more affluent areas of Surrey where his parents embodied the classic old-money archetype. He'd done piano lessons, he'd sang in the choir, and had been treated to a few drum lessons. Through drumming, he'd obtained some gigs with Surrey bands 'The Spoken Word,' and the 'Millords.'

Banks had attended a private boarding school in Hurst Green, East Sussex, which was another 'feeder' school for Charterhouse. Banks and Gabriel formed Garden Wall with Chris Stewart, who was born in Crawley and grew up in Horsham, Sussex. The trio would be Gabriel on vocals, Banks on keys, and Stewart on drums.

Garden Wall's one and only concert took place in December 1965, on the stage at Charterhouse School. They shared a double bill with Anon. Both bands broke up after the school concert, but from the remnants sprouted an idea: Genesis.

Phillips and Rutherford started writing together in 1967. They even attempted to make a demo (demonstration) tape in their home studio. The sessions included members of Anon as invited participants. It's worth reminding ourselves, at this stage, that these musicians were school lads, the oldest of them 17, the youngest, just 15. Perhaps, retrospectively, we might cringe at their *next* decision, but it made complete sense to them at the time.

———

Born in Marylebone, London, in 1944, Kenneth George King had a rich New Jersey industrialist for a Father and a famous actress for a Mother. The family moved to Surrey, where Kenneth and two brothers were raised in a fabulous mansion, at Ewhurst, Surrey. Not surprisingly, Kenneth King was sent to boarding schools, one being a 'feeder' for Charterhouse. Kenneth King started living as a border at Charterhouse in 1958. He'd secretly listen to Radio Luxembourg on a transistor radio hidden under the bedclothes in his dorm-room.

Due to his lackadaisical approach to academic studies, King was encouraged to depart the hallowed towers of Charterhouse in 1962 to intensively prepare for the exams he'd need to pass if he wanted to gain admission to a reputable university. Instead of swotting, he landed a job stacking shelves and he produced a couple of demo recordings. Brimming with misplaced confidence, he schlepped around town, promoting himself as an up-and-coming rock 'n' roll singer. At around the same time he became the manager and middle-man for a band called The Bumblies in nearby Cranleigh, occasionally singing for them.

While taking a gap year before starting at Cambridge (he failed the Cambridge scholarship exam, but somehow managed to sweet-talk his way onto a course), he crossed paths with Brian Epstein. His meeting with the Beatles boss galvanised his ambition to get into rock 'n' roll management. When he came back to Britain, he presented two Bumblies numbers to several record labels to have them recorded. The second of these, "*All You've Gotta Do*," was even produced by Joe Meek, but nothing came of either. He contacted the Oh Boy! show host and label executive Tony Hall, and offered his services, and through *that* call, Hall connected him with The Zombies with whom he'd been working. King presented them The Zombies with six songs he'd been working on, one of which was '*Everyone's Gone to the Moon.*' The band rejected the song, so it ended up being an A side for King (his debut.) The Zombies suggested he changed his name: he chose Jonathan King.

'*Everyone's Gone to the Moon*' was released in August 1965 and King relentlessly plugged it. Mainly due to his relentless plugging, the song became a massive hit.

In 1967, King was invited to an old boys' reunion at Charterhouse School. He turned-up rather pleased with himself, advising staff he was the 'most famous' of all Old Carthusians (he wasn't.) King listened to the Anon numbers being performed. Legend has it that he produced a new name for their band, 'Genesis' after the lads asked for his assistance. He organised a short-term recording deal for the schoolboys.

King produced the first three singles for Genesis, including '*The Silent Sun*' (1968) and an album, '*From Genesis to Revelation*' (1969). The King-produced album sold just 649 copies: the singles, even *less*. After the failures, Stewart decided to leave the band, so *another* Charterhouse student, John Silver, took his place as drummer.

Thankfully, Genesis parted ways with King quite quickly after and joined forces with Tony Stratton Smith, in 1969. Their album 'Trespass' (1970) was recorded with Smith in the stunning Surrey village of Wotton, at a cottage owned by Macphail's parents. Genesis gained a Tuesday night residency at Ronnie Scott's Jazz Club in Soho where they met prog-rockers Rare Bird (interesting side note: the Rare Bird keyboards player was Dave Kaff, better known to rock fans as Viv Savage of the spoof-band Spinal Tap). Anyway, the Rare Bird musicians recommended they communicated with Charisma Records since the label already signed similar bands: The Nice, the Bonzo Dog Band and Van der Graaf Generator.

After *Trespass* was released via Charisma, ill-health and stage fright caused Phillips to leave Genesis. John Mayhew took over from John Silver as the 'touring' drummer for the band, although his position in the lineup was always uncertain. He was older and more experienced than the other members, a working-class carpenter by trade, and a seasoned musician who'd played with several bands before Genesis. Probably, for all these reasons, the other band members decided to part ways with him in July 1970.

The hunt for a guitarist and drummer started by the band placing ads in Melody Maker. Wandsworth born Middlesex-raised drummer Phil Collins, previously with a relatively unknown band called Flaming Youth, noticed the advert. Collins had attended the Barbara Speake stage school and, through the school, and had played the Artful Dodger in two West End runs of the musical Oliver. Roger Taylor, subsequently of Queen, turned down an invitation to audition. Collins and Ronnie Caryl, both from Flaming Youth, attended an audition at Gabriel's parents' house in Chobham, Surrey. Collins was taken on by Genesis to be their new drummer and backing vocalist, while Caryl didn't make the cut.

Genesis started writing and practicing as a quartet in Farnham, Surrey. Genesis invited Steve Hackett, who was a guitarist with Quiet World at the time, to join their line-up as the lead guitarist, in January 1971. Immediately following his joining, Genesis began a major tour with Lindisfarne and Van der Graaf Generator.

Gabriel's parents' home served as the inspiration for the manor house on the *Nursery Cryme* album cover, painted by Paul White-head, 1971. The lifestyles of the Charterhouse Set were far removed from mine on the St Helier estate in Carshalton, or my friends' lives at Merland Rise, in Tadworth, or the daily routines of the people who were educated in Sheerwater, close to Woking. I'll address Sheer-water soon, but first, let's take a peek into the life of the first successful *freelance* recording engineer in rock history; and as you might assume, he was *also* from Surrey!

———

Note: In 1968, bassist Jobe joined the Savoy Brown Blues Band (then, just Savoy Brown), taking over from Robert Brunning who had left to pursue a career in teaching. Richard Macphail established himself as a highly regarded sound engineer.

27

THE SOUND CHAMPION

Glyn Johns, the older brother of Andy Johns was born in Epsom, Surrey, in February 1942. Andy went on to produce and engineer the Rolling Stones' *'Exile on Main Street,'* but *Glyn* is the subject of this chapter.

By all accounts, Glyn Johns was a superbly behaved chorister and a wonderful boy soprano. He received expert instruction at St Martin's Church in Epsom from the renowned organist and concert-arranger Felton Rapley who, it seems, was also gainfully employed by Epsom's Odeon as a cinema organist (albeit Rapley took on the identity of Peter Barrington for this less revered but no less honourable employment.) The young man's musical journey was likely shaped by his involvement in the church choir, and through the influence of Rapley's notable pipe-organ performances and his teacher's ability to create incredibly *expansive* soundscapes. (Rapley later achieved recognition as a successful sound recording artist in his own right)

When Johns' voice finally 'broke,' as they all must, he became unfit for the church choir, so as an alternative, began attending the church's Wednesday night youth club. There he observed Jimmy Page playing guitar. He'd later befriend the guitarist and was persuaded to buy a guitar of his own. Johns began to play the tea chest bass for a local cheapjack jazz ensemble, and started hanging out with a group of music-loving friends, among them was Ian Stewart (who'd go on to become the Rolling Stones' boogie-woogie keyboardist until he was demoted by Andrew Loog Oldham).

At the age of 17, Johns dropped out of school to establish a little band (The Presidents) to stumble into a job at the IBC Recording Studios, an establishment that had been founded in the 1930s and specifically set-up to disrupt the BBC's dominance in sound recording. The IBC Studios, located in London's Portland Place, operated a fully transistorised desk, one of the first of its kind, built around 1958.

John's introduction to the music industry was through his role as a recording engineer's *assistant* for a track laid-down by the renowned Skiffle-monger Lonnie Donegan. Radio Luxembourg's Alan Stagg was master of audio at IBC, (he later became better known as the General Manager of Abbey Road studios) and Stagg became Johns' primary educator. According to his biography, Johns recorded Joe Brown, as a *fully qualified* engineer, in the year that followed.

Due to his relationship with Stewart, (they shared a flat) he was able to persuade The Rolling Stones to utilise the IBC equipment on a weekend in March 1963 when the studios were not open. Oldham disliked the arrangements and made a fuss. Consequently, and to avoid bad feeling developing between Stewart and Oldham, Johns allowed the scheme to slip and *instead* convinced Georgie Fame and the Blue Flames to perform at the IBC outside of regular hours, using the *same* makeshift arrangements he'd offered the Stones. Fame wholeheartedly embraced the offer and invited Shel Talmy, the famous Chicago producer, to be part of their session.

Georgie Fame's album 'Rhythm and Blues at the Flamingo' (1964) marked Johns' first full album credit.

Through *this* extracurricular activity (authorised and approved by IBC, I should add) Johns began to establish his influence and expand his network of music-business contacts, while also honing his skills as a producer and engineer. As Johns' reputation flourished, he started working with ever-more prestigious clients and artists.

Johns soon became known as a 'must have' freelance engineer and producer, open to working with *anyone* and not tied to any specific brand. He did work for Pye, for Decca Records, and for the

Immediate label, that had been founded by Andrew Loog Oldham with the Surbiton (Surrey) talent agent Tony Calder. The Immediate signings included Billy Nicholls, John Mayall, Savoy Brown, The Small Faces, The Nice, and Fleetwood Mac.

In 1965, Johns collaborated on engineering and mixing The Rolling Stones' fifth album, 'December's Children', which featured a handful of cover songs. However, the album *also* included the band's self-penned superhit, 'Get Off of My Cloud,' which was written by Jagger & Richards as a response to the unrealistic expectations that people outside of their *circle* had of the band's trajectory. The *album*-title came from Andrew Loog Oldham, who thought it sounded sufficiently surreal and romantic to be considered intellectual and 'beat poetry' inspired. The album earned certified gold sales in the U.S., no doubt driven by the track, 'Get Off of My Cloud', but the disc also sports a much-loved song written alongside the session guitarist Big Jim Sullivan, titled 'As Tears Go By' which had been a reasonable hit for Marianne Faithfull a full year before the album came out, and the singer had established a romantic relationship with Jagger. (In 1966, Faithful was infamously found wearing *nothing but* a fur rug when the drugs squad conducted a search at Keith Richards' home in West Wittering, Sussex.)

Glyn Johns received his first co-production credit for The Pretty Things' second album, 'Get the Picture?' (1965). This recording had a number written by Jimmy Page (*You Don't Believe Me*) and also several covers including material written by American songwriters Ike Turner and Tim Hardin. An interesting side-note: my second cousin, John Alder, who goes by the name Twink, played drums on two tracks on this recording.

Perhaps as a result of his previous positive encounter with producer Shel Talmy, Johns was given the opportunity to engineer a number of early Kinks and Who records, including the well-known numbers 'You Really Got Me' by the Kinks and 'My Generation' by The Who.

Throughout the 1970s, Johns worked as an engineer with the Who and contributed to parts of *Quadrophenia*, in 1973. Additionally, Townshend enlisted him to engineer Clapton's 'Rainbow Concert' the same year (recorded using Ronnie Lane's Mobile Studio.) Clapton was joined on the famous Rainbow Theatre stage, by an all-star lineup that included Ron Wood (guitar), Ric Grech (bass), Steve Winwood (keys), Jim Capaldi (drums), Pete Townshend (rhythm guitar) and soon to be Traffic (and Can) percussionist Rebop Kwaku Baah.

———

Led Zeppelin's inaugural studio album was engineered by Glyn Johns at Olympic Studios, in October 1968. It's encouraging to think that those two Epsom schoolboys ultimately collaborated to create history-making music. Page has since claimed that the majority of the album was recorded live, and they didn't use overdubs. Johns valued the pure intensity and passion of a live performance, so was pleased to comply with Page's request to experiment with what he described as 'natural room ambience.' The distinctive echoing sound you hear today on this recording lent the album a remarkable sense of expansiveness and reverberance. Amazingly, this would be among the very first album to be issued *exclusively* in stereo.

Johns was in popular demand on both sides of the Atlantic in the late 1960s and early 1970s, collaborating with American artists like The Eagles and the Steve Miller Band. Johns engineered the live recordings of Bob Dylan's 1969 Isle of Wight Festival performance (with The Band) at the request of producer Bob Johnston. Johnston, who'd been Dylan's (and Simon & Garfunkel's) producer of choice, had been made head of Columbia, at Nashville, but shortly after the Isle of Wight Festival he followed Johns' example to become a freelance producer, working (without royalties) with Lindisfarne in 1972 (on *Fog On The Tyne*). He later worked in a freelance capacity with Jimmy Cliff, Willie Nelson, Pete Seeger, and The Waterboys. Perhaps through *this* valuable connection, Johns was invited to record songs for Billy Preston, Howlin' Wolf, Spooky Tooth, and the Ozark Mountain Daredevils.

Following an evaluation of Joan Armatrading's second album's underwhelming sales, A&M appointed Johns to produce the artist's next three albums. *'Love and Affection'* was Johns' immediate response.

Johns worked with The Clash and contributed to the recording of the album that became known as *'Combat Rock.'* He collaborated with Paul McCartney on the *'Pure McCartney'* album, and he recorded for Linda Ronstadt, and Bill Wyman's Rhythm Kings, and worked on David Bowie's *'Nothing Has Changed'*, which is the very highly praised compilation 'showcase' published in November 2014. Johns has long believed that the emotional connection between musicians is a *vital* yet often overlooked element in the recording process. Most recording artists attempt to capture rare 'sunlight in a bottle,' in the studio environment, though few achieve it. Johns had long suggested that connection between artists on an emotional level could be the missing component.

Johns also invented a technique for recording drums in stereo using a variety of carefully placed mics around the kit (a technique now referred to as the 'Glyn Johns Method.') It gives his tracks a brightness and rhythmic saturation that is seldom heard in other recordings. Glyn Johns must be among the top candidates to be recognised as a primary creator of the modern rock 'n' roll sound.

28

A JUG OF SPIDERS

It is hard for an outsider to comprehend just how utterly *quiet* and incredibly *dull* it was to grow up in Surrey in the heyday of rock 'n' roll.

I joined everything I could. I went to church. I enrolled in extra activities at school. I joined the drama group. I joined the church youth club. I joined the Cub Scouts (which I loathed.) I did all these pursuits because we were properly *cut-off* and, of course, there was *nothing to do!*

To provide an insight into what it was like to travel across the County of Surrey – and the sense of isolation we *all* had – let me tell you about my girlfriend named Gill. She lived in Mogador, which, although it sounds like a place-name made-up by J.R.R. Tolkien, it is actually a bland sub-village (part of Lower Kingswood) just 5 miles from my home on Epsom Downs (or nine minutes by car.) But in the rock 'n' roll years, to see Gill, I had to make an *epic* journey across *Middle Earth*. First, I'd have to stride to the main Brighton Road from Tattenham Corner – which was a brisk hike of twenty minutes. At the main road I'd wait for a Green Line bus (a single-decker coach) that would, hopefully, take me towards Lower Kingswood. The coach would take me past the haunted Tadworth Court and beyond the prefab housing estate nestled near the Chipstead Valley. The coach eventually rattle its way into Lower Kingswood. I would have to 'allow' about an hour-and-a-half for this stage of the journey.

These coaches (known as Green Line buses) were introduced in 1953 with the explicit purpose of linking-up the umpteen new settlements that sprung-up around the suburbs. The theory was that Green Line buses would operate in areas that were, on average, 30 miles from London. Green Line buses were operated by the Country Bus and Coach division of London Transport who also ran double-deckers painted in green livery on what they described as the London Country Bus routes, which, theoretically, were London Transport services that ran outside the G.L.C transport area. Note: the G.L.C. (Greater London Council) replaced the London County Council (L.C.C.) in 1965 as the principal local government body for 'metropolitan' London.

The Green Line coach that I took to Gill's house was a number 80 (or, possibly, a number 80a, I've never been a bus anorak, *sorry*) and it delivered me into a semi-residential area. At this point, the driver would stop the engine, kick out the passengers and eat a snack. I'd have to walk the remaining part of my journey (a further twenty minutes) to my girlfriend's house.

When we eventually got together, we'd escape into the country. Gill and I would stroll over Margery Downs or trek to Colley Hill. At that time, I really thought that Reigate was the end-of-the-world. You literally couldn't see anything *beyond* the hill. On the far side was unspoilt countryside. It was *so* different to the suburban areas of the County, to Morden, Sutton, and Cheam, that I recognised and had been raised in. Yet, both *bits* were, and *are*, Surrey! At Colley Hill I had the feeling we couldn't proceed further because we were at the rim of *everything*.

Years later, the massive M25 motorway was built. This thorough-fare not only spoilt the view from Lower Kingswood– but also created a tarmac buffer between countryside and suburbia. When the London Orbital was planned, people thought it might harness the diffusion and leakage of Surrey into London. That's because most people assumed that everything *within* the 'M25 zone' would be in possession of Greater London, and everything 'outside' the motorway would be *country*. Even the Metropolitan Police thought they'd be getting a bigger policing area as a result of the M25. (This didn't turn out like that, in fact the 'Met' got their wings pruned.) But the M25 rim is not as clear-cut as it *should* be. The vast road did *not* become the outer edge of London... and *thank heavens for that*. I can take you to places right now where Greater London *has* extended beyond the M25 gyratory and gurgled into outer districts like syrup from an over-filled pie. On the other hand, I can also show you places, well *within* the M25 gyratory, that remain wilderness areas – remote valleys, wild heaths, magical woods, and tumbling hills. This is the contradiction that I have pointed out over-and-over about Surrey living: the County is both a municipality *and* a rural area *at the same time*. Growing up in Surrey was like being a major character living on the edge of a novel you are never allowed to enter. It's cynical to think so, but I think our parents probably *did* prefer it that way. I suspect they wanted us to be safely tucked away from the ugly and seductive aspects of the Big City, cocooned in the comforts of semi-rural living.

Back in the rock 'n' roll years we didn't have the luxury of the M25 motorway. We didn't *even* have the luxury of cars. But that didn't stop town planners from laying out huge roads. Car ownership would soon become a "social necessity" and an "expression of men's (sic) sense of independence and self-respect," according to Patrick Gordon Walker, M.P., who made these remarks in April 1960 and added a recommendation: "We must rebuild our whole environment of working and living in terms of the motor car." And that's exactly what they set out doing. Based on U.K. government statistics, between 1951 and 2010, the percentage of households having access to a car or van increased from 14% to 75%. Even more British households have had access to two or more cars since 2002. Britain's car ownership rate exploded in the rock 'n' roll years, and soon we surpassed all other developed nations in terms of vehicles per mile.

The A3 Portsmouth Road is one such 'rebuild of the whole environment.' The super-road split the County all the way to Putney Vale. The incision created a separate 'limb' of Surrey, severing Worcester Park from New Malden, Chessington from Long Ditton, Oxshott from Esher, Cobham from Byfleet, Godalming from Elstead, and so forth, all the way to the County boundary. The idea of a *major* Kingston bypass road was originally raised in 1911, and the current route was inaugurated in 1927. Roadway upgrades began in the 1920s. So, this radical car ownership programme wasn't a 'new-fangled' idea, it had just been postponed because of the two world wars. Those drivers who speed along the A3 to London probably don't care that the head of our County has been adroitly guillotined by their grey asphalt serpent of death.

———

During the late 1930s, numerous homes were constructed in and around the Epsom & Ewell area, to form very large, and also very *bland*, residential areas. Two of the blandest were West Ewell and Stoneleigh. In the past, this region was farmland and a few cottages and barns scattered here-and-there but many acres of housing were developed in the 1930s. And when town planners developed estates in those days, they thought about the residents that might someday live in the homes, so added schools, clinics, parades of shops, churches, and other useful social amenities. One of the most notable amenities on the Stoneleigh / West Ewell estate was the medium-sized Rembrandt Cinema, built for the new population. According to the Epsom and Ewell History Explorer, using memories compiled by local historian Derek Phillip, it seems the Rembrandt cinema was opened in 1938 by screen actress Claudette Caulbert and the pantomime actor / horse-racing fanatic Tom Walls, (who owned a stable at his home in Ewell.)

During the 50's suburban cinemas like the Rembrandt typically included cafes and bars where they served teas and refreshments. However, the Rembrandt's restaurant closed, to be repurposed as a dance studio. One of my fondest memories from my rock 'n' roll childhood was going to the Granada Sutton (formerly the Plaza) to have a birthday tea with friends. According to the Granada advertisement, their cafe was open daily from 10 a.m. to 10:30 p.m. and served meals *at prices to suit everybody*.

Anyway, when a movie didn't arrive at the cinemas in Sutton or

Epsom, we kids from Banstead or Epsom Downs had to go on an adventure to the Rembrandt at Stoneleigh. Often we were obliged to wait outside the cinema in chilling colds because the bus travel seemed to take forever, so we usually set forth early. And because they didn't have any cafeteria, we were stuck *outside*. That's why I have such strong and painful remembrances of the Rembrandt. Those who know Stoneleigh Hill will recall that there weren't many shops, cafes, or shelters where we could hide from the wind. The worst part of any trip to Stoneleigh was having to worry about returning home after the movie. There were few buses, lengthy queues at the only bus stop, and a significant probability that the bus we were using might abruptly withdraw from service *before* we reached our destination. Remember that there were no mothers waiting to pick us up and ferry us around. Teenagers were expected to make *their own* travel arrangements if they wanted to go somewhere during the rock 'n' roll era! These factors meant that West Ewell was the *extent* of our range from Epsom Downs and Banstead. The 'Rembrandt' cinema was about as far 'North' as we'd dare travel. That's why me and my pals *never* schlepped all the way to Tolworth.

———

Despite its less-than-ideal location (for us bus travellers) situated opposite the Tolworth Tower, on the fast and dangerous A3 Portsmouth Road, (though well-placed for motoring patrons) the Toby Jug gained recognition as one of the most important music venues in suburban Surrey during the 1960s and 1970s. The place was built by the brewery company Charrington, in 1934, to serve an influx of motorists that were *expected* to use the new Portsmouth Road and so would need a place to guzzle beer before continuing an onward journey. The venue began hosting jazz evenings, then R&B nights in the mid 1960's, and towards the end of the decade, the venue specialized in rock shows. Most of the 1970's bands played the nearby Kingston Poly, the St. Marys College Strawberry Hill, the Ewell Tech, and the Digby Stuart College in Roehampton (Teachers Training) but bands nearly always added the Toby Jug to a touring schedule. One of the earliest remembered rock gigs at the Toby was the Yardbirds visit in January 1964. Fleetwood Mac played the Toby in 1968, the Jeff Beck Group (with Rod Stewart, Ronnie Wood, and Mick Waller) played the Toby in '69,

For those who are unaware, by the way, a Toby Jug, sometimes called a *philpot*, is a type of ceramic jug shaped like a sitting man who is typically sculpted holding a jug of beer. The sitting man often carried the head of a well-known individual. The original drinking man (likely based on Shakespeare's Sir Toby Belch from the play Twelfth Night, hence the name,) smoked a long pipe and wore a tricorn hat. These jugs became extraordinarily collectible (nearly every British home owned one in the Seventies), and the most popular pots were those that portrayed a grizzled pirate visage (a guy that looked a lot like Keith Richards does *now*) or a bull-doggish Winston Churchill, cigar between lips. London's Charrington Brewery utilised the Toby Jug as a hallmark.

———

With a confident tone in their voice, Surrey people—and Kingston residents in particular—will tell you that David Bowie's debut performance took place at the Toby Jug in Tolworth. Occasionally, they will modify this assertion by stating, 'Well, at least he performed his first Ziggy Stardust show at the Toby.' Although neither claim is accurate, it does show how well-known the location is in the Surrey collective memory.

In 1955, David Jones' family moved to Sundridge Park, Kent, where young Jones attended Burnt Ash Junior School. Kent is often spoken about as if it were a world apart from Surrey. But Surrey has suburbs in Kent's backyard; Shirley, Addiscombe, and Selsdon are just a short bus ride from Beckenham, Shortlands, and Bromley. The two Counties *merge* on the south-east border of the Capital. And that's probably why this region was absorbed by Greater London in 1965.

By the end of the next year, Jones had started playing the ukulele and tea-chest bass, joined skiffle sessions with friends, and began playing the piano. He rehearsed a stage presentation of numbers made popular by Elvis Presley and Chuck Berry—complete with gyrations in tribute to the original artists—and presented his one-lad show to his local Wolf Cub group. Jones attended Bromley Technical High School (now Ravens Wood), where he studied art, music, and design. Notably, Peter Frampton and Siouxsie and the Banshees co-founder and bass-player, Steven Severin, also attended the same school. Jones suffered permanent eye damage when his friend, George Underwood, who went on to become a well-known album-cover artist, punched him in the eye. Underwood designed album covers David Bowie (*Hunky Dory*) and T. Rex (*Futuristic Dragon.*)

Jones formed his first band, the Konrads, in 1962 at the age of 15. Playing guitar-based rock and roll at local youth gatherings and weddings, the Konrads had a varying line-up of between four and eight members, Underwood among them.

His first single, '*Liza Jane*' (by Davie Jones with the King Bees) was a commercial flop. After the failure, Jones joined a blues outfit known as the Manish Boys, who covered Bobby Bland's '*I Pity the Fool*' (pro-duced by Shel Talmy) in March 1965. Jimmy Page played guitar on the recording. The B-side of the single was a number composed by Jones: '*Take My Tip.*'

That single didn't do much better than '*Liza Jane*' so Jones moved on to another blues outfit, this one known as the Lower Third, with songwriter and producer Tony Hatch (who'd already seen some success working with Petula Clark.) Their first release was a single titled '*Can't Help Thinking About Me*' produced by Hatch but written by Jones, who had since decided to use the surname Bowie so consumers wouldn't muddle-him-up with the *much more* famous English born actor/musician Davy Jones of the television-show band The Monkees (1966–1968.) Interesting side-note: Davy Jones and Phil Collins *both* appeared in the original London production of Oliver! They played the role of the Artful Dodger. Steve Marriott played 'a workhouse boy' in the same musical.

'*The Laughing Gnome*,' the artist's novelty single (still widely and deservedly mocked) was released in 1967. It was produced by none other than Mike Vernon with Woking record producer Gus Dudgeon, who'd later produce many of Elton John's best-loved hits. Dudgeon is also renowned in the record industry for being the first producer in history to use a "sample" during production; though, for 'The Laughing Gnome' recording all he delivered was some excruciating gnome-prattle. Fun side-note: *The Smurf Song* by Pierre Kartner, a.k.a. Father Abraham, wasn't released until 1977, that's around ten years after Bowie's 'Laughing Gnome,' thus presenting more motivation, if any more was needed (along with Terry Jacks, Brotherhood of Man, and Demis *bloody* Roussos) to backflush the U.K. record charts with the carbolic acid that *punk* would bring.

————

Following the commercial failure of 'The Laughing Gnome' and two further singles, the artist's manager (Kenneth Pitt at the time) proposed that Bowie changed producers and was referred, via a mutual contact, to Tony Visconti, a New Yorker who had experience working with the Move and Manfred Mann. By producing 'Ride a White Swan,' Visconti had transformed T.Rex's hippy-folk sound into something electric and wondrous, propelling them into the early glam rock movement. The release of the Visconti produced album *Electric Warrior* (1971) thrust Marc Bolan and T. Rex into the superstar stratosphere. Could he do the same with Bowie?

Bowie met Angie Barnett (the inspiration for 'The Prettiest Star') in 1969. Angie attended Kingston Polytechnic. By around 1970, Bowie had begun to assemble a loose-knit community of likeminded musicians around his vision. He'd nicknamed these collaborators as the Hype, and his Hype included Mick Ronson on guitar, Visconti on bass, and John Cambridge on drums (to be replaced by Mick 'Woody' Woodmansey) with Benny Marshall on harmonica. In April 1970, Ronson, Woodmansey, and Visconti started recording Bowie's 'The Man Who Sold the World' album. The album was to change Bowie's fortunes, but most importantly, it would bring about the Spiders From Mars.

Amongst the subsequent 'Spiders' touring line-up would be members of Bowie's Hype plus the South African-born Tucky

Buzzard keyboardist Nicky Graham; the jazz-fusion Brand X keyboardist Robin Lumley (a cousin of Joanna Lumley); the Croydon-born 'Whiter Shade of Pale' Hammond organist Matthew Fisher; John Mayall's Bluesbreaking drummer Aynsley Dunbar; and Warren Peace who provided backing vocals for the band (real name Geoffrey MacCormack), and had been a long-time pal of Bowie's since his Bromley days. With Ronson's deft arrangements and under the spell of David Bowie —who created a complicated stage persona named Ziggy Stardust — this group of gifted individuals came together to create a theatrical production that is *still* considered to be an iconic cultural landmark in British popular music. Certainly, it captured the *Geist* of the *Seventies*.

Norman Carl Odam, the rockabilly outsider known profession-ally as the Legendary Stardust Cowboy, is said to have been the inspi-ration behind Bowie's 'Stardust' moniker. Despite being completely self-taught, Odam was able to land a record deal with Mercury Records, despite his frantic and, at times, garbled uniqueness.

The majority of the Ziggy album was recorded between October 1971 and February 1972, and a tour of the album was set to begin in February the same year. Brian Ward captured the famous album cover photograph on January 13th '72, at Soho's Heddon Street. Bowie and the Spiders recorded tracks for Bob Harris's 'Sounds of the 70s' at the Maida Vale Studio, on January 18th. When Bowie performed for John Peel in the same month, he introduced *the persona* of Ziggy with a few songs from *The Rise and Fall*. The session was taped at the BBC's Broadcasting House in central London and aired on 28th January. The show debuted on February 7th. Bowie and the Spiders played a gig at The Friars, Market Square, Aylesbury, in the County of Buck-inghamshire on Saturday, January 29th, the day after the BBC show. This would be the inaugural warm-up performance for an upcoming tour, though no one can confirm with any certainty whether *any* Star-dust songs were performed at the Friars' gig. On February 10th, Bowie made an appearance at the Toby Jug Tolworth with other Spiders; however, this was another *warm-up* event, and it's unclear how many (if any) Stardust songs were played at the show. On Satur-day, February 12th, 1972, London's Imperial College hosted the formal debut of Ziggy Stardust and the Spiders From Mars. Bowie and the band donned dramatic stage attire and wore makeup for the album's debut public performance, and Bowie changed costumes multiple times. The band played the Dome venue in Brighton, with the same or a similar set, on Monday, February 14th. As a result, the Toby Jug is just one location that may lay claim to the opening performance of Ziggy Stardust and the Spiders From Mars.

Regarding his Surrey shows, Bowie and the Spiders played Wallington Public Hall on February 24th. The set list for *this* show, just days after the Toby appearance, most likely *matches* the Tolworth set; of 14 songs reportedly played at Wallington, *Five Years, Moonage Daydream, Starman, Lady Stardust, Hang On to Yourself, Ziggy Stardust, Suffragette City,* and *Rock 'n' Roll Suicide* were from the new album. The remaining songs were taken from previous recordings.

In March Bowie and the Spiders performed the same show at the Croydon Greyhound and, in May the same year, they performed the piece at Kingston Polytechnic. On May 27th they played the show at Ebbisham Hall, Ashley Road, Epsom (*my* local venue.) The last 164 bus back to Banstead left at Epsom at 11.20pm... if we weren't on it, we would have been stranded!

29

GHOSTS AND STRUGGLES

In 1958, John Weller was born in Woking, Surrey, to parents John and Ann Weller. Although his birth name was John, his parents chose to call him *Paul*. His Father held jobs as a taxi driver and a builder, while his Mother worked part-time as a cleaner.

Situated near the River Wey, Woking began as a village that expanded around St Peter's Church, one of the oldest churches in Surrey, during the Norman era. The construction of the London and Southampton Railway began in October 1834 and the first trains were running between Nine Elms and Woking by May 1838. Before the advent of the railway, the area had been a scattering of cottages and small-holdings. But the railway brought about gigantic transformations.

Woking, originally known for agriculture, but with a healthy brick-making sector too, saw the rise of heavy industry during The Great War of 1914-18 when the Martinsyde Aircraft Works opened on Oriental Road. Due to limitations, the founders, Martin & Handasyde, couldn't expand their factory at Brooklands so established a new factory they called the Lion Works, on the former Oriental Institute site. The Lion works were the biggest employers in Woking by 1939.

The first council housing in Woking was constructed following the end of the First World War, and by the summer of 1921, around 100 families had moved into new properties in Old Woking, Horsell, Knaphill and the Westfield suburbs from slum sites in London. London County Council acquired 230 acres in Sheerwater in 1947 and built 1,279 homes (the project completed by 1951) to address the housing shortages on the Capital caused by bomb damage and population growth.

Bishop David Brown School, formerly known as the Sheerwater County Secondary School, was established in 1954 and built to address the population of the Sheerwater estate. Once settled into this school, Weller started playing guitar.

———

The year 1972 marked a significant turning point for the British boogie blues and shuffle band Status Quo, because it was the year they landed a major hit with *'Paper Plane'*, a chart buster that revived an otherwise flagging career.

Francis Rossi (vocals, guitar) and Alan Lancaster (bass) both pupils from Sedgehill Comprehensive School in Catford, South London, formed a band called The Paladins, which later changed its name to The Spectres and then Traffic Jam when John Coghlan (drums) joined their line-up. They began to write their own material. One night they met Rick Parfitt, a Woking born guitarist, who was playing with a cabaret band known as The Highlights. *His* ensemble had been triumphantly performing (and gaining income) at one of the holiday camps on Hayling Island (Captain Harry Warner's first camp was on Hayling Island as well as at least two other similar camps.) From this sparkly show-biz 'step up' Parfitt's Highlights were invited to perform at the even more impressive camp of Butlins, Minehead. Parfitt befriended Traffic Jam, and their manager at the time, a gasfitter named Pat Barlow, invited him to join *their* line-up.

In order to avoid confusion with Steve Winwood's project 'Traffic,' they renamed themselves The Status Quo (later dropping the *The*). The band then released a psychedelic number called *'Pictures of Matchstick Men,'* written by Rossi. This single achieved remarkable success in the domestic charts and became a Top 40 hit in the United States. The other Surrey musician in the Quo line-up at that time was keyboardist Roy Lynes, from Redhill who had been around during the Spectres period and the Traffic Jam incarnation, and had, *himself*, replaced The Paladins keyboards player, Jess Jaworski. Though he too would eventually be replaced by Peter Frampton's Andy Bown, in 1970.

But it wasn't until '*Paper Plane*' (released on Vertigo) and the accompanying album, '*Piledriver*', (featuring the band in their iconic 'heads-down, guitar necks-at-the-ready' pose on the cover) that the band gained recognition as the uncompromising, and *consciously* simplistic rock 'n' rollers they'd be for years to come. Back in the early 1970's, you'd catch the band's live performances at popular (though, smallish) venues like Wallington Town Hall, Winning Post Twickenham, Toby Jug Tolworth, Greyhound Croydon, and the Civic Hall Guildford. It's likely that Weller caught the band's performance at the Guildford show, because, from 1973 onwards (after Paper Plane) Quo were being packaged with bands like Slade, Caravan, and Lindisfarne to play bigger shows at grander venues, many of them overseas.

―――――

Shortly after watching the Status Quo show, Weller formed a band with his closest friends, including Steve Brookes on lead guitar and Dave Waller on rhythm guitar, and with Rick Buckler on drums. They tended to rehearse and perform Beatles covers. Later, they enlisted Bruce Foxton, another Sheerwater student, as a lead guitarist, but he soon replaced Brookes on bass guitar, thus freeing-up Weller to become the band's lead guitarist.

When Weller heard Shel Talmy's 1965 hit '*My Generation*' by The Who and connected with its rebellious lyrics, he began immersing himself in 1960s mod culture, even riding a Lambretta scooter and styling his hair like Steve Marriott of The Small Faces. Weller and Foxton opted for Rickenbackers, instruments that were favoured by The Who and Beatles, and the band started donning mohair suits on stage. In terms of artistry, their music was starting to emulate the soul and R&B mod sounds of the 1960s too, performing stage shows that were similar to those of The Small Faces around 1965. However, an awe-inspiring and *tumultuous* explosion was looming in the realm of rock 'n' roll. The entire popular music ecosystem was about to be altered.

───────

Rhythm and blues, be-bop, electric blues, big band swing, trad jazz, jump blues, doo-wop, Skiffle, and British Beat all underwent evolutionary phases, genetic drifts, and natural selections, carrying their artistic traits with them across generations and producing musical variations through mutations (like Johnny Kidd & the Pirates) to inspire new artists and adjust and modify the original 'shape' of the sounds.

Yet, evolution has its own set of consequences. When inspirational concepts are replicated, too many repetitions (even repeats of a clever design) will eventually impede innovation; expanding 'popular' sounds can lead to surplus overlapping; when financial considerations determine success instead of an openness to explore ideas, precious talent can be overlooked; and, although conflict is a necessary in cooperative endeavours, rivalry always produces winners and losers, so fosters vulnerability, exploitability, and weakness.

The fate of once-popular genres, such as Skiffle, serves as a reminder of how quickly popular ideas fade away. Given how many thousands of bands there once were in the Skiffle craze, we must ask: where are they now? The answer is that the strong of them transmuted into something *else*. This is the survival of the fittest in a popular music context. Hence, an upheaval was needed to make space for *new* organic elements. Yes, a revolution was required to clear the palette of rock 'n' roll. We definitely desired it!

While Weller was performing in the Surrey clubs with his mod revival band, the pop charts were overflowing with *bosh*, such as:

Paper Lace

Terry Jacks

Peters and Lee

Donny and Marie Osmond

In all honesty, I thought Andy Williams' voice was splendid, and I thought the Andy Williams Show was terrific because it popularised Elton John. But, honestly, was Williams' rendition of Neil Sedaka's ballad '*Solitaire*' the best that record companies could come up with? Really?

I remember Johnny Rotten once explaining: 'Of course we hated Yes and of course we hated Pink Floyd and of course we hated *every-thing* those bands stood for... but what we *really* hated, what *actually* made us want to bring about revolution was the bloody Wombles!'

———

Malcolm McLaren, an East London native with an art school background, recruited Glen Matlock, another art-school graduate, to assist in his vintage clothing store on the fashionable King's Road, in Chelsea, which he ran with partner Vivienne Westwood. The anarchic styles offered in their provocatively named S.E.X. shop attracted like-minded anti-authoritarian 'art school types', such as Chrissie Hynde, Siouxsie Sioux, and Steven Severin.

John Lydon, born in North London, was a Kingsway College student when he became another shopper and part-time 'helper' at McLaren's S.E.X. boutique. He auditioned for a role in a band that McLaren was, allegedly, putting together. In November 1975, at Saint Martin's School of Art, *this* band played their first ever show. The band took the name Sex Pistols. John Lydon adopted a new name, Johnny Rotten

McLaren orchestrated the Sex Pistols to ignite a rebellious movement of discontent, to shift the depleted narrative of rock 'n' roll: and the Pistols certainly succeeded in this ambition!

The Jam rose to fame around the same period as the Sex Pistols, who gained popularity with hits like '*God Save the Queen*' and '*Pretty Vacant*.' The Jam's breakout single '*In the City*' was written by Weller and produced by Vic Coppersmith-Heaven, the same sound engineer who'd worked for the Nashville Teens (with Polydor A&R man Chris Parry.) Parry had, apparently, been 'tipped-off' about The Jam by Shane MacGowan he liked what he saw.

Yet, despite the best efforts of the Pistols and The Jam, and The Clash, Siouxsie and the Banshees, X-Ray Spex, The Slits, and Bolton's Buzzcocks, the revolution had not *yet* begun in earnest. Among their competitors, the punks faced solid resistance from the likes of the Brighouse & *bloody* Rastrick Brass Band, David *bloody* Soul, Brotherhood of *bloody* Man, Manhattan *bloody* Transfer, and *bloody* Baccara! But the general mood and appetite of the record-buying public, the *teens*, was *adjusting to New Wave*; though it wouldn't just be The Jam from their *Town Called Malice* or, in fact, the *out to lunch* Sex Pistols that were about to overthrow the establishment. No, help was about to come from *another* new wave band, and they *too*, came from Surrey!

30

THE GUILDFORD JACKPOT

Kingston was Surrey's county town when I was growing up. Either Kingston or Croydon, to be *unprecise* (do you see how confused we'd get?)

Every year on a 'day out' (because travelling 'all the way to Kingston' from Epsom Downs was considered some kind of crazy pilgrimage that only unbalanced people would dare make) my siblings and I would go to Bentalls department store in Kingston because my Mother said that it was *the only place* she could obtain towels and curtain material 'outside the West End'. Part of our annual pilgrimage included visiting the 'Coronation Stone' where at least two tenth century kings were crowned, possibly even Frithuwald, who was the aforementioned King of Surrey, though if he were, it would have been a lot earlier, in around 673 A.D. (We're not completely sure if he was ever crowned King of Surrey or *even* a 'true' King. Some historians suggest Frithuwald was a 'sub-king' who operated under the jurisdiction of King Wulfhere of Mercia.) In any case, because this would be a special 'day out' we'd eat lunch by the ancient stone in the shade of the grand Guildhall in Kingston. And it was *that* grandness and a sign that read 'County Hall' in gold lettering that convinced the younger *me* that Kingston was the principal town of the County. Indeed, starting in 1893, Kingston upon Thames *did* serve as the County's administrative hub. However, the notion of a county town is not only fuzzy, but also unregulated. Cornwall is a prime illustration: which is the county town—Launceston, Bodmin, or Truro? And Surrey already 'had' Southwark and Newington inside it's 'lines' before it 'decided upon' Kingston! And then there was Croydon!

Like most families from Epsom and Banstead, we travelled to Croydon once a year to purchase 'overcoats' from Allders or C&A. C&A had been doing business in the town since 1946 but a 'linen draper and silk mercer' named Joshuah Allder, originally from Walworth, London, established a Surrey institution: his department store opened in 1862. In the rock 'n' roll era Croydon boasted one of the biggest shopping districts in the South-East (second only to London's West End) so, to us teenagers, it seemed like the 'centre of Surrey shopping.

Many parts of historic Surrey, notably Kingston-upon-Thames and Croydon, were annexed by Greater London in the boundary modifications of 1965. Since then, Guildford has been *informally* recognised as the historic county town (which it *isn't* or ever has been, either officially or unofficially.) It even established a university (earning a royal charter in 1966) and a cathedral (consecrated in 1961), but the place never developed into a city (it needs a charter for that), it isn't the most populous settlement in Surrey (that distinction belongs to Woking); nor does it serve as the county's administrative hub (that designation went to Reigate, in 2021.) Therefore, what does Guildford have that other places haven't?

On the map, Guildford is located somewhat left of centre of Surrey, so I guess it's location is beneficial. Guildford has a river: the town is traversed by the Wey, a tributary of the Thames. The railways date back to 1838. The town's markets date back to 1276. And, of course, Guildford has its famous Guild Hall and once operated its own corn exchange. It also has a castle (rare in Surrey.) Manufacturing existed in the town since the *before* the industrial revolution; though the nation's first purpose-built car factory, Dennis Brothers Limited, was located on Bridge Street and is best known for its ambulance and firefighting vehicles. Several multinational organisations have their headquarters in Guildford these days, and the town's Research Park is home to a number of leading international tech companies. The town has the *second* largest suburban population in the County and it's *that* flourishing suburban population that interests next. But first we must take a Camel ride!

––––––

Andy Ward, a drummer from Epsom, went to City of London Freemen's School in Ashtead and started playing with a rock band called Brew, along with Jim Butt, Doug Houston, Colin Burgess, and Jan Obodynski. Aged fifteen, he met Geoff McCelland who'd recently been ousted from the fledgling John's Children by young Marc Bolan. Seeking a drummer, the Shades (Champion Jack Dupree's backing band) placed an ad in Melody Maker, and Ward was the musician who answered it.

Meantime, the Bym Art School educated keyboards player Peter Bardens had been tapping keys on his Hammond organ with The Cheynes and a few gigs with Van Morrison's Them. After Them, the musician formed Peter B's Looners which eventually morphed into Shotgun Express, a soul band that featured Rod Stewart, Peter Green, and Mick Fleetwood.

The Village was formed by Bardens in 1968, and featured the future Attractions bassist Bruce Thomas, with Bill Porter on drums.

In 1970, Bardens collaborated with Peter Green and Andy Gee to record The Answer album.

––––––

A trio consisting of Andrew Latimer, Ward, and Doug Ferguson, who had previously been working with Guildford based songwriter/keyboardist Phillip Goodhand-Tait, placed an ad in Melody Maker seeking a *new* keyboard player. Bardens responded and easily aced their audition. This decision turned out to be one of the best career moves for this group of musicians.

They needed to travel to Ireland to complete Bardens' previous outfit's contractual obligations, but after that, he was able to work with them without restrictions. They decided to go by the name Camel.

Camel made their live debut at the Waltham Forest Technical College in December 1971. They supported Wishbone Ash.

Camel's instrumental concept album *The Snow Goose*, which drew inspiration from Paul Gallico's short story of the same name, was released in 1975 and served as their breakthrough album, garnering them the recognition they deserved. Nevertheless, Gallico filed a lawsuit against the band claiming copyright infringement. To avoid the anticipated brouhaha Camel agreed to add the words: *music inspired by...* to the front cover and liner notes.

Camel's music, blending prog-rock, jazz-blues, folk, and classical elements, heavily influenced the emergence of what was to be known as the neo-prog subgenre of the 1980s. This subgenre saw the rise of bands like Marillion, Solstice, Twelfth Night, and Pendragon. However, we must redirect our focus from Camel to another Guildford band.

———

Before heading to Guildford for one last time, we must take a quick day trip to Ilford. It's the birthplace of Brian John Duffy, a jazz-influenced Essex entrepreneur with a thick-set wide-jawed appearance. His Irish-born educationalist father sent him to Holy Cross Residential Open-Air school in Broadstairs, hoping the 'sea air' would improve his son's asthma.

The lad's encounter with the violin at this boarding school sparked a curiosity for jazz, leading him to explore the genre. An epiphany struck while visiting a club in Essex, leading him to pursue a career as a jazz drummer. It's essential to keep in mind that this occurred prior to the emergence of rock 'n' roll in Britain, hence his idol was the swing bandleader Buddy Rich. Through his job as an apprentice cabinet-maker in London, Duffy was able to save enough money to buy himself a drum kit.

He played gigs in Essex and London with his band, the Omega

Dance Orchestra. Until his seven-year apprenticeship ended, he played as a semi-professional musician on a regular basis. Subsequently, he dabbled in a variety of temporary jobs before venturing into the ice cream trade. Following his time as an ice cream van operator, he became a depot manager in Guildford, Surrey. He organized the ice cream supply for events such as Royal Ascot and the Farnborough airshow.

He continued to gig at weekends and evenings, and once performed for the renowned music-hall performer Barbara Andrews, who is a Chertsey born native and mother of legendary superstar Julie Andrews (the Andrews family relocated from Beckenham to Hersham a little while after Julie was born).

To broaden his entrepreneurial ventures, Duffy ventured into home brewing and made a deal with a brewery to purchase The Jackpot, a sizable Guildford property that came with an off-licence. He made upgrades to the space and arranged his own setup. Before long, he was making ever-greater profits and building a prosperous wholesaling business. But his first marriage failed because of his obsession with his many businesses. During this period of frantic money-making his music-making ambitions were also put on hold.

Following a time of introspection, Duffy tried his hand at auditioning local musicians with some kind of project in mind. At one of these interviews, he met a guitarist and vocalist named Hugh Cornwell, who had previously played with the Anglo-Swedish band Johnny Sox.

———

Cornwell grew up in Tufnell Park, Kentish Town, and went to William Ellis School in Highgate. It was there he met Richard Thompson, who would later join Fairport Convention, and together, they formed a band called Emil and the Detectives, with Cornwell on bass and Thompson on lead guitar. Interesting side-note: William Ellis School had a reputation for fostering jazz talents, with Ken Colyer and Gerry Conway among a stellar array of musicians who received an education there.

Upon earning a bachelor's degree in biochemistry from the University of Bristol, Cornwell proceeded to undertake post-graduate research at Lund.

Young Cornwell went to Lund, in Sweden, in 1972 to pursue his doctorate. He secured a job at the university hospital. While in Sweden, he encountered Hans Wärmling, a nurse at the same hospital, who also played guitar in a band called The Jackie Fountains. In line with what you might anticipate, they formed a partnership and swiftly commenced planning a project they called Johnny Sox. While Wärmling wanted to remain in his native country, Cornwell decided to conclude his academic activities in Sweden and return to London, in 1973. He managed to persuade the other members of 'Johnny' who, by then were Jan Knutsson, Gyrth Godwin, and 'Chicago Mike' to come to Blighty with him.

Johnny Sox continued to play on the London circuit until mid-1974, when Duffy joined the line-up as drummer (going by the name Jet Black), replacing 'Chicago' Mike.

———

Jean-Jacques Burnel, who'd been educated at the posh Royal Grammar School, Guildford, joined the band as bass player. He'd initially trained as a classical guitarist and had studied history at the University of Bradford. The Johnny Sox name was abandoned, and the outfit rebranded themselves as the Guildford Stranglers due to their focus on the Surrey town. Cornwell's old pal, keyboardist & saxophonist Hans Wärmling, on holiday from Sweden, joined their line-up on a temporary basis towards the end of 1974, though was replaced by Dave Greenfield, who answered an advert for a keyboardist, in 1975.

In the mid-Seventies The (Guildford) Stranglers were situated in a squat in the delightful village of Chiddingfold, near Godalming. Occasionally, they'd go by the nickname The Chiddingfold Chokers while performing small local shows. They often visited The Crown Inn. Side note: In the early 1980s, Genesis had built The Farm studio (also known as Fisher Lane Farm Studio) in Chiddingfold. Eric Clapton, David Crosby, and George Harrison all used the studio. Genesis recorded their studio albums at The Farm between *Abacab* (1981) and *Calling All Stations* (1997). The Chiddingfold village cricket green served as a filming location for the 1995 smash song "*Over My Shoulder*" by the Genesis side project Mike + The Mechanics, while Genesis rehearsed at the Chiddingfold Ex-Servicemen's Club.

But back to The Stranglers: In the early days, they'd travel to gigs in one of Black's ice-cream vans! Black functioned as their management and took the unusual step of registering The Stranglers as a company in September 1974. Black was forever the shrewd businessman.

––––––

The Ramones made their international stage debut in England about four months after their influential self-titled debut album was released. They supported The Flamin' Groovies at The Roundhouse in London, July 1976. Sharing this bill were The Stranglers.

In October the same year, Patti Smith performed at the Hammersmith Odeon. Her show was *also* supported by The Stranglers. The Stranglers' reputation as British punk heroes was undoubtedly cemented by these notable performances.

In October 1978, during a performance at the University of Surrey that was scheduled to be filmed for the BBC TV show Rock Goes to College, The Stranglers stomped off stage because an agreement to make tickets available to non-university students had *not* been honoured. In my opinion, this choice showed their fair-mindedness beliefs, which would later become ingrained in their character and disposition, in addition to reflecting the cool-headed financial acumen that Jet Black had emphasised right from the start.

The 1977 studio album *Rattus Norvegicus* (sometimes known as *Stranglers IV*) was one of the best-selling albums of punk era Britain. It achieved platinum sales.

No other punk band has as many songs licensed for commercials as The Stranglers. However, Burnel perceived the band as something *separate* from punk. Considering their shared affection for jazz, blues, and even classical music, I think it's a valid observation.

Jet Black died in 2022, aged 84. Hans Wärmling died in a boating accident in 1995, aged 52. Dave Greenfield died in 2020, aged 71. Hugh Cornwell is still performing.

31

APPENDIX: SURREY ROCK CONCERTS

This is by no means a comprehensive or authoritative list of *every* rock performance that was held in Surrey during the rock 'n' roll era; rather, it is a representation of the grandeur & abundance of performances during the period. I have focused especially on bands that are well-known, musicians from Surrey, and sometimes on rare yet fascinating performances. Please send me a direct message on face-book.com/rockingsurrey if you believe I have overlooked a crucial location or event, and I will try my best to include your suggestion in future editions. Neil Mach.

Croydon Fairfield Halls
   Johnny Kidd and the Pirates (1962)
   Muddy Waters and Sonny Boy Williamson (1963)
   Jerry Lee Lewis (1963)
   The Rolling Stones (1963 + 1964)
   Beatles (1963)
   Freddie and the Dreamers (1964)
   Roy Orbison (1964)
   Willie Dixon (1964)
   Carl Perkins (1964)

Howlin' Wolf (1964)
Bill Haley and his Comets (1964)
Manfred Mann (1964)
Chuck Berry (1965)
The Moody Blues (1965)
The Byrds (1965)
John Lee Hooker (1968)
T-Bone Walker (1968)
Big Joe Williams (1968)
Pink Floyd (1969)
David Bowie (1969 and 1973)
Joe Cocker (1969)
Delaney & Bonnie (1969)
Al Stewart (1970)
Derek and the Dominos (1970)
Free (1970)
Genesis (1971)
Elton John (1971)
E.L.O. (1972)
Ralph McTell (1974)
Procol Harum (1974)
Gryphon (1974)
Black Sabbath (1974)
Davis Theatre, High Street, Croydon (demolished in May 1959)
Slim Whitman (1956)
Guy Mitchell (1957)
Bill Haley and his Comets (1957)
The Crickets (1958)
The Montanas (1958)
Gary Miller (1958)
The Louis Armstrong All-Stars (1959)
Gene Krupa Quartet (1959)
Top Rank, London Croydon 1966-1974 (aka Cinatras)
Love Affair (1968)
Pink Fairies (1970)
Slade (1972)

Manfred Mann's Earth Band (1972)
Purley Ice Rink (aka Orchid Ballroom and Tiffanys et al)
The Animals (1965)
The Yardbirds (1965)
Stevie Wonder (1966)
Small Faces (1966)
Spencer Davis Group (1966)
The Troggs (1966)
The Who (1966)
The Hollies (1966)
The Searchers (1966)
The Easybeats (1966)
Small Faces (1967)
Jimi Hendrix Experience (1967)
Status Quo (1968)
Sly & the Family Stone (1968)
Marv Johnson (1969)
The James Gang (1970)
Deep Purple (1971)
Family (1972)
Sweet (1972)
Slade (1972)
Croydon Rec, Beckenham
David Bowie (1969)
Wallington Hall
David Bowie (1972)
Ashcroft Theatre, Croydon (Fairfield Halls)
Medicine Head (1972)
Osibisa (1975)
Prelude (1976)
The Gun, Church Street, Croydon (closed 2012)
Them (1966)
John Martyn (1969)
David Bowie (1969)
Croydon Art School
Thunderclap Newman (1971)

Kilburn and the High Roads (1971)

The Granada, Clarence Street, Kingston (closed in 1987)

Cliff Richard and the Drifters (1959)

Gene Vincent (1960)

Adam Faith (1960)

Dickie Pride (1960)

Vince Eager (1960)

Duffy Power (1960)

Joe Brown (1960)

Tommy Steele (1961)

Helen Shapiro (1961)

Bobby Vee (1962)

Gary 'U.S.' Bonds (1962)

Johnny Burnette (1962)

Bruce Channel (1962)

Del Shannon (1962)

Little Richard (1962)

The Crickets (1962)

Brenda Lee (1963)

Roy Orbison (1963/64)

The Searchers (1963)

Gerry and the Pacemakers (1963)

Tommy Quickly (1963)

Johnny Kidd and the Pirates (1963)

The Fourmost (1963)

The Rolling Stones (1963)

Joe Brown and the Bruvvers (1964)

The Crystals (1964)

Manfred Mann (1964)

Freddie and the Dreamers (1964)

The Hollies (1964)

The Kinks (1964)

The Honeycombs (1964)

Herman's Hermits (1964)

Dusty Springfield (1964)

The Tremeloes (1964)

Adam Faith (1964)

Yardbirds (1965)

Marmalade (1967)

The Herd (1967)

Traffic (1967)

The Who (1967)

Johnny Cash (1968)

Carl Perkins (1968)

Chicago (1969)

The Cellar Club, Kingston upon Thames (first at Ashdown Road then relocated to a boathouse off the High Street. Closed as a music venue in 1967)

The Nashville Teens (1962)

Mike Berry and the Outlaws (1962)

Screaming Lord Sutch (1962), The Roosters (1963)

The Rolling Stones (1963)

Steve Marriott and the Moments (1963)

Gene Vincent (1964)

The Animals (1964)

Jerry Lee Lewis (1964)

The Yardbirds (1964)

Small Faces (1965)

John Mayall and the Bluesbreakers (1965)

The Moody Blues (1965)

The Steampacket (1965)

Joe Symes and the Loving Kind (1966),

Jimmy Winston and his Reflections (1966)

Pinkerton's Assorted Colours (1966)

Shirley Collins (1966)

The Troggs (1966)

Jo Jo Gunne (1966)

Cream (1966)

The Mojo Club, Merton

Steampacket (1966)

Kingston Polytechnic, Kingston upon Thames

Wishbone Ash (1970)

Elton John (Tumbleweed Connection tour 1971)

Yes (Yes Album tour, 1971)

Queen (1971)

Mott the Hoople (1971)

David Bowie (Ziggy Stardust tour 1972)

Genesis (Nursery Cryme and Foxtrot tours, 1972)

Velvet Underground (Loaded tour, 1971)

MC5 (1972)

The ABC cinema, London Road, Croydon (formerly the Savoy and later The Cannon. Demolished in 2005.)

Cliff Richard and The Shadows (1962)

The Everly Brothers (1962)

Billy Fury (1962)

Eden Kane (1962)

Helen Shapiro (1962)

Tommy Roe (1963)

Chris Montez (1963)

The Beatles (1963)

Dickie Pride (1963)

The Tornados (1963)

Billy Fury (1963)

Del Shannon (1963)

Gerry and the Pacemakers (1963)

Bobby Rydell (1963)

Carl Perkins (1963)

The Animals (1964)

Chuck Berry (1964),

The Toby Jug, Tolworth

Chicken Shack (1968)

Fleetwood Mac (1968)

Black Cat Bones (1968)

John Mayall and the Bluesbreakers (1968)

John Dummer Blues Band (1968)

Family (1968)

Jeff Beck Group (1969)

Freddie King (1969)

David Bowie (1972)

Genesis (1972)

The Coronation Hall, Kingston

The Yardbirds (1964)

The Zombies (1964),

Gene Vincent (1964)

Wizzard (1972)

The Wooden Bridge Guildford

The Rolling Stones (1963)

John Mayall and the Bluesbreakers (1963)

The Artwoods (1966/7)

Jeff Beck Group (1967)

Fleetwood Mac (1967)

Champion Jack Dupree (1968)

The Plaza Ballroom Guildford aka the Ricky-Tick Club

Gene Vincent (1961)

The Yardbirds (1963/4)

The Moody Blues (1964)

Goldie and the Gingerbreads (1965)

Long John Baldrey (1965)

John Lee Hooker (1965)

The Who (1965)

The Odeon Theatre, Guildford

Cliff Richard and the Drifters (1959)

Terry Dene (1959)

Duane Eddy (1960)

Bobby Darin (1960)

Gene Vincent (1960)

The Shadows (1961)

Adam Faith (1962)

Billy Fury (1962)

The Beatles (1963)

The Everly Brothers (1963)

Bo Diddley (1963)

Mickey Most (1963)

The Flintstones (1963)

The Rolling Stones (1963/4)

Manfred Mann (1964)

Joe Brown and the Bruvvers (1964)

The Crystals (1964)

Johnny Kidd and the Pirates (1964)

The Hollies (1964)

Dave Clark Five (1964)

The Kinks (1964)

Billy J Kramer and the Dakotas (1964)

Yardbirds (1964)

The Harvest Moon, Bridge Street, Guildford

The Creation (1966)

John Mayall and the Bluesbreakers (1966)

The Stoke Hotel Guildford

The Amboy Dukes (1966)

Shotgun Express (1966)

The University of Surrey

Led Zeppelin (1968)

Yardbirds (1968)

David Bowie (1970)

Faces (1970)

Genesis (1970)

Bridget St John (1970)

May Blitz (1970)

Patto (1970)

Yes (1970)

The Who (1971)

John Martyn (1972)

Camel (1973)

Caravan (1974)

Gong (1974)

Magma (1974)

Hatfield and the North (1974)

Curved Air (1974)

St Mary's Church Guildford

Budgie (1970)

Royal Stoughton, Guildford

The Stranglers (November 1975)

Guildford Town Hall, Ricky Tick London Road (later to be built as G Live)

The Rolling Stones (1963)

Railway Tavern Redhill

The Stranglers (1975)

The Cure (1977)

The Star Inn, Guildford

The Stranglers (1974)

The Bluesette Club, Leatherhead

John Mayall and the Bluesbreakers (1966)

The Artwoods (1966)

The Creation (1967)

John's Children (1967)

Pink Fairies (1972)

MC5 (1972)

Refugee (1974)

Ebbisham Hall, Epsom

Gene Vincent (1961)

Gentle Giant (1972)

Pink Fairies (1972)

David Bowie (Ziggy Stardust tour 1972)

Camel (1972 + 1973+ 1974)

Thin Lizzy (1973)

Gryphon (1975)

The Walton Hop, Walton-on-Thames

Sweet (1969)

The Cricketers, Chertsey (aka the Riverside Club)

Goldie and the Gingerbreads (1965)

John Mayall and the Bluesbreakers (1965)

Jeff Beck Group with Rod Stewart (1967)

Peter Green's Fleetwood Mac (1967, 1968?)

Eddie Floyd (1967)

Dorking Halls, Dorking

Van der Graaf Generator (1971)

Genesis (1971)

Epsom Baths

The Rolling Stones (1963/4)

Fairport Convention (1971)

Queen (1971)

Genesis (Nursery Cryme tour, 1972)

Ewell Technical College Ewell (aka Ewell Tech and since 1975 NESCOT)

Cream (1967)

Band of Joy (1968)

Led Zeppelin (1968)

King Crimson (1969)

Nick Drake (1969/70)

Deep Purple (1970)

Comus (1970)

Black Sabbath (1970)

Caravan (1970)

Queen (1971)

Kevin Ayers (1971)

Genesis (Trespass tour 1971)

Hawkwind (1971)

Sutherland Brothers and Quiver (1974)

Thin Lizzy (1974)

Seventh Wave (1974)

Baths Hall Sutton

Cliff Richard and The Drifters (1959)

The Who (1966)

The Granada Cinema, Sutton

Adam Faith (1960 + 1962)

Gene Vincent (1961)

Eden Kane (1962)

Helen Shapiro (1962)

Billy Fury (1962)

Billy J Kramer and the Dakotas (1964)

Gene Pitney (1964)

Swinging Blue Jeans (1964)

The Searchers (1964)

Badfinger (1970)

Faces (1973)

Wizzard (1974)

Wallington Public Hall

Tony Orlando (1962)

Bruce Channel (1962)

Gene Vincent (1962 + 1964)

The Kinks (1964)

The Zombies (1964)

The Who (1965)

Status Quo (1971 + 1972)

Uriah Heep (1971)

Hawkwind (1971),

E.L.O. (1972)

The Red Lion Pub, Sutton

The Rolling Stones (various dates as the house band)

John Renbourn (1965)

The Surbiton Assembly Rooms Kingston upon Thames (now part of Surbiton High School)

Guy Carawan (1966)

Steve Benbow (1966),

Alex Campbell (1963)

Jesse Fuller (1967)

King George's Hall Esher

The Yardbirds (1964)

Weybridge College, Weybridge

The Moody Blues (1964)

The Stranglers (1976)

Brooklands Technical College

Barclay James Harvest (1968)

Dando Shaft (1972)

Richmond Athletic Ground, Richmond

National Jazz and Blues Festival (1961, 1962, 1963, 1964, 1965)

The Rolling Stones (1963)

Yardbirds (1964)

Pink Floyd (1968)

The Nice (1968)

Canned Heat (1968)

Writing on the Wall (1968)

Fleetwood Mac (1968)

Yes (1969)

The Groundhogs (1969)

Station Hotel, Richmond (the Crawdaddy Club)

The Rolling Stones (1963)

Balme's Dance Club Chobham

Genesis (1969)

The Star Hotel, Broad Green, Croydon

Genesis (1970)

David Bowie's Hype (1970)

Angel Hotel, Farncombe

Genesis / Fusion Orchestra (1970)

Black Sabbath (1971)

Kingston Hotel, Kingston-upon-Thames

Genesis (1969 + 1970)

Al Stewart (1970)

Mott The Hoople (1970)

Carshalton College

Genesis (1970 + 1972)

Queen (1971)

Farnham, the Maltings

Genesis (1970 + 1971+ 1972)

The Greyhound, Park Lane, Croydon

Faces (1969)

Deep Purple (1970)

Love (1970 + 1974)

Free (1970)

Black Sabbath (1970)

Yes (1970)

Status Quo (1970)

Elton John (1971)

Leon Russell (1971)

Argent (1971)

Thin Lizzy (1971 + 1975)

Rory Gallagher (1971)

Genesis (1972)

David Bowie (1972)

E.L.O. (1973)

Camel (1974)

Black Oak Arkansas (1975)

Motörhead (1975 + 1976)

AC/DC (1976)

Judas Priest (1976)

The Stranglers (1976)

The Jam (1977)

Ramones (1977)

John Cale (1977)

Buzzcocks (1977)

Siouxsie and the Banshees (1977)

The Slits (1977)

The Civic Hall, Guildford

Yardbirds (1963)

Rolling Stones (1963)

Fleetwood Mac (1967)

Episode Six (1968

Freddie King (1969)

Quintessence (1969)

T.Rex (1971)

Genesis (1971 + 1972)

Rory Gallagher (1971)

The Doors (1972)

Status Quo (1972 + 1973)

Camel (1972 + 1973 + 1975 + 1976)

Byzantium (1973)

David Bowie (1973)

John Cale (1975)

Renaissance (1976)

Thin Lizzy (1976)

Judas Priest (1976 + 1977 + 1978)
AC/DC (1976)
Stranglers (1977)
The Slits (1977)
Elvis Costello and the Attractions (1978)
Buzzcocks (1978)
Iron Maiden (1978 + 1979)
Saxon (1978)
Muddy Waters (1978)
Boomtown Rats (1978)
The Police (1979)
The Undertones (1979)
The Hive Club, Wooden Bridge Hotel, Guildford
Elton John Bluesology (1966)

32

TALKING TO SURREY BANDS

Chat with: **TRUTH ABOUT VEGAS**

In your online presence you describe yourselves as coming from South London, yet you originate in Walton-on-Thames... if you were you born and raised in Surrey, why say you're from London?

Yeah, we were all born and raised in Surrey. Originally it was Sean and Jacob who knew each other through their school in Walton — they shared the same passion for music. They jammed with a few people in 2009-2010 before meeting Jack from down the road in Molesey who became the bass player. It never worked out and the band went into exile.

A couple of years later, Sean met Joe at college, and they became friends once they discovered that they live round the corner from each other and that they shared the same influences. So, they started up a new band and invited Jacob and Jack to join which became Truth About Vegas. We described ourselves as coming from South London because that's where we played our first bunch of shows and to also to appeal to a wider audience — instead of just labelled to one town.

Do you have any difficulty in finding local venues where you can perform??

Yes and no. We have played an equal share of London and local gigs. We've found it's a lot easier getting a show in London than it is getting a local show ... which isn't actually surprising if you think about how many venues and promoters there are based in London. In our opinion, the amount of decent local venues and promoters in Surrey is quite limited. We have played a bunch of local shows before for example The Holly Tree in Addlestone or The Peel in Kingston, but it's not as available as it is in London, which is a shame.

What is your favourite *local* live music venue?

For us, probably The Peel in Kingston. Great sound and decent stage. Loads of great bands have played there... although The Peel seems quite dead at the moment.

(Author's note: The Sir Robert Peel, Cambridge Road, Kingston announced closure 2014.)

Do you think that it can be a struggle to be a musician in surrey?

We think it depends on the type of music you play. For example, Indie is quite a big thing in Surrey. There's definitely some sort of genres that struggle in Surrey... [possibly because] it's just not the time nor the place. There's definitely a lot of potential to become a great musician in Surrey — with vast opportunities. There are loads of great studios and quite a few decent venues all over Surrey. It all depends on what you make of it.

How often do you get to play Kingston, Guildford and Croydon shows?

We've played in all those towns before... but not recently. Our first gig was actually put on by Theory Project Revolutions (TPR) in Guildford's community centre supporting a Kerrang! featured band called "My Favourite Runner Up." That was a good first gig. I think TPR are struggling to keep everything running at the moment and are fund-raising so check them out as they put on really good shows in Guildford for young bands across Surrey. We played in Kingston supporting another Kerrang! featured band called Hey Vanity, who were touring at the time. We were going to play in Kingston again a couple of weeks ago for Banquet Records' New Slang, which is an amazing bill to be able to get on to but unfortunately the headline band had glandular fever, so pulled out last minute, which was a shame. We've played at the Scream Lounge in Croydon too which is an okay venue, just a bit far away for us.

Are you saying a journey to these towns is difficult for you?

It's not difficult to get to Kingston or Guildford ... it was only difficult for the Croydon show... as it's miles away from us and only Joe could drive us (at the time) with all the gear in his tiny car. It was extremely cramped and the suspension on it is totally knackered now! But luckily Jacob also drives now, so we've got two cars. For London shows it's a totally different story though. We mainly use Jacob's dad as our taxi/roadie for London shows. We've had to hire vans before and for some London gigs we've even had to catch the tube with all our gear. Not fun!

Where do you get your largest & most energetic crowds?

In Surrey it's The Holly Tree in Addlestone, probably the most energetic and largest crowd we have. A pretty packed-out venue and overall a really fun night. Lots of moshing and encores with good vibes.

(Author's note: The Cave at the Holly Tree, Addlestone is still putting on gigs.)

Would you say you have a large local following?

We definitely have a loyal fan base that travels wherever we go. We have people who are there for every gig... even the ones uptown in London. Our fan base is definitely growing every gig which is always a good thing.

How do you make sure you keep local fans loyal?

Keep pleasing them. We keep our promise that every show will be a new and even better experience then the last. We never play the same set twice and we never stop writing new material. We always keep them up to date and informed on our websites too about any opportunities and shows coming up.

Do you think it's helpful to be in the suburbs for gigging purposes etc. or would you prefer to be based in London?

I think it totally depends on the band again... Yeah, some bands would benefit [from] being based in London but then again some would benefit more in the suburbs. It does seem like more bands based in London have a higher chance of going a lot further in music than suburban bands... but there's also a lot of bands based in London that don't go anywhere too. But I think we're in an ideal location. I wouldn't say we are based in the Suburbs (although we live in Walton) because for us getting to London is easy. It means we can play a mixture of shows locally and in London and construct a following in both areas, which is happening.

What does the County of Surrey offer up-and-coming musicians?

There's a good wide-spread of venues and promoters all over Surrey, although it's limited to a degree, there are still great opportunities. There's a load of really cool rehearsal studios such as Tweeters and Powerhouse Studios which offer relatively cheap and decent rehearsals for bands. Also, there are so many nice recording studios too, for example Masterlink Productions located in the countryside [near] Guildford. It's an amazing little studio. It's where we recorded our EP '*Alcoholiday.*'

https://www.masterlinkproductions.co.uk/

Do any of your 'music heroes' come from Surrey?

You Me At Six are obviously the most well-known band from Surrey, they came from Weybridge which is just up the road from us. We hope to follow in their footsteps. You Me At Six have been a great example for young bands. They prove you don't have to be based in London to get anywhere and you can still become a professional artist even from suburban Surrey.

(Author's note: The Surrey band You Me at Six released their eighth album *Truth Decay* in February 2023)

———

Chat with: **LITTLE GRIM**

'Little Grim' is a rock group based in Kingston. The band-members came together in 2012, each bringing with them elements from eclectic musical backgrounds; Progressive rock (Joe and Jeremy), indie pop (Chris) and punk (Roger). The band merges these influences into a wholly unique class of music: which is extraordinary, exemplary, and darkly toned.

I chatted to Joseph Murphy, lead vocals & rhythm guitar, about what it meant to be a music maker in Surrey:

Do you think Surrey has ever been part of a musical revolution?

In my time, I haven't thought of Surrey as a host to any music 'revolutions,' though I would say it has always been a good passing point for revolutions, welcoming new ideas and fads. I'd say that Surrey encourages creative revolutions that originated *elsewhere*.

What do you think living and working in Surrey has to offer young musicians ?

Surrey offers a safety net for young musicians with friendly and accessible local music venues as well as a relatively calm atmosphere; it can be intimidating in places like London... where there are a thousand events on every night. It warms them up to those, more intense shows.

What was your first experience of hearing live music in Surrey?

My first experience was at Carshalton's Rockstock... I suppose it's not technically part of Surrey so as an alternative to that, Nescot Live (which has recently shut down) and my school hall, was where I first experienced live music. There are A LOT of *screamo* bands in Surrey... I found that out pretty soon!

Where did you meet band-mates and other music contacts?

We met at School (Glyn Technology)

What's your favourite surrey band?

Are Arcane Roots from Kingston? I'm a big fan of their first EP. I don't know if the artists I love came from Surrey... I haven't ever thought to look their origins up.
(Author's note: Arcane Roots *do* come from Kingston. They formed at Reigate College in Surrey but ceased performing in 2018.)

What is your favourite Surrey music venue?

I'd say that one of the most receptive gigs we ever played was at Nescot Live at the Nescot centre. I find the shape of any venues we've played has been their main downfall, as you can't connect with the audience if half of them are stuck round the corner of the venue! I do love McClusky's in Kingston... but it has a similar issue.

(Author's note: McClusky's on the Riverside at Kingston announced closure in 2015 but *had* hosted The Maccabees, Mystery Jets, Franz Ferdinand, You Me At Six, George Ezra, Royal Blood, Frank Turner, Catfish and the Bottlemen, amongst others.)

Do you use any recording studios / rehearsal spaces in Surrey?

We have used Skyline in Epsom... and Venti Venti (Ewell) but we've been self-recording since.

––––––––

Chat with: **THE TONIKS**

Guildford band The Toniks play what they define as "Quintessentially British" sounds: unabashedly bold and bright. Their loyal audiences enjoy the band's empathic lyrics, catchy hooks, and similarities in style to The Beatles and The Jam.

I chatted with Jez Parish, guitar & vocals, about what it means to be a hard-working musician in Surrey.

You promote yourselves as *quintessentially British*, do you think it helps that you come from Surrey?

Yes, I think it *does* help coming from Surrey, as it is such a middle-class area... the trappings of middle class surround you. I came from a working-class background, grew up on a council estate in Woking but, that said, we would go with my mate to watch his dad play cricket ... eating cucumber sandwiches on a summer's day! I would say I love our quirky Britishness and I'm very proud of it: I still love the image of a red phone box (which there still are few around), bowler hats, boating blazers, strawberries & cream...

Do you think that the music scene in Guildford is healthy and vibrant?

I think if you want to learn music, and start a band, then Guildford has is it all... a great music school, which has produced lots of independent highly skilled music teachers / players. A hand-full of great live music venues and fantastic location... close to London only 30/40 min away... The flip-side to all this is that it is over-saturated with musicians... so it's harder to get rehearsal slots. Competition for gigs, and [getting] bums on seats is harder than it's ever been before!

What is your most important local music venue?

If I want to go and see a band on tour, then G Live has the bigger bands, but for a more diverse musical treat - where you will see in my opinion a more interesting array, we'd go to the Boileroom, Guildford. [www.theboileroom.net] They have up and coming touring bands, and sometimes an older band who are on tour who were big in their day. This usually couples with a local support slot, so from a punters point of view, you get to see new music, that you may not have heard of before. From a band's point of view, exposure to a new audience, and possibly music industry if press or the touring bands manager. But these are rare, as labels often like to choose the support bands rather than the venue supply one.

Where did The Toniks first meet?

The Toniks project was formed by me (Jez Parish) and (Mark Taylor) just writing in Mark's studio... well it was more of a shed in the early days... we would write and craft pop tunes that we liked ... we uploaded a demo onto myspace, where we got lucky, as we had interest within the first 6 months from a guy called Dan Moore, who unknown to us at that time, was working for Supervision Management... We found this out later as he left this detail on his e-mail thread ... He was asking where were we playing? What we were about? Do we have more song etc.... so, we sent him a demo of other song ideas, but at that time we did not even have a band!!

So, we put one together very quickly and got out there. Dan

Moore loved our tunes, and later came to see us play a set in Camden –North London. He thought it would be a struggle to get a major signing as they were not signing many bands during the recession, but suggested we go down the publishing route. So, we did, and got a publishing deal with FPM publishing. But we still needed a record label, so we set that up to become Smile Records. The next stage was to get more reliable band members in. (We've found that a lot of musicians are flaky and transient. We all have our own agenda. So, when it gets tough, we found band members loose heart in this tough industry.) As we are in Guildford, there were plenty of musicians to choose from. We auditioned and have now the current line up Tom Yates, lead guitar, Jess English on Keyboards, and most recent Colin Marshal on drums. And all from Surrey - which helps with logistics.

How useful have events such as Jakefest been for you? Have you participated in other festivals or major events in Surrey ?

Events like JAKEFEST and other charity events are a god send to bands in Surrey, as bands get exposure to brand new audiences; there are normally a few bands on the bill, so it allows for networking opportunities too. But above all it gives the feeling of doing something worthwhile... Musicians are normally skint, but they can offer services free, and contribute in some small way to the community.

I know you have been broadcast on Brooklands Radio, how helpful have Surrey-based radio stations been for you?

Local radio is a lifeline for bands, as this still is one of the best ways of getting your music out there. Brooklands Radio have been amazing for us. We have also had a lot of help from 96.4 Eagle Radio, they have a live Sunday session which we have been on a couple of times, which includes a quick 10 min interview, and they record a live acoustic track to air. Recently we have been extra lucky in that Eagle have set up a new subsidiary DAB and online radio station called 'eagle3' which will play new chart releases, and they intermingle local bands on the play list, which is great for local exposure.

We all aspire to getting our records played on regular rotation... If you get this on say XFM, Absolute, Radio 2 etc.... unless you are terrible, you are only *then* truly on your way. So, it's great that 'eagle 3' has been set up. I spoke to a contact at Eagle, as we sent our début album out for review to get on the main play list, and what we found out is that they only normally play it if a major label sends material or if the artist is already established!! Which basically means a closed door for any new band trying break through. Same with the National radio stations, you would have to employ a Radio plugger for £4-10,000 just to get the ear of the programme scheduler, which not a lot of new bands or independent labels have the capital to facilitate. We also had another lucky break as BBC Surrey /BBC Sussex as they played a track on our album "rise and shine' during a drive time show with Mark Carter. If we can get continued support from our local radio stations, this can only up our profile.

Where did you play your first gig as The Toniks ?

I am not sure because it all seems like a bit of a blur... but probably the remix bar in Woking... (sadly, not there anymore.)

What is the furthest you have travelled for a gig?

The furthest we have travelled was the International Wine Festival in Canada! We got a lucky break, as our drummer Colin Marshal, knows one of the organisers, He tried this with previous bands he was in but had no joy. Lucky for us they liked our sound, and we got paid enough to go out there and support 'The Sheep Dogs.'

While we were there we played the Horseshoe Tavern in Toronto, where another radio presenter (also at the gig) loved the band so much that he put us on regular rotation on his station "rtds.ca." We could only carry 70 CD albums in our suitcase, and we sold out in 3 days... so for us it was very worth it.

What is the most important thing that Surrey has to offer a musician or band?

The networking opportunities with other Surrey musicians

Have you made a video on location in Surrey?

We have not made a video as yet - we have plans to make one... Surrey does offer some beautiful scenery as well as some cool urban spaces... so location will not be too hard to find.

The Jam started their career playing local working men's clubs, though it means they had to compromise their sounds to 'fit' their audience... would you be interested in playing venues that might be 'outside' your comfort zone?

We already played some strange and unusual gigs. so, playing outside the comfort zone is part of the journey for bands, or should be! We recently played the YMCA in Woking...never even knew it was there! We played a birthday party where there were only two microphones and we have 3 vocalists, so I shared a mic with Jess, which was not too pleasant as I had just eaten raw onion earlier! We also did a great gig which was uncomfortable as it was in the bandstand in Woking Town Centre... normally the reserve of Brass Bands. When in Canada we played a charity gig where they did not have *any* microphone stands. I used a broom handle and lots of gaffer tape ... you learn to improvise when you're in these situations!

Do you ever get a sense of detachment or isolation being based in Surrey?

Yes, you do feel a bit out of it as London is where we hear all the action is... but in reality the action is where you make it happen, you don't go to the action, you make the action *go to you*. Surrey is great as it's well placed to travel to London, or Brighton. The biggest issue we find is parking... as bands need drop gear of at a venue, then find a spot to park.

33

SOURCES

https://voyager.jpl.nasa.gov/mission/spacecraft/
https://www.smithsonianmag.com/science-nature/what-is-on-voyagers-golden-record-73063839/
https://www.surreyi.gov.uk/census-2021/ethnic-group/
World Health Organization, past pandemics report
The Complete Beatles Chronicle. London: Chancellor Press
The Beatles: The Biography, Spitz
www.keithflynn.com/recording-sessions
Oxford Dictionary of National Biography
Lost Hospitals of London, ezitis.myzen.co.uk
Museum of Modern Art, www.moma.org/
Ravel: Man and musician, Orenstein
America's Greatest Depression, Chandler
First Blitz: The Secret German Plan to Raze London, Hanson
The Subterranean Railway, Wolmar
www.sutton.gov.uk
www.heliermemories.org.uk
Rural Rides, Cobbett
Outlaws and Highwaymen, Spraggs
Who are the baby boomers of the 1960s? King's College London
The Family Allowances Act 1945

www.striking-women.org
The Virgin Encyclopaedia of Fifties Music, Larkin
Teddy Boys: A concise history, Ferris
A brief history of the Teddy Boys, Mitchell
The Chess Story, Callahan, Edwards
Skiffle: The Roots of UK Rock, McDevitt
AllMusic at www.allmusic.com
Jelly Roll Morton, Yanow
www.mudrock.org.uk
www.visitsurrey.com
The Office of National Statistics
Tommy Steele Biography, Eder
Tommy Steele, a lifetime, Lassandro
2iscoffeebar5670.blogspot.com
Peter Grant, Welch
recordcollectormag.com/
Blues Singers Biographies, Dicaire
www.erikoest.dk/
www.surreycomet.co.uk/
music.si.edu
http://www.45-rpm.org.uk
NME Rock and roll years, Frame et al
Rock and roll, an unruly history, Palmer
The Restless Generation, Frame
Roots, Radicals and Rockers, Bragg
Discogs.com
A Concise History of Jazz, Brown
Skiffle: The Roots of UK Rock, McDevitt
The Virgin Encyclopaedia of Sixties Music, Larkin
Surrey in the Sixties, Davison
www.originalquarrymen.co.uk/
www.cliffrichard.org/
My Life My Way, Richard
Cliff Richard & the Shadows, Ellis
britishlocalhistory.co.uk
www.enteclive.com/

The History of Live Music in Britain, Frith
Hybrid Children of Rock, Hoffman
Greatest guitarists, Gibson Guitar Company
Eric Claton biography, Kemp
Jimmy Page biography, Prato
Peter Grant, Welch
The Secret History of Rock 'n' Roll, Knowles
Sonic Boom, Reddon
The Rolling Stones: in the beginning, Rej
With the Beatles, Erlewine
www.beatlesbible.com/
bigsixties.blogspot.com
https://www.kingston.gov.uk/
Independence Days Ogg
The Virgin Encyclopaedia of Seventies Music, Larkin
Surrey in the Seventies, Davison
Rock Atlas, Roberts
UK Census (2011)
Genesis: Chapter and Verse, Banks
Genesis: A Biography, Bowler and Dray
Sound Man, Johns
www.biography.com/
Teenage Wildlife, Doggett
Strange Fascination, Buckley
The Complete David Bowie, Pegg
Steve Hoffman Music Forums, stevehoffman.tv
Working Class Heroes, Simonelli
Are we not new wave, Cateforis
The Jam, Harris
themeninblack.co.uk
www.punk77.co.uk
www.thechiddingfoldarchive.org.uk/
The Stranglers, Hughes
A Multitude of Sins, Cornwell
www.discogs.com/
www.allmusic.com/

GRANADA — KINGSTON

STAGE ● ONE DAY ONLY ● Sat March 18 at 6.30 & 9 o'c

Kennedy Street Enterprises Ltd. and Peter Walsh present

THE HOLLIES

THE TREMELOES

RICHARD KENT STYLE   DAVE BUTLER

SPENCER DAVIS Group

THE YOUNG IDEA

PAUL JONES

SEAT PRICES   7/6   10/-   15/-   All bookable

POSTAL BOOKING SLIP

HOLLIES SHOW

To Box Office Manager, Granada, Kingston

Fairfield Hall, Croydon   SATURDAY 7th SEPTEMBER

JOHN SMITH presents

THE BEATLES

"PLEASE PLEASE ME"   "FROM ME TO YOU"

Compere—TED KING

MIKE BERRY and the Innocents

ROCKING HENRY and the Hayseeds

IAN CRAWFORD and the Boomerangs (MANCHESTER)

FREDDIE STARR and the Midnighters

TWO PERFORMANCES 6.15 AND 8.45

Seats   10/6   8/6   6/6   5/-

RICHMOND ATHLETIC ASSOCIATION GROUNDS
KEW FOOT ROAD · RICHMOND · SURREY

THE NATIONAL JAZZ FEDERATION present the

4th NATIONAL
JAZZ FESTIVAL

7th, 8th & 9th AUGUST, 1964

Nº 1023

10/-

FRIDAY
EVENING

THIS PORTION TO BE GIVEN UP ON
FRIDAY 7th AUGUST
7.30 to 10 p.m.

GUILDFORD
Civic Hall

Asgard
Sunday Concerts !

30th APRIL
GENESIS + ben

21st MAY
BREWERS DROOP and
CLIMAX CHICAGO

11th JUNE
KINGDOM COME
ARTHUR BROWN
swaztika

Street Publicity ASCOT 70884

start 7-30.   BAR   50p Tickets on door only.

HAROLD DAVISON PRESENTS

"AMERICAN FOLK-BLUES FESTIVAL '68"

FEATURING

JOHN LEE HOOKER
T-BONE WALKER
BIG JOE WILLIAMS

JIMMY REED • CURTIS JONES
EDDIE TAYLOR BLUES BAND

PRODUCED BY LIPPMANN & RAU

THURS • 24 OCT • HAMMERSMITH
ODEON
SAT • 26 OCT • MANCHESTER
FREE TRADE HALL
SUN • 27 OCT • LEICESTER
DE MONTFORT HALL
MON • 28 OCT • BIRMINGHAM
TOWN HALL
TUES • 29 OCT • BRISTOL
COLSTON HALL
WED • 30 OCT • CROYDON
FAIRFIELD HALL
FRI • 1 NOV • SHEFFIELD
CITY HALL
SUN • 3 NOV • NEWCASTLE
CITY HALL

FOX at **TOBY JUG**
1 HOOK RISE SOUTH,
TOLWORTH SURREY

THURSDAYS at 8 pm

FEBRUARY 10th
David Bowie
FEBRUARY 17th
Pink Fairies
FEBRUARY 24th
Manfred Mann
MARCH 2nd
Argent
MARCH 9th
Atomic Rooster
MARCH 16th
Status Quo

Licensed Bar - Snacks • D.J. Rick Hawkins

ABOUT THE AUTHOR

Neil has spent over three decades in music journalism. He has contributed to Raw Ramp, Ramzine, Blues In Britain, Classic Rock and other established publications. Neil is *"one of the UK's best writers,"* according to Peter Noble, the publicist for Paul Weller, Peter Frampton, Hugh Cornwell, and Joe Bonamassa. Neil is an enthusiastic & successful podcaster and has broadcast over 120 hours of material to podcast hosts. He has reported for radio and television and has contributed to music documentaries. He has written several rock artist biographies and is the author of more than twenty highly rated books. He has received numerous writing honours. He's a well-respected public speaker. Neil lives in Surrey with his spouse, Sue. He is the father of two adult daughters and grandfather to grandchildren.

Printed in Great Britain
by Amazon